CONTENTS VOLUME TWO

Preface

In Part 2 of this work we continue the story of Great Western Goods Cartage, at a time when the haulage of goods by rail was essential to the economic welfare of the railway company.

As before in Part 1 the emphasis is on continuing the chronological development of the goods and cartage services. Nowhere was this more pronounced as with the horse and cart giving way to mechanised transport and also with the Road-Motor operations of the railway becoming more efficient in the face of competition from outside hauliers.

In reality the GWR had little option but to modernise its fleet, as outside individual private operators were keen to exploit any gap in the market that might present itself.

Competition increased as years passed resulting in the development of the concentration schemes as are described in detail in Chapter 10. The GWR were very keen to offer the customer a literal 'door to door' service, whether this meant from manufacturer to customer or in the case of livestock with the collection of animals by GWR lorry, transport to the nearest appropriate railhead, movement by rail, and then a final delivery by road to the market, fair or show.

On occasions this also could mean economy of movement, such as when the goods concerned – whether deadstock or livestock - was not necessarily taken to what was geographically the nearest station but instead taken on a slightly longer road journey to be trans-shipped at a railhead which had perhaps better connections to the destination point. The principal governing factor here was the state of the roads themselves, in country areas many remaining unmetalled and so almost impassable in winter or during times of extreme weather.

As years passed so we also see the start of what would become a container revolution, small boxes by comparison with todays' monstrosities but a foretaste of what was to come. Again none of this would have possible without the motor engine.

To complete this second part a number of admirable books listed in the bibliography have been referenced. Whilst study of the GWR New Work Orders, vehicle Diagram Indexes, fleet lists, and contemporary operating documents has enabled the history of GWR cartage to be explored even deeper than before. Why certain developments took place in the prevailing context of the time is explained, such as the reluctance of the broad gauge GW to become involved in collection and delivery (C&D), and hence the need to rely on cartage agents. Also, for the first time, carriers employed as agents by the GW at different stations and the dates during which they operated are listed. The relative costs of cartage by the railway and by agent are investigated.

None of this study would have been possible without the kindness and generosity of many people. Once more first and foremost is David Hyde without whose generosity in letting me use his cornucopia of photographs and documents, and his general advice and guidance, this book would not have been possible. David has asked me to record his thanks to his evening class students and audiences whose memories have contributed

Petrol pump at Alfred Road garage in 1936. Mechanical horse still has pre-shirt-button lettering. Filler cap is over bonnet. To the left is a Thornycroft lorry, registration GY3047. To the right an Associated Daimler '428' van, fleet 1922, registration UU5001, that was new in September 1929. Horse lorry fleet 2251 at extreme right. ***GWR/D J Hyde collection***

Churns being loaded at Shrivenham under the watchful eye of the Station Master. (For full details of the vehicle, etc., see page 179.) ***Author's collection***

over the years to produce a wider picture of the GWR: in this connection, those to be thanked are David Colcombe, Keith Ettle, Paul Gilson and the late Trevor Saunders. Equally I am extremely indebted to Philip Kelley for letting me go through his collection of photographs and documents, again without which this book would not have been possible. I am also very grateful to all those who have helped with photographs, in particular to Elaine Arthurs and her team of volunteers at STEAM Swindon, and to the Great Western Trust at Didcot for sight of the horse-drawn vehicle Diagram Index. I have tried not to use illustrations already published, except where necessary to highlight a particular point; to help the reader I cross-reference photographs and engineering drawings in other sources when appropriate. The late Gordon Mustoe sent me his research notes on GWR Cartage Agents in general, and the firm of Thomas Bantock based at Wolverhampton in particular, and I gladly acknowledge that very important source of information. Some of the information on distribution of cartage vehicles by Goods District is down to John Copsey. Chris Turner has provided information on the pioneering Zonal Scheme that was the last reorganisation of the GWR C&D service, and which was copied by all regions of British Railways after nationalisation.

As goods cartage is the principal topic, GWR buses are not discussed except mostly in relation to the period before WW1 when there were only a few goods road motors that had to be maintained by the bus repair system, and which was a period when motor staff were moved and promoted across both passenger and goods sides. At that time, buses, vans and lorries were given sequential running numbers as they joined the fleet and that requires interpretation. The motor vehicle Fleet List, from the first two buses on the Lizard to the 1930s, compiled by the late John Cummings, and kindly made available by Philip Kelley, is reproduced. It should be recognised that GW buses conveyed parcels and packages of goods up to 1cwt in the early days, and played an important role in C&D. We note that up to the 1930s and beyond, in Parliamentary Acts and other documents, the term 'car' was employed for any type of 'mechanically-propelled' vehicle such as motor buses, motor lorries and even steam wagons. Because the book has little to say about rail vehicles (already covered in detail in our other books), we spell 'wagon' for road vehicles rather than the alternative 'waggon'. We also note that the word lorry — nowadays meaning a vehicle driven by an internal combustion engine — originally applied to horse-drawn goods drays.

Research and sources of information relate to GWR public and private documents; MacDermot's *History of the Great Western Railway*; the *Railway Magazine*; the *Railway Gazette*; and the *Great Western Railway Journal*. In the text, references to books listed in the bibliography are mostly via the name of the author without the title of the book. Where dates are given for introduction of horse-drawn, and motor, vehicles it may sometimes refer to when authorisation was given in GW documents for construction or purchase of the vehicles; or it may mean when completed at the Road Wagon shop in the Carriage Works at Swindon; or delivery of motor chassis from the makers – it is not always clear from the records. Similarly, for scrapping dates and for approval, completion and opening of buildings and works.

Anglicised spelling of Welsh place names is used throughout as it was by the GW. Mistakes are down to me and I should be grateful to hear about any.

pp Tony Atkins

Publishers note: *We are sad to record the passing of Tony Atkins in the autumn of 2018, just a few short weeks before Part 1 of this record was published. Fortunately, Tony had not just completed the first volume but in fact the whole book, what would turn out to be Parts 1 and 2 being passed to the publisher in the summer of 2018. Thus with the kind co-operation and consent of his widow Mrs Margaret Atkins, we are delighted to be able to publish the rest of the manuscript.*

CHAPTER SEVEN

REPAIRS, GARAGING AND MANAGEMENT OF MOTOR VEHICLES

The drivers of the earliest GW motor vehicles were their own mechanics, and a half-day a week was devoted to basic maintenance and adjustments. The first GW bus route was in Cornwall in August 1903. By that December, so successful were the services that the GW decided to purchase 25 more buses, and the original Helston-Lizard route was followed by others from Penzance to Marazion; to Land's End; and to St Just; and between Saltash, Callington and Albaston (Gunnislake), all by June 1904. Meanwhile services had been introduced from Slough to Burnham Beeches; to Windsor; and to Ascot, in March, April and May 1904 respectively. So, to carry out complicated repairs within a driver's ability, one motor repair depot was established in Penzance and another at Slough. The Penzance garage was at 'Old Serpentine Works' rented from the town council but, in 1914, in anticipation of celebrations of the tercentenary of the Borough, the GW premises in Leskinnick Place became the garage. The Slough repair shop, opened in 1905, was 80ft long by 30ft wide, and in 1910 an extension 45ft by 45ft was added as the GW decided that this was the depot at which all 'heavy repairs' (ie those requiring the use of a machine shop) should be carried out. Slough became the headquarters of the *Road Motor Car Department* (1909-1922) and of its successors, the *Road Transport Department* (1922-1942) and the *Road Motor Engineer's Department* (1942-1947).

Vehicles requiring attention were sent to and from Slough by rail on well wagons. An interesting piece of 'worker demarcation' is seen by notice E65727 of January 1909 regarding the responsibility for loading, securing and passing under the loading gauge of road motors when conveyed by rail. At Slough and Penzance, road motor car staff would undertake only loading and securing under the guidance of the station staff, the latter being responsible for passing under the loading gauge, but at all other stations chaining and securing, as well as load gauge testing, was carried out by the station staff, the road motor staff being responsible only for placing the vehicles on the trucks.

By 1909, GW bus services had been introduced in to Devon, Wales, the Cotswolds and other areas, and additional local garages and minor-repair depots had been established at 23 bus centres, for example in 1907 at Trowbridge in former stables in Castle Street. By this time, there was at each centre a 'leading driver' (foreman at the larger depots) who was responsible for maintenance, regular running repairs and making good all small defects. In addition, local leading drivers and foremen were responsible for stores records and organisation of relief driving requirements.

That each vehicle was in good order before being taken out in those days was ensured by the 'Certificate of Efficiency' which was filled up and signed by the leading driver, driver and cleaner daily, and again signed when one driver took over from another. An article in the May 1910 *GWR Magazine* likened the certificate to the 'train staff' of single-line working. Leading drivers were ultimately responsible to the Superintendent of the Line at Paddington (who had a 'Motor-Car Assistant' in charge of both the traffic and mechanical work), but were supervised day-to-day by the Divisional Superintendent and local Station Master. For mechanical work, the system was divided into three districts, each under a Mechanical Inspector who visited his depots weekly as far as was practicable, and reported monthly on cards to the Motor-Car Assistant on the condition of every vehicle. This 'split management' came about because when motor bus services first started, the arrangements followed the traditional GW practice where the mechanical side was supervised from Swindon and the traffic side from Paddington. Grant, who was Superintendent of the Plymouth Traffic Division when the first GW bus service opened between Helston and the Lizard, relates that "....... While the motors and drivers were under the control of a motor manager in London, I had to arrange for substitute vehicles when a motor failed....." According to an article by F C A Coventry in the 1910 *Swindon Engineering Society*, the operation of the rapidly-growing bus fleet (just 3 vehicles in 1903; 63 by the end of 1905; 82 by the

Penzance –

Adaptation of Premises in Leskinnick Place, Penzance (at present let by the Company) for use as a motor Garage, in lieu of premises known as the Old Serpentine Works, which are now rented by the Company from the Corporation, but will be required by the Corporation for the celebration of the Tercentenary of the Borough		2/13	1914 Mch	12	1,200
Amount included in estimate for erection of Motor Garage.	£1,028	2/13	Mch	12	
Contract let to Mr A. N. Coles for	991	Tender 599	June	11	
					37
Additional Expenditure in provision of slate roof in lieu of galvanized iron roof and in provision of urinal for workmen		E10	1915 July	29	95
					1,258

Slough –

Extension of the accommodation at Slough for overhauling and repairing Road Motor Cars. Removing and refixing Steps, Inspector's Office, Stores Huts, etc.	T6	1910 June	30	1,250

General view of Slough motor repair shop in 1911. The nearest chassis is a Milnes-Daimler; that behind is a Straker-Squire with details of weight distribution painted on (seen behind steering column of Milnes-Daimler); and behind that is a Goodchild Auto Carrier. Work benches to the right equipped with leg vices. ***GWR/A G Atkins collection***

end of 1909) proved that the method of management was very inefficient; it led to a great deal of duplication of work, delay and considerable expense. Therefore, a separate *Road Motor Car Department* was formed to deal with both the traffic and mechanical sides. By 1909 all clerical work had been taken over from the Superintendent of the Line and the whole of the management of the Motor Car Department became concentrated in one administrative headquarters at Slough, with Mr Coventry as chief. He had originally been Assistant to the Manager of the Carriage Works at Swindon and, under him, 'responsible for road motor work'. A single department got away from the 'two department syndrome' where the traffic department aimed to raise its receipts and the mechanical side always struggled to reduce its costs. For the first half of 1911, the *GWR Magazine* reported that seven of the motor centres did not record a single failure. In one instance this involved the running of 44,000 miles over difficult country roads (it should be remembered that few roads were covered in tarmac in those days). The average mileage per failure for the whole service was 11,230.

The simplification and efficiency of having one department for all *cartage* work was not possible in the early years of the 20th century, since the number of motor vehicles on parcels and goods cartage was insignificant compared with horse transport (only 8 goods motors in 1905 but over 3,000 horses). So motors had to fit in with the management arrangements for the horse-drawn cartage fleet. Headquarters staff in the so-called *Horse Department* were concerned with the cartage of goods and parcels, the fixing of cartage rates, and the supply and maintenance of horses and vehicles. They were housed in separate sections at Paddington under the control of the Chief Goods Manager and of the Superintendent of the Line, with horse-drawn vehicles being constructed on order at the road-wagon shop at Swindon. The few motor vehicles that were employed on parcels and cartage duties were repaired and maintained by the Road Motor Car Department at its various out-stations, and motor drivers at that time might transfer between buses and cartage vehicles on promotion.

After the 1910/11 extension to the Slough repair depot the shed became 130ft long by 40ft wide. It was equipped with

Belt-driven machinery in the Slough workshop including lathes, shaping machines and drill presses. ***GWR/A G Atkins collection***

appropriate machine tools, the power for which was provided by electrically-driven shafting. The depot had the capacity to completely overhaul one chassis per week on average, in addition to all the heavier work required to keep the fleet of motor vehicles across the system in working order. Chassis were brought in for overhaul after about 30,000 miles. Fifty men were employed at the Slough depot in 1911, comprising fitters, turners, blacksmiths, coppersmiths, tinsmiths, patternmakers, carpenters, painters and labourers. Since a large variety of different motor vehicles had been bought by the GW from a wide range of manufacturers at different stages of development of the motor fleet, an extensive stock of spare parts (over 2,500 items) had to be kept in those early days at Slough in order that replacements for practically any damaged or defective part could be supplied by return train after receipt of a telegram from one of the centres running motor vehicles. According to Coventry's 1910 *Swindon Mechanics Institute* article, connecting rod and big-end failures caused most trouble and expense, followed by magnetos. (The Swindon loco factory had made up big-end roller bearings in 1906-7 for eight

Outside the corrugated iron structure at Slough in 1911 is shown the chassis of fleet 50, LC1171, at that time a Milnes-Daimler bus, later a lorry. On the chassis is painted the weight distribution 'faw 3t' (to the left of fleet 50 below steering column) and 'raw 4t' towards the rear live axle. ***GWR/A G Atkins collection***

210

(830) O.S. 15k—1/05

Westbourne Park -

PARTICULARS.	Authorized by Directors		
	No.	Date.	Amount
Construction, upon land owned by the Company and formerly forming part of the Locomotive Depot, of a Garage for 36 Motor Vehicles employed for Goods & Parcels Cartage	11	1911 March 16	2225
GWR Contract for construction of new Roadways, Drainage, and Earthwork for the Motor Garage let to Messrs Caffin &c for £361 Amount included in Estimate 384	Tender 313 F11	1911 May 24 March 16	23
Contract for the Erection of Corrugated Iron & Steel Framed Buildings for Motor Garage let to Messrs. J. Morton &c for £1044 Less Amount included in Estimate 938	Tender 328 F11	June 29 March 16	106
GWR Contract for erection of Garage let to Messrs Caffin &c for £848 Less Amount included in Estimate 760	Tender F11	1911 Sept 6 March 16	88
Equipment of Garage	18	Dec 14	292
			2691

GW accounts for the construction of the original 1911 Westbourne Park (Alfred Road) garage "for 36 motor vehicles employed for goods and parcels cartage.......upon land owned by the company and formerly forming part of the Westbourne Park locomotive depot". *GWR/D J Hyde collection*

Westbourne Park: Extension of Motor Garage. No 336 — Correspondence L. G. B. 50/207 — Feb 20. 8 — 127

PARTICULARS	Authorised by Directors: Minute	Date	Amount	Allocation – Capital: Engineering	Capital: Signals	Revenue: Engineering Department	Signal Department: Signals	Signal Department: Telegraphs	Collection & Delivery	Cartage of Parcels
			£	£	£	£	£	£	£	£
Extension of Motor Garage at Westbourne Park. to meet present day requirements (forming part of a larger scheme based on observations of the principal London public garages)	T5	1918 July 4	9,074	9,074						
Temporary entrance.	5	4	30						15	15
Alterations to existing Building	5	4	886						443	443
Raising height of roof of present overhauling shop.	5	4	160						80	80
Original Cost of portions of existing Building displaced, not reproduced. £272				272					136	136
			10,150	8,802					674	674
Electrical Engineer:– Lighting Garage and provision of Cables from Royal Oak Sub-station to Garage.	5	4	586						293	293
			10,736	8802					967	967
The original Garage was constructed in 1912 at a cost of £2,707. See old series Book 8/218										
Contract for construction of extension let to Messrs Holliday & Greenwood for. £10,998 / Amount included in estimate 9390	B8	1919 May 9	1608	1608						
Provision of hut for wheelwright	T4	Oct. 9	90	90						
Final settlement with Messrs Holliday & Greenwood:– Add. cost of Labour & Material (provided for in Contract) £1,945; Additional Works 1050; Settlement of claim, made by Contractors 526	S13	1920 Aug 7	3521	3521						
			15,955	14,021					967	967

Durkopp buses bought for the GW fleet in 1905 which had poorly designed engines; the GW would have preferred to purchase Milnes-Daimler chassis but owing to the London and country-wide boom in bus services, it was a seller's market and the GW had to put up with what was available.) All magnetos were sent to Slough once a year and thoroughly cleaned, repaired, re-magnetised and tested. It is amusing to read that ".....one great difficulty in reducing working costs is the fact that motor car manufacturers charge high prices for spare parts. It is usually only possible to obtain good quotations for spare parts from outside firms not directly connected with the manufacture of new cars......" It was at Slough before WW1 that improvements in the GW motor fleet were carried out, such as the replacement of plain metalled bearings by ball bearings in the earliest motor vehicles, and the fitting of more efficient brakes (up to the mid-1920s, most vehicles were equipped only with rear-wheel brakes).

To cater for the growing number of motors employed for goods and parcels cartage in London, a steel-framed corrugated garage for 36 vehicles (with provision for extensions up to 100 vehicles) was erected in 1911 on the site of the old BG locomotive yard at Westbourne Park (later to be called the Alfred Road depot). There was no space at Paddington Goods Depot at that time to keep motor lorries, and the situation did not change until after the depot was rebuilt in the late 1920s (see vol 2A *GW Goods Services*).

During WW1 Slough repaired Army Service Corps lorries, and overhauled Berna chassis (made by Saurer in Switzerland) before they were sent to Swindon to have charabanc bodies fitted to transport munition workers in various parts of the country. The GW's Mr G V O Bulkeley from Slough acted as consulting engineer for the Fisheries Board in fitting appropriate auxiliary engines to vessels.

In 1917 the number of goods motors across the system had become greater than the number of passenger buses. To minimise the labour and rail transit involved in sending motor vehicles to Swindon for what were only minor body repairs, it was agreed between Churchward and Coventry in 1919 that slight repairs followed by painting and varnishing could be done locally throughout the system by CME staff upon request from the Motor Car Department. After WW1, outstations where road motors were based gradually became better equipped, e.g. an inspection pit was dug at Bilston in 1919.

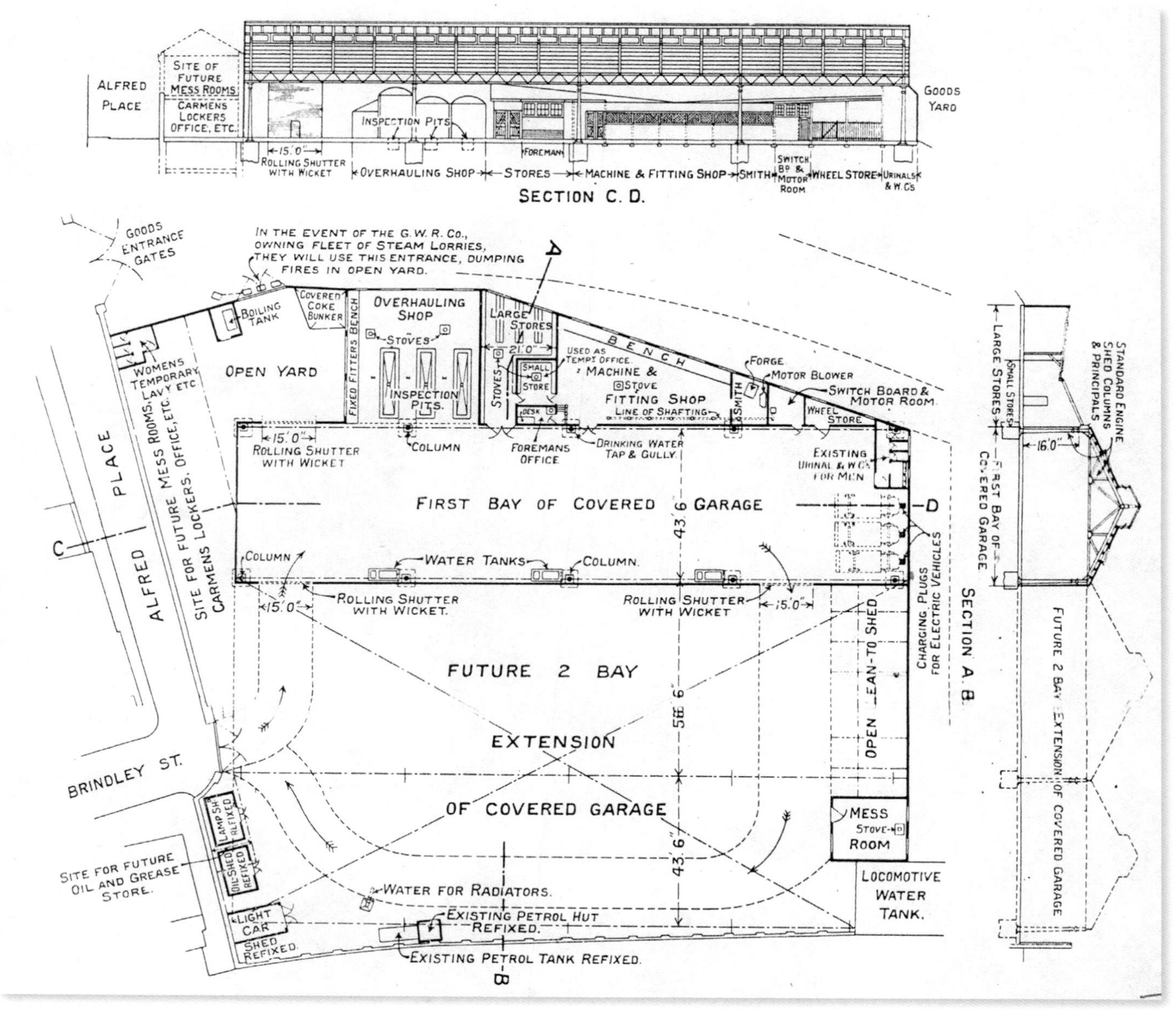

Map of Westbourne Park garage. ***Author's collection***

The Westbourne Park/Alfred Rd structure was extended in 1920 as part of a larger scheme to have three bays, each 43ft 6ins by 188ft and each accommodating 36 vehicles, together with stores, offices, a mess room and a machine shop. At first only one bay would be built until the fleet increased. Details included roller-shutter doors and three pits for inspection and repair. Vehicles were examined for repairs (a) monthly; (b) every three months in a partially-stripped state; and (c) every six months completely stripped down. In the outside yard, petrol was supplied to vehicles by gravity from a calibrated 40-gallon tank on the roof of the petrol shed, having been pumped up from an underground tank (see below). There were also facilities for charging the batteries of electric parcels vans, current being taken from the GW power station at Park Royal which supplied the Hammersmith-Bishops Road line. The state of charge was determined from the specific gravity of the battery acid. In 1921 the different types of vehicle served by Westbourne Park were: sixteen 1-ton, eleven 1½-ton, and eleven 3½-ton petrol parcels vans; fifty-nine 3½-ton and two 5-ton petrol goods lorries; four 2½-ton and two 3½-ton electric parcels vehicles. This totalled 44 parcels vehicles and 61 on goods C&D. By this time there was also a small garage at South Lambeth where goods lorries were based but that did only running repairs, vehicles being brought to Alfred Road for periodical inspections and overhauls.

In July 1920, railway arches Nos 60 and 66 at Bristol Temple Meads were adapted to be used as garage accommodation 'for lorries *loaned* by the government' (presumably the early ex-army AECs discussed in Chapter 5).

This is the original repair shop at Alfred Road looking from East to South and the pits provided. Short Period inspections in 1919. Notice board on right saying 'FIRE NOTICE/ the position of cars/in this shop must be head/towards the doors/Back all cars into the shop'. Chain block and tackle hitched around roof stanchion. Lock-up (toolroom?) on right. Letters A, B and C to pick out vehicles being dealt with. *Author's collection*

Another view of the three inspection pits in 1919 at Westbourne Park. Far left is LH9244, the first type of THORNYCROFT of 1914 30-cwt chassis 1758, Fleet C3 (later 503), with engine taken out; middle is Y2629 Straker-Squire 1-ton parcels van of July 1914 (fleet 311); nearest is a recently-acquired AEC ex-army lorry. *Author's collection*

Alfred Rd/Westbourne Park garage extension of 1920 showing various vehicles in the yard including two Ransomes electric vans [notice 'Express Parcels Services' (plural)]; and the end of a horse lorry on which 'CO-112' is painted. Was it a trailer for the 2nd GW motor lorry? Vehicle under shed to right. *Author's collection*

Road Transport Department

In February 1922 the opportunity was taken to set up a separate GW *Road Transport Department* for both passenger and all goods vehicles (including horse-drawn cartage), as it made sense to embrace the mechanical, commercial and operating sections all in one department. The head of the Road Motor Car department at Slough, Mr Coventry, became the new Superintendent of Road Transport with a new office at 53 Eastbourne Terrace, Paddington. Mr A Twist was Horse Superintendent, B Humphrey Motor Assistant and B F Tee Commercial Assistant and Chief Clerk. By 1924 the new department had 847 staff, including 13 from constituent and subsidiary lines after the Grouping. As Superintendent of a separate department, Coventry reported to both the Chief Goods Manager and the Superintendent of the Line. A board minute stated that the new Superintendent would be responsible "......(a) for the supervision of the whole of the company's transport arrangements including those carried out by cartage agents; (b) for securing that the equipment provided is adequate to the requirements and economically and efficiently used; (c) for compiling financial and operating statistics with the object of demonstrating that the vehicles are adequately used and that arrangements with cartage agents are satisfactory and commercially justifiable; (d) for overhauling the present stock of all descriptions of road vehicles and of horses; and (e) preparation of a schedule of the company's equipment and the submission of an annual programme of renewal......" The new department had

Repair shops in the arches at Temple Meads in 1922 just after electric lighting had been installed (previously gas and oil lighting). Reconditioning a Tylor engine from an ex-army AEC. Pistons on bench. ***Author's collection***

its own District Officers who exercised local control across the system; roving inspectors would visit garages in their areas about every three months and report on how motor vehicles were being maintained. Reports from the new department begin to appear in GW literature after 1925.

As far as ease of maintenance is concerned it is worth recalling that engines in the earliest days had the cylinder head integral with the engine cylinder block (so-called monobloc construction) in which valves could only be ground-in from within the cylinders. The 4/5-ton Thornycroft forward control lorries of 1926 were the first on the GW to be equipped with engines having detachable heads. Their engines had 4⅜ins x 5ins cylinders giving 45hp, and were very advanced for the time also having automatic ignition and thermostatic control of the cooling water.

The original 5ins bore of the Tylor engine fitted to some of the ex-army AEC vehicles was reduced to 4½ins at Slough and, with alteration of the choke and jet size of the carburettor, an equivalent power was obtained at lower petrol consumption.

The question of who was responsible for the condition of road vehicles, and who paid for the work, arose in 1923. A letter from Collett to his CME staff across the GWR stated that "In future, Station Masters and Goods Agents will advise this Department of any repairs necessary to road vehicles; that is to say that the responsibility for the good condition of the vehicles for service will not rest with this Department. Further, they [CME staff] will undertake the work of greasing." The letter went on to say that the only work CME staff should carry out locally was "........ Repairing floor boards, broken futchels and carriage bars (light running repairs). Also changing shafts, tail doors, foot boards, heel boards, rave rails, wheels, springs, scroll irons, shaft pins and door pins and any spare parts that can be obtained from Swindon. Also painting the vehicles after they have been out about two years, if required, when there are not enough heavy repairs to necessitate forwarding to Swindon....." The intention was that all vehicles should be dealt with locally before (if necessary) being sent to Swindon. Coventry's reply was that "It was not the intention that any alteration in the present arrangements with regard to large depots, where the Carriage and Wagon Department employ staff who do the greasing of the vehicles, should be made. The whole object of the arrangement was to save the expense involved where men of your department were required to travel about from station to station to do the work." Handbags at ten paces!

Slough: Extension of Road Motor Depôt

NO. 70

Correspondence L. G. B. 64 / 28.

PARTICULARS	AUTHORISED BY DIRECTORS			ALLOCATION							
				CAPITAL ([illegible])			REVENUE				
	Minute	Date	Amount	Engineering	Signals		Engineering Department	Signal Department Signals	Signal Department Telegraphs	Collection & Delivery 3/4	Passr. Road Vehicles 1/4
			£	£	£	£	£	£	£	£	£
Extension and reconstruction of Road Motor Depôt at Slough											
Extension of accommodation (Buildings)	T.8.	1924. Oct. 30	10693	10.693							
Reproduction of and alterations to existing works. Buildings £ 2.370; Heating, Gas & Water 600; Lighting 630; Alterations do. 207; Road Transport Dept: Incidental works 1.500			5.307							3980	1327
Original cost of works displaced & not reproduced £ 25				25						19	6
			16.000	10.668						3.999	1333
Contract for the building work estimated to cost £12863 let to G.D. Peters & Co: who will convey to the G. W. Co: 1R. 11p: of land required for the extension in consideration of their being allowed access over the up-side approach road.											
Additional payment to G.D. Peters & Co: £1.082. for extra work.	E 14.	1925. Dec. 17									
Contract with W. Freer for heating Stores & Offices £274; Estimate T.C.M. 8 of 30/10/24 300.	E. 8.	1925. Oct. 8	26							20	6
			15.974	10.668						3979	1.327
Additional expenditure for making up Approach Road; Telegraphs	E. 10.	1926. Mar. 25	1123 ~~1250~~ 127	1123 ~~1250~~					~~127~~	95	32
			17224	11.791						4074	1359

S U M M A R Y.

	1921	1922	1923	1924	1925	1926	1927	1928	1929
GRAND TOTAL (Road Transport Department Staff) ...	-	806	840	918	984	1,074	1,144	1,296	1,478

ROAD TRANSPORT DEPARTMENT.

GRADE.	1921.	1922.	1923.	1924.	1925.	1926	1927.	1928.	1929.
SALARIED STAFF, WEEKLY PAID CLERKS AND SUPERVISORS.									
Officers and other Staff in receipt of £500 per annum, and upwards	-	7	7	7	7	7	8	8	8
Male Clerical Staff - Adults	-	17	22	23	24	32	32	36	47
" " " Juniors	-	3	4	4	3	2	4	5	4
Unappointed Clerks ...	-	3	3	3	3	3	3	3	3
Technical Staff ...	-	2	2	2	3	3	3	3	3
Railway Supervisory Staff...	-	32	34	35	37	38	44	47	52
Workshop	-	19	21	22	22	23	21	22	24
Women Clerks - Adults ...	-	8	10	12	12	13	12	15	16
" " Juniors ...	-	1	2	1	1	1	-	1	2
TOTAL - Adults ...	-	88	99	104	108	119	123	134	153
" Juniors ...	-	4	6	5	4	3	4	6	6
CONCILIATION STAFF.									
'Bus Checker	-	-	-	-	-	2	2	3	-
'Bus Conductor, Motor - Adults	-	77	76	81	60	46	41	45	52
" " " Juniors	-	2	3	12	38	41	73	110	163
'Bus Driver, Motor, Public Omnibus 'A' rate	-	84	88	101	132	177	202	268	256) 330
" " " " 'B' "	-	-	-	-	-	-	-	-	74)
" " " Private Omnibus	-	1	5	11	11	11	12	13	13
" " " Leading, Class 1 'A' rate	-	14)	12)	10)	14)	20)	18)	21)	22)
" " " " 'B' "	-	-) 20	-) 16	-) 13	-) 16	-) 26	-) 31	-) 34	1) 23) 36
" " " " Class 2	-	6)	4)	3)	2)	6)	13)	13)	13)
'Bus Controller ...	-	-	-	-	-	-	1	-	-
Carter	-	8	10	7	7	7	9	10	10
" Leading	-	-	-	1	1	1	1	1	1
Motor Driver Instructor ...	-	-	-	-	-	-	-	-	2
Cleaner, Motor Omnibus - 'A' rate	-	26	41	41	42	49	51) 57	39) 73	39) 74
" " " 'B' "	-	-	-	-	-	-	6)	34)	35)
" " " Juniors	-	3	7	7	8	27	27	35	48
Motor Driver (Petrol or Steam) 'A' rate	-	-	-	-	3	3	6	4	1) 2
" " " " " 'B' "	-	-	-	-	-	-	-	-	1)
Stableman-in-Charge ...	-	8	7	11	13	13	14	14	14
Stableman (not in charge) 'A' rate	-	270	270	278	283	286	268) 284	243) 268	208) 247
" " " " 'B' "	-	-	-	-	-	-	16)	25)	39)
Stable Boy	-	13	12	13	14	16	14	12	11
Storekeeper	-	1	1	1	1	1	1	-	-
Stores Issuer	-	1	1	1	1	2	2	-	-
Storesman	-	1	1	1	1	1	1	-	-
Stores Lad	-	-	-	1	1	-	-	-	-
TOTAL - Adults ...	-	497	516	548	572	625	664	733	781
" - Juniors ...	-	18	22	33	61	84	114	157	222

SHOP AND ARTISAN STAFF.

*	1922.	Revised Grades.†	1923.	1924.	1925.	1926	1927.	1928.	1929.
Apprentice - Adults	6	Apprentice ...	12	10	7	6	10	14	13
" Juniors	6	Carpenter, Grade 1	1	1	1	1	1	1	1
Blacksmith ...	1	Fitter, Chargeman	13	17	17	17	14	15	14
Carpenter ...	1	" Grade 1	30)	42)	44)	49)	48)	59)	80)
Chargeman ...	16	" " 2	19) 67	21) 78	22) 85	21) 93	20) 88	23) 107	25) 136
Coppersmith ...	1	" " 3	18)	15)	19)	23)	20)	25)	31)
Doorman ...	20	Fitter's Mate ...	10	15	12	6	8	4	7
Fireman ...	17	Improver ...	3	-	4	-	-	-	4
Fitter ...	22	Labourer, Grade 1	-	-	1) 4	1) 7	1) 2	1) 3	1) 5
Fitter's Mate ...	25	" " 2	1	4	3)	6)	1)	2)	4)
Improver ...	5	Machinist, Grade 1	-)	-)	-)	2)	2)	2)	3)
Labourer ...	8	" " 2	3) 4	2) 4	2) 4	2) 4	2) 4	2) 5	2) 6
Machine Man ...	4	" " 3	1)	2)	2)	-)	-)	1)	1)
Night Watchman ...	1	Metaller ...	1	1	1	-	-	-	-
Painter ...	2	Painter, Chargeman	-	-	-	1	1	1	1
Radiator Repairer	1	" Grade 1	1) 2	1) 2	1) 2	1) 1	1) 1	5) 5	5)
Repairer ...	20	" " 2	1)	1)	1)	-)	-)	-)	1) 14
Repairer-in-charge	3	" " 4	-	-	-	-	-	-	8)
Saddler ...	17	Patternmaker,							
Sheet Metal Worker	2	Chargeman	1	1	1	1	1	1	1
Shop Cleaner ...	11	Saddler ...	19	20	23	23	23	22	21
Turner ...	4	Shop Lad ...	-	1	-	2	2	2	2
Wheel Man ...	1	Smith, Chargeman	-	-	-	1	1	1	1
		" Grade 1	2	2	2) 3	-) 2	2) 2	2) 3	1) 2
		" " 2	-	-	1)	2)	-)	1)	1)
		Smith's Doorman	21	23	24	24	25	24	21
		" Fireman	19	21	23	22	21	22	23
		" Striker	3	3	3	3	3	3	4
		Stores Checkers	-	-	-	-	-	2	2
		" Issuer ...	-	-	1	1	1	-	-
		Storesman ...	-	1	-	-	1	1	1
		Tester ...	-	-	-	-	-	-	2
		Tinsmith, Chargeman	-	-	-	1	1	1	1
		" Grade 1	3) 4	3) 4	3) 4	2)	2)	4)	4)
		" " 2	1)	1)	1)	1) 5	1) 5	1) 6	1) 6
		" " 3	-	-	-	2)	2)	1)	1)
		Turner, Chargeman	-	-	-	1	-	-	-
		" Grade 1	5	12	12	11	11	11	10
		Watchman ...	1	1	1	1	1	1	1
		Wheelwright ...	-	-	-	-	3	2	5
TOTAL - Adults	188	TOTAL - Adults	177	210	225	226	218	241	289
" Juniors	6	" Juniors	12	11	7	8	12	16	15

MISCELLANEOUS GRADES.	1921.	1922.	1923.	1924.	1925.	1926	1927.	1928.	1929.
Male Staff -									
Messenger, Adult ...	-	-	-	-	-	1	2	1	1
" Junior ...	-	1	3	3	3	3	2	3	4
TOTAL (Male) - Adults	-	-	-	-	-	1	2	1	1
" Juniors	-	1	3	3	3	3	2	3	4
Female Staff -									
Caretaker	-	1	1	1	1	1	1	1	1
Charwoman	-	3	4	4	4	4	4	4	6
TOTAL (Female) ...	-	4	5	5	5	5	5	5	7

The new workshop at the Slough Road Transport Department in October 1926. Various moveable hoists with overhead chain-operated blocks and tackle, under the nearest of which is a company car with another over at the left. Different wheels, tyres and inner-tubes against wall at right, including a 'cushion' solid rubber tyre off an ex-army AEC lorry (the circumferential groove gave increased flexibility). Belt-driven machinery in the background with foreman's cabin to the left. ***GWR/P J Kelley collection***

Another view of the repair shop looking in the same direction towards the foreman's cabin. The bench is equipped with bench vices (as opposed to leg vices in the original repair depot). Fitters performing various tasks – the nearest using a hacksaw is left handed. *GWR/P J Kelley collection*

Inside the stores at the Slough repair shops in 1926. To the left, boxes of nails, nuts, bolts and special items such as 'paper glass'. At the right a sprung-load tow bar lies on the floor, on top of which are a steering column and hydraulic damper (shock absorber), with revolving brushes from a road sweeper. Behind are pre-painted 'G.W.R.' signs that, at the time, fitted on the outside of vehicle scuttles. ***GWR/P J Kelley collection***

Once again reflecting the rapid increase in fleet numbers, an additional brick-built repair shop was erected at Slough in 1924/5 close to the site of the original heavy repair shop that itself had been enlarged in 1911. The new shop was 228ft long by 81ft wide, with additional smaller bays accommodating the smithy and engine-testing rigs. All the work, from stripping and cleaning to final painting and varnishing, was done under one roof. Equipment provided included a cylinder grinding machine that could re-bore any engine in the GW fleet, a vulcanising plant for repair of (pneumatic) tyres and various lifting gantries (designed and manufactured at Slough). In 1928, engines in older lorries were retrofitted at Slough with newer carburettors to give easier starting in cold weather. Ease of starting engines and breakdowns had been a problem from the earliest days. Grant writes that ".....In December 1903 an experiment was made with a parcels van [bus?] between St Austell and Megavissey to start at 9am, but the engine could not be made to work until 1pm. That experiment occupied a day of 15 hours......" Leslie King told the author that when he went to Bridgwater Goods in 1927, the depot had two goods motors: a solid-tyred ex-army AEC lorry and a smaller 2-tonner. The AEC had "hazardous starting arrangements" with much swinging of the starting handle, backfiring, etc and sometimes having to be towed by the two-tonner before the engine fired. Fitters had to travel from Taunton when breakdowns occurred.

The machinery in all GW workshops was kept up to date as the years passed. In 1931 it was proposed to put in electric dynamometers at Slough to test engines, and a new and quicker cylinder boring and sleeving machine was installed in 1933 which could re-bore an engine in 8 minutes compared with 20 previously. By 1934 all new types of vehicle brought into the fleet were tested on a standard route around Slough using the 'Tapley Performance Meter' by which its tractive effort was determined; and exhaust gas analysers were installed in repair shops during 1935. C&D motors ran a relatively limited daily mileage with numerous stops and starts that made it difficult to keep the engine warm, so that carburettor settings were not 'normal'. A 'jet scheme' was in place to ensure that the best size of carburettor jet was fitted to engines depending on their working conditions (hilly/flat country, heavy/light loads, etc). Expenditure was also approved in 1935 to enable all motor vehicles working in districts where there was no street lighting to be fitted with electric lamps: previously they had had oil or acetylene lamps, with the latter only for use in country districts.

Associated Daimler '428' chassis and cabs, as originally fitted with solid rubber tyres and in works grey, loaded on Scorpion carriage trucks at Southall station for delivery from AEC to Swindon for fitting of bodies and painting. Station buildings at left background and, going to the right, an advert for Waverley cigarettes, the 'Elite' shop with sunblind down and a crenelated building. During the rail journey the vehicles were kept in place with cross bars and strapped to the hinged side rails. On the nearest Scorpion, the Dean-Churchward cross-cornered brake handle down and 'on'. *British Commercial Vehicle Museum*

Batch of six Brockhouse 6-ton pole trailers (16ft short wheelbase) being painted at Slough on 9 February 1934. Those furthest away are most advanced with 'G.W.R.' already painted on the central cream panel on telescopic beam (shirt-button not introduced until later that year). 'GWR PADDINGTON STATION LONDON' on forecarriage. Coded Vibo A after 1935. *GWR/P J Kelley collection*

PAMPHLET No. 202.

G.W.R.

Swindon Engineering Society.

"FURTHER NOTES ON ROAD TRANSPORT MAINTENANCE"

BY

A. E. C. DENT, A.M.I.A.E. (Member).

EXCERPT OF TRANSACTIONS, 1934-35.

PUBLISHED BY THE SOCIETY:
2, EMLYN SQUARE, SWINDON.

ALL RIGHTS OF PUBLICATION ARE RESERVED.

G. H. E. BOND, *Hon. Secretary.*

Chassis of A1 Thornycroft damaged by collision in 1939. The frame was straightened at Temple Meads repair shops and the vehicle put back into service. *Author's collection*

When a motor vehicle broke down in the street, a fitter with his bag of tools would come along and, providing the failure was not really serious, would soon send the vehicle on its way. Such jobs were carried out by mechanics from the short-period overhaul teams.

Of the total operating costs of GW road transport in 1938 (wages principally), only 14percent was allowed for repairs and overhauling of all sorts.

During WW2, the headquarters of the GW Road Transport Department were moved to the countryside away from London to Beenham Grange near Reading (GW postal address Aldermaston), to and from which staff trains ran daily, with some staff finding accommodation locally. Immediate jobs to be done were to limit the areas of headlights that were illuminated, and to paint the edges of mudguards white, both owing to blackout restrictions. Headlamp masks for the fleet of road motors were purchased in November 1939 at a cost of £450. Bombing and strafing caused destruction and damage to garages and to the fleet of road motors. In 1941, temporary electric lighting was installed following the destruction by bombing of the Goswell Road garage (Smithfield). The electrical power circuit in the garage at Exeter also had to be repaired following bomb damage. For the Cathays workshop in Cardiff, the road-wagon shop at Swindon was asked to provide 33 black-out curtains in December 1942. On 13 February 1943 a bomb fell on the site of the old Millbay goods shed (previously bombed in 1941 – see Chapter 3) and penetrated No 11 arch that was used as a garage; two 3-ton Scammell lorries were damaged. 'Open-type' hand inspection lamps were a danger and were replaced by 'gas-tight' lamps in road motor repair shops in numerous locations during 1943-44. In 1943, the road-wagon shop constructed a new body to replace the original body of Scammell AL trailer T1493, damaged by enemy action.

Cartage Controller and Road Motor Engineer

The operation of cartage services across the GWR was in the hands of the local Goods District Transport Officers, but the supply and maintenance of both horses and motors came under the direct supervision of the Road Transport Department set up in 1922. This arrangement was different from what happened on the other main line railways. When Mr Coventry retired in November 1942, his post was abolished and a 'split' arrangement was

Machine shop at Alfred Road garage on 28 May 1942. Woman worker at centre left. Men elsewhere. Lathes belt-driven from overhead shafting running along wall. Smaller machines in centre driven by individual electric motors. *STEAM Swindon*

Body repair shop during WW2. Woman worker with tenon saw at right centre. Man at left centre with brace and bit attending to a cab roof on which lies a hand drill. Trailer body being reconstructed at back centre right. To the right of the woman is number plate GJ 2326, fleet 2507, belonging to a Morris 25-cwt van. *STEAM Swindon*

Cirencester (Watermoor) ~ Road Motor Repair Shop

No.
CORRESPONDENCE L.G.B. 97/165
18
15H

PARTICULARS	DIRECTORS' MINUTE No.	Date		Amount	TOTAL	ALLOCATION CAPITAL Name of Account	Amount	REVENUE Road Transport Dept.			SUNDRY ACCOUNTS Name	Amount
				£	£		£	£	£	£		£
Purchase of R.A.F. hangar and adaptation as repair shop accommodation for road motor vehicles.												
Purchase of R.A.F. hangar				110		Garages, Stables &c.	110					
Clearing site etc.				22				22				
Provision of access from road to repair shop				12		do.	12					
Additional concrete floor, timber framing, corrugated cement-asbestos sheeting, glazed and painted lights, doors and frames				191		do.	191					
Water service, washing facilities and drainage				25		do.	25					
Lighting				110		do.	110					
Dismantling, loading up and re-erecting hangar		1947		100				100				
Chief Engineer	T.2	May	22		570							
					570		448	122				
(Appropriation remains unchanged as the bulk of the expenditure was incurred prior to 1.1.48)												

Thursday, 26th April 1945

New Work Order	CORRES. C.M.E's.	Works
5928	65213	

Mr. [illegible]
Carry out the undermentioned work at Swindon.

2 Van Bodies and mount on Austin 4-ton Chassis Nos. 4382 and 4383.

Lot No.830 – Renewals.

Charge Lot 830/13/90.

Vote £	Est. Cost £	Allocation Statement No.	Drawing No.	Date completed
			Slough Drg. D/1068 Swindon Drg. 122144	6.10.45

Order signed by FCH

Authority General Manager's G1/2795/56, 26/4/45.
Mr. Dent's Order E.507, 20/4/45.

Division of Estimate		Appropriation
	£	Departmental New Work Lots 13/90

The papers in this case were passed to Order Office by HJS
2,500 pads, 5 diff. lvs.—Est. 701—8-41—(37-1)

instated. Thus W H E Humphrey, as *Cartage Controller*, became responsible for the operation of all goods and parcels services while A E C Dent, the *Road Motor Engineer*, was responsible for the supply and maintenance of road vehicles. Both reported to the Chief Goods Manager and to the Superintendent of the Line and, additionally, the Road Motor Engineer advised the General Manager on all technical matters. Cartage services were thus brought under the direct control of the chief officers of the goods and traffic departments. This closer coordination resulted in improved depot working and was vital during WW2 when considerably greater volumes of traffic had to be handled with limited supplies of petrol.

An article in the August 1942 *GWR Magazine* aimed to remind drivers of the ways they could play their part in keeping GW vehicles on the roads in difficult times. Reducing petrol and oil consumption was obvious but rubber for tyres also had to be imported, so under-inflation of tyres and hitting kerbs was to be avoided, as was overloading of vehicles and excessive speed. Needless damage to vehicles was important at a time when the motor maintenance staff were handicapped by the difficulty of obtaining new parts. Want of care at loading banks was highlighted as a frequent cause of damage (backing with the tailboard down; 'sandwiching' other vehicles that caused the sides of a vehicle, the driving mirrors, the door handles, the mudguards, etc to be damaged in drawing out). Many hundreds of difficult-to-replace side and tail lamps had to be repaired every month and it was pointed out that a lot of the damage was avoidable if drivers were more patient and careful. Heed must have been taken because, as discussed in Chapter 5, the performance of the GW goods cartage services was outstanding by the war's end.

In Chapter 3 it was noted that a grounded condemned horsebox was used as a stable at Melksham, and in 1946 the body of condemned V12 goods van No 16429 of 1912 was put down at Worcester for storage of oils and greases; in another case, grounded van No 85457 became the foreman's office at Treforest (a new building for repairs being erected at the end of WW2). Use of grounded bodies continued with X1 meat van No 47963 of 1889 going to Oxford's motor repair shop and Z1 gunpowder van No 16981 of 1904 being placed at Kidderminster; there were many other examples. On a larger scale, an RAF hangar was purchased in 1947 and adapted as a repair shop at Cirencester

GREAT WESTERN RAILWAY.

INSTRUCTIONS

to

TEMPORARY MOTOR DRIVERS.

Road Transport Department,
Paddington.
23rd September 1935.

S.7181/1.

GREAT WESTERN RAILWAY.

INSTRUCTIONS TO TEMPORARY MOTOR DRIVERS.

1. Motor drivers on duty must have with them their Driving Licence, Driver's Docket, Tool Kit and where driving a Heavy Motor Car (i.e. exceeding 2½-tons unladen weight), Articulated Vehicle or Motor Tractor, their Licence to drive a Heavy Goods Vehicle. They must also see that the following certificates, etc. are carried when their vehicle is on the road :-

On the Car Road Fund Licence, Identity Certificate (two in the case of Articulated Vehicles) Certificate of Deposit, Log Book, and where Livestock is being carried, Livestock Register.

- 2 -

On a trailer Identity Certificate, and where Livestock is being carried, Livestock Register.

2. Motor drivers, before taking their cars out of the yard or repair shop, must satisfy themselves that the radiator is filled with water; that there is sufficient petrol in the tank for the day's working; that the oil level in the engine base is correct; that registration number plates are clean and properly secured and the horn in working order and secure.

ON NO ACCOUNT MUST A MOTOR VEHICLE BE TAKEN ON THE ROAD WITH EITHER INEFFICIENT BRAKES OR STEERING.

Care must be taken before starting an engine to see that the change-speed lever is in neutral position and the hand brake on. Where variable ignition is fitted, this should be retarded before starting up.

3. Should a car stop with-

- -

out apparent cause, the driver should endeavour to get it running again quickly. If he is unable to do so within a reasonable time, he must at once telephone to the Repair Depot stating what is wrong, the street in which the car is standing, the most direct way of reaching it, full particulars of any load that may be on the car at the time, and what portion of his collection or delivery work he is unable to complete. He must afterwards telephone similar information to the Station Master or Agent. Should he, after doing this, remedy the trouble, he should again telephone, and if assistance has already been sent, wait until it arrives, or leave certain means of notifying those sent. Motor Drivers whose cars are being temporarily repaired on the road must assist in the repair work. In cases of mechanical failure, the driver must take steps to get the car off the main road or to the side of it and cause as little obstruction as possible.

- 4 -

4. Motor drivers must not bring their cars to the repair depot for repair until so instructed by the Station Master or Agent who should telephone to the Road Transport representative upon receiving the driver's report of the breakdown and obtain his advice as to the course to be pursued.

5. Any damage done to a car or fittings, or loss of any part of the car (other than by street accidents) must be reported on a Damage and Loss Form (kept at the Office); the driver must hand his report to the Station Master or Agent, who will forward to the Road Transport Department's representative.

6. The driver is required, when taking over a vehicle, to enter up in the LOG BOOK the car number, date and time. Any defect observed must be entered in the Log Book and brought to the notice of the Station Master

-5-

or Goods Agent or his authorised representative, who will be responsible for advising the Road Transport Department (by telephone, if necessary). The driver when finishing duty must fill up the remaining columns of the Log Book. Should a driver make an entry of what he believes to be a defect on the car, but which on examination by the maintenance staff is proved not to be sufficiently serious to prevent the car running, he must accept the ruling of the Road Transport representative, who will make a note of his decision in the Log Book.

7. If a driver is asked for his Insurance Policy by a Police Officer, he must point out to him the "Certificate of Deposit" which is exhibited in every vehicle and which covers the Company's responsibility in regard to Insurance.

8. During winter months or such time as side lamps are required, Drivers must see that they are

- 6 -

equipped, before leaving the Yard or Repair Depot, with the necessary lamps. Motor drivers must make themselves familiar with the notices posted at the depots concerning the removal of lamps from cars.

9. The use of naked lights in or near oil or petrol stores or for the purpose of examining cars is forbidden.
SMOKING ON DUTY IS FORBIDDEN.

10. Motor drivers must not drive with the foot resting on the clutch pedal.

11. Motor drivers must be thoroughly conversant with the working of the fire extinguishers fitted to the cars, and will be held responsible for seeing that their cars are fitted with extinguishers in proper order before they leave the depot.

12. Pneumatic tyres must be kept inflated to the required pressures and examined daily for cuts, or for

- 7 -

nails, etc. which may have become embedded therein, also to see that the valve caps are on.
Driving on tyres which have become deflated is strictly forbidden.

13. Windscreens must be kept clean, and when vision is in any way reduced or obstructed owing to bad weather conditions (such as fog, falling rain or snow, etc.) or through the glare of lamps, failure of the car lights, or any other cause, drivers must not drive with the windscreen closed. Even when cars are fitted with windscreen wipers, occasions arise when visibility may be restricted and it is necessary to open the windscreen to obtain maximum visibility.

14. Before taking a vehicle and trailer on the road, the Driver must see that the coupling gear and the trailer brake gear are in good working order. He must also see that the trailer registration plate and Identity Certificate are in position

- 8 -

on the trailer, (N.B. The Identity Certificate referring to the trailer is carried on the tractor portion of Articulated Vehicles).

When applying the brakes of a trailer outfit, the trailer brake must be applied first, to prevent the trailer overrunning the vehicle.

15. A MOTOR DRIVER IS NOT PERMITTED TO CARRY ON HIS VEHICLE ANY PERSON OTHER THAN HIS VANGUARD OR SUCH OTHER COMPANY'S SERVANT AS MAY BE ON BUSINESS WITH THE VEHICLE.

16. PETROL MUST NOT BE USED FOR CLEANING OR OTHER UNAUTHORISED PURPOSES AND ITS UNAUTHORISED REMOVAL FROM A VEHICLE PETROL TANK IS FORBIDDEN.

17. MOTOR DRIVERS ARE FORBIDDEN TO PARTAKE OF INTOXICATING LIQUOR WHILST ON DUTY.

18. Temporary Motor Drivers are expected to be acquainted with the legal requirements of the Road Traffic Acts 1930 - 1934, and the

- 9 -

Rail Traffic Act 1933, including -

*(1) Drivers' Hours of Duty.
(2) Procedure in case of accident
(3) Maximum loads and safe loading.
(4) Drivers' Docket to be compiled currently.
(5) Speed Limits.

*A break of at least half an hour must be taken after a continuous driving period of 5½ hours, and the aggregate driving time on any day must not exceed 11 hours except on two days per week when the aggregate driving time may be extended to 12 hours.
Any time spent on work in connection with the vehicle or its load is classed as driving time.

10. Employees may only drive the types of vehicle for which they have been passed by the Company's Road Transport representative as indicated in the following certificate.

- 10 -

MOTOR DRIVER'S CERTIFICATE.

Name.................................
(in full)

Station..............................

Department...........................

Types of vehicle passed to Drive	BY (signature)	DATE.
....	....	....
....	....	....
....	....	....
....	....	....

Mechanical and Electrical work done by the CME for the Road Transport Department

Installation and connecting up of equipment at GW repair shops and garages around the system was performed by members of the Chief Mechanical Engineer's staff – either locally or sent from Swindon or the other loco works. At Slough and other repair shops, machine tools were belt-driven at first, then equipment had individual electric motors. Starting in the late 1920s when mains electricity became available across the country, electric lighting, power points, electric drives and heating were variously installed or improved in stables, garages and repair shops across the system. For instance, in 1934 electric light was installed in offices at the Mint Stables Paddington, and at Coton Hill, Shrewsbury; and Aberystwyth, Taunton and Goswell Road (Smithfield) in 1935. In 1934/5 rectifiers for battery charging were installed at a number of locations, such as No 7 Arch, Clock Tower Yard, Bristol Temple Meads; and at Paddington, Oxford and Exeter. Cullompton received attention in 1938, at the time when a new garage was built at Kidderminster. The work at Kidderminster was completed at a cost of £303 that was £105 over the authorised sum; a memo of November 1939 to explain the discrepancy said that the estimate was actually for gas lighting, that the soil excavated was very heavy and that there was difficulty in obtaining suitable labour. Similar work was carried out during and after WW2, with electric lights being installed in the paint shop at Foxes Lane (Wolverhampton); power points at the sub-depot at Southall Goods; and alterations to the repair shop at Thingley Jct sidings,

~~Record~~ Office, SWINDON.

G.W.R. (6755)

Chief Mechanical Engineer's Dept.

Reg. No. PM ~~MM~~. 3688.

Desc. To be Tested: Portable Hand Gantry

RECORD OF TESTS AND EXAMINATIONS.

Date	Station	Record to Superintendents: Loco.	Eng.	Elec.	Signal	Marine	Docks	Copy in Tissue Book	No. of Report	Report Filed	Test.	Exam.
30/10/33	Slough Rd. Tpt. Works	✓						22/3	1185	✓	✓	✓
26-8-43.	Rd. Motor Tpt. Shrewsbury	✓							F. 3208	✓	–	✓
23.2.45	do	✓							E. 4831	✓	–	✓
13.2.46	do	✓							E. 4463	✓	–	✓
29.4.47	do	✓							E 8862	✓	–	✓
14.9.48	do	✓							H 618	✓	–	✓
9.11.49	do	–							E.130	✓	.	–
5.12.50	do	✓							E.1094		–	✓
2.5.52	"	✓							D165		–	✓
18.6.53	"								D 1339	✓	–	✓
7.12.55									D 2752	✓	–	✓

See other Side for Remarks. PTO 1,000—B.M./56. 1941.

(Stamp: R. TRANSPORT)

Reg. No. M.M 3688

Remarks	Date	Corres.
Transferred to Shrewsbury	6/11/33	1914
29.12.56 Shrewsbury em Dept.	D. 4093	✓ – ✓
12.1.57 " "	D. 5510	✓ – ✓
19.3.58 " "	D. 7114	✓ – ✓
19.1.59 " "	D 8464	✓ – ✓
3.2.60 " "	D. 9989	✓ – ✓

All equipment in garages and repair shops was tested by the CME department. This record card relates to a portable hand gantry crane originally installed at Slough on 30 October 1933, but moved to Shrewsbury garage in 1934. ***D J Hyde***

Karrier Cob tractor fleet C4104, DLT227, photographed on 23 February 1937 painted on the bonnet with a simple shirt-button design consisting of a cream circular disc having a brown 'GWR' without any thin circular surround, unlike the shirt-button at the top of the cab which is encircled. Vertical windscreen, divided into two with three licence discs. *Author's collection*

When the contractor J T Younghusband & Son hired to the GW at Paddington some 70 vans in 1876 (Chapter 3), every vehicle had to have 'Great Western Railway Co (Owners)/F G Saunders Secty' painted on each side in a conspicuous manner. [Saunders was company secretary between 1863 and 1886, succeeded by J D Higgins 1886-1892; G K Mills 1892-1910; A E Bolter 1910-1926; and F R E Davis from 1926.] The name of the secretary was painted on the forecarriage of GW-owned horse-drawn vehicles, although it is not always visible in photographs. However, on GW *motor* vehicles, the practice soon became standard in the form of 'Great Western Railway/name of Company Secretary/Paddington Station'. The inscription was most often on the nearside of the vehicle. [There was no fleet number on the first Milnes-Daimler lorry of 1904 when it appeared, nor legal ownership in terms of the name of the GWR secretary, but both were present on the second lorry in 1905, see Chapter 4.] After 1933 the name of the secretary no longer appeared, to be replaced by 'GWR PADDINGTON STATION LONDON' painted in white; after WW2, even this disappeared.

In the 1920s, tare weight was painted in white on the black chassis of motors (originally in italics, later in block letters) and 'load not to exceed' values, along with the maximum speed. Following the Traffic Regulation Acts of the early 1930s (Appendix 5), additional information had to be written on the chassis such as the unladen weights of vehicles and axle loadings. It took the form of white block lettering, in the abbreviated form of UW, FAW, BAW (or RAW), and MAW, meaning unladen weight, front axle weight, back (or rear) axle weight respectively, with MAW for middle axle weight on 6-wheeled vehicles. (Some of this information was already on the early GW buses.) However, this seems to be absent at the end of the 1930s, possibly owing to regulations that came into force in October 1938 affecting the legal lettering on vehicles and trailers. Those regulations also stated that maximum tyre sizes were to be indicated on 'heavy motor cars'.

Tractors, trailers and articulated vehicles introduced in the 1920s followed the same general pattern of the brown and cream livery and eventually displayed shirt-buttons where there was space. Back raves and tailboards of some lorries and trailers, and the whole rear of some vans, were painted cream in 1938 and later (this was before blackout regulations came into force).

Although some GW buses carried commercial advertising from the beginning, advertisements appearing on contemporary C&D cartage vans related only to GW matters such as facilities for luggage in advance, excursions, steamer routes, etc. In 1930, however, the GW agreed to display national advertisements on its cartage vehicles.

Vertical windscreen 6-ton mechanical horse with brown-encircled GWR shirt-button on cream circular disc on brown bonnet. Photographed 28 January 1940 in blackout guise. Three licences on split windscreen. *Author's collection*

Standard two-horse 4½-ton tilt van to Diagram D11 showing 'A E BOLTER SECY GWR PADDINGTON' on side of forecarriage. *Author's collection*

GREAT WESTERN RAILWAY.

CHIEF MECHANICAL ENGINEER'S DEPARTMENT,
BRIDGWATER G.W.Z. STATION,
February 3rd 1931.

FEB 4 1931

Your reference :– 246131.

Please quote this reference :—
G 55/312.

Dear Sir,

Advertising on Company's Road Vehicles – Provinces.

With reference to your letter and enclosure of the 19th ulto, I hereunder give particulars of the road vehicles which are suitable for the display of posters:-

Station.	Number.	Class.		If suitable for display of posters.	Size of Poster board required.	
Barnstaple	2615	Covd	Lorry.	Yes	3'6"	x 2'4".
"	3012	"	"	"	"	"
Bridgwater	1736	"	"	"	"	"
	2615	"	"	"	"	"
	2100	"	"	"	"	"
Taunton	1867	"	"	"	"	"
	3397	"	"	"	"	"
	2659	"	"	"	"	"
Tiverton	2396	"	"	"	"	"
	1572	"	"	"	"	"
Wellington	2543	"	"	"	"	"

Yours truly,

W Satunley

A.W.H.Christison, Esq.,

Newton Abbot. 10.

Provincial advertising. *Author's collection*

Vehicle Numbering

Horse-drawn vehicles were usually numbered sequentially, the greater the number, the newer the vehicle, but there was some grouping of numbers for special vehicles such as large floats which in later years were found in the 1200s and 1300s. It is not known how the numbering of existing horse vehicles at Hockley fitted in with the numbering of the first products from the Swindon road-wagon shop when it opened in 1870. Horse vehicles not only had the number painted on in various locations, it was also incised on removable parts of the wooden bodies. Vehicles taken over from Agents were added to the horse wagon fleet and numbered. In some cases on scrapping of old vehicles, previous fleet numbers of horse vehicles were re-used.

Before motors were introduced, horse-drawn vehicles were used by the Chief Mechanical Engineer's department and by the Chief (civil) Engineer's department – and even much later it seems; Order 1812 of December 1944 instructed Mr Dent the Road Motor Engineer .'to take cost of renumbering Horse-Drawn vehicles in Engineering and CME's departments' service.'

The original numbering scheme for *all* GW road 'cars', irrespective of being motor- or steam- bus, traction engine, van, lorry, car or motorcycle was also a single sequential fleet list. Numbers 1 and 2 were the Lizard buses of 1903 and more buses took succeeding numbers until the first goods lorry of October 1904 became number 37 in the list; the second lorry was fleet 44 of February 1905. The first parcel van was fleet 40. Although having a lower fleet number than the second lorry, the parcel van did not appear until June 1905. Appendix 1 gives the fleet list compiled by the late John Cummings.

From January 1904, it was decreed by Government that all motor vehicles that ran on the public highway should be registered and display number plates (Appendix 2). At first, registration of GW vehicles was done locally where vehicles were allotted to work. The Lizard buses (that predated the regulation) eventually received County of Cornwall AF numbers. The first GW lorry had a London 'A' number, but the second had a Plymouth 'CO' registration. Where to position the number plates was not clear at first and there are pictures of registration plates attached to the sides of GW vehicles and to the chassis, rather than at the front and rear which later became standard. Sometimes there was a dash between letter(s) and number; even full stops between letters. Most had white letters and numbers on a black ground, but the second GW lorry CO-112 (with a dash) was black on white (Chapter 5). Some have zeros in front of the number as in 'BH 020' rather than BH 20 for the 1908 electric parcels van.

Number plates tell us where vehicles were first stationed, eg Straker & Squire parcels vans at Birkenhead (CM plates), Birmingham (O), Cardiff (BO), Liverpool (K), Bristol (AE) and Manchester (N). The only makers to register vehicles at the factory before handing over to the GW were the Yorkshire Steam Motor Company (the Teme Valley 3-ton steam wagon in 1905 with Leeds number plate U 308, Chapter 4) and Ransomes, Sims & Jefferies for their electric vans of 1919, all of which had DX (Ipswich) numbers. After the formation of the Road Transport Department in 1922, new vehicle registration was done centrally and all new vehicles received London number plates. Non-London registrations appear thereafter in the fleet list only (a) on vehicles absorbed at the Grouping, (b) from purchase of second-hand vehicles, and (c) from those taken over from cartage agents. Whatever changes there may have been with different bodies on the same chassis, or changing of fleet numbers, the registration number always remained with the chassis.

'Mixed' consecutive fleet numbering continued until 1914 when some attempt at grouping together similar types of vehicle was made; in 1913 three Maudslay buses had been bought and given the next available fleet Nos 178-80 in the usual way. But when a dozen more were delivered in 1914, it was decided to group them all under fleet numbers 201-215, the earlier three being re-numbered 201-3, suggesting that the 200s numbers were intended to be allotted to new buses. (Until the 1600-series of 1929, '-00' numbers were not used, unless they were vehicles later transferred from elsewhere.) Similarly, when 24 Milnes-Daimler 1-ton parcels vans arrived in 1914, they were given 301-24, suggesting the use of the 300s for parcel vans. Later, in 1920, the 400s series for lorries was commenced. However, this separation was not always maintained.

When motor vehicles were re-numbered, withdrawn or sold on, their fleet numbers would become vacant. Up to the mid-1920s, policy was to re-use the old numbers, so that there are 'second users' of some numbers. Thus when the three Munnion-bodied Clarkson steam buses were found to give considerable boiler trouble, the GW sold them in 1907 (see Chapter 4). This left fleet numbers 34-6 vacant at the beginning of 1908, at a time when a dozen 20hp Milnes-Daimler buses were being purchased: three of the new vehicles were given the old fleet numbers with the other nine given the next 'new' fleet numbers 96-105. A Liversidge-bodied Durkopp bus of 1905 was got rid of in 1910, and its fleet number 48 was given to a Milnes-Daimler 30hp 5-ton lorry in 1911; another Durkopp (fleet 62) was similarly de-listed in 1911, and the number assigned to another Milnes-Daimler.

The old numbers of the first 3 Maudslay buses that had been moved to the 200s were subsequently assigned as follows: 178 to a new Straker & Squire 1-ton parcel van in 1916; 179 to the Knox tractor in 1918 (Chapter 5); and 180 to another Straker & Squire 1-ton parcel van in 1918. However, this last van was soon re-numbered to fleet 95, the former number of the just-withdrawn early electric parcels van BH 020 of 1908, in order to create space for the first ex-army AEC 45hp vehicles that arrived in 1919. Eleven lorries were given the next available new fleet numbers 180-190; and 191-99 became nine GWR-bodied buses on the same AEC army chassis. But to keep all new buses together, 191-199 soon were renumbered to 225-217 (reverse order) and added to the Maudslays with fleet 216 in between being another GW-bodied bus on an AEC MY-type chassis. The rest of the 200-series were given to buses bodied at Swindon to fit AEC ex-army chassis. To keep the ex-army lorries together, fleet 180-190 were re-numbered 401- 411 in 1920 to start the 400 series, which was filled up by the autumn of 1923. Since interchange of bodies was done relatively easily on vehicles with simple, straight-sided chassis, many AEC lorries were given Swindon-built bus/charabanc bodies for summer use, as listed in Appendix 1.

In January 1922 the GW *Road Motor Car Department* morphed into the *Road Transport Department*, now to include horse-drawn vehicles. By this time numbering had reached about 258 (the most recent bus); 330 (newest parcel van); and 461 (latest motor lorry), and different categories (bus, van and lorry) of newly-acquired vehicles were numbered according to this scheme, except that the 300s later became a bit of a rag-bag of all sorts of vehicle rather than just parcels vans.

The vacated fleet numbers caused by transfers of buses to the 200s were eventually allocated to Austin 20hp buses (193/6-8); an Austin 12hp car (195); a Willys-Overland 15-cwt van ex-Cardiff Rly (194); and the GW's first Fordson tractor (199) delivered in September 1922.

The first Thornycroft vans (originally fleet C1-10, see later) became 501-510, the rest of the 500s being Burford 30-cwt chassis dating from August 1922 through November 1924 (mostly lorries or vans, but some were buses). Some of the Burford vans were replacements for Straker & Squire parcels vans dating from 1911/2. In 1923 the 400s were used up, so the 600s and 700s were allocated to ex-army AEC 45hp YC vehicles, some having been bought from dealers as late as 1927. They were nearly all lorries, some of which, as noted in the Fleet List, having bus/charabanc bodies in the summer. The 800 series began with another AEC YC type XB 9847 of 1921, but it was moved back to fleet 709 as a van, and replaced as 801 by a Buckingham-bodied Burford 30-cwt bus of 1924. The rest of the 800s were all vehicles on Burford 30-cwt chassis, a mixture of buses, lorries and vans. The 900s were all Thornycroft A1 chassis from 1925-7. Fleet 901-40 were buses, many of which would later transfer to the new national bus operators between 1928-30. The rest were lorries and vans; a number of the vans were for the Special Contract Delivery scheme (MacFarlane Lang and so on, Chapter 10). Fleet 945 of 1926 started life as a lorry, but had a GW bus body between 1931-2 and in that form was transferred to Bristol Tramways in 1932 (when the Corris Rly came into the GW fold from the Bristol company).

The 1000 series started with eleven Burford 30-cwt lorries of 1926, followed by 18 Ford 1-ton lorries, then four Thornycroft A1 lorries of August 1927 (fleet 1030-3). The latter were part of a much bigger order of 100 vehicles delivered up to the year 1930, of which in 1929 twelve were A2-type. Rather like the Maudslay buses of 1913/4, the 1400 series was started for these Thornycrofts and fleet 1030-3 became 1400-3. The vacated numbers were quickly filled by three more Ford 1-tonners (1030/2/3) and by a Thornycroft rigid-chassis '6-wheeled' lorry (fleet 1031 of 1928). Fleet numbers 1037-48 were to have been GW buses but were delivered directly to the new Western National/Devon General companies in 1928, leaving the numbers spare. Thereafter the 1000 series becomes a haphazard mix of makers (Chevrolet tippers; a Thornycroft J-type; Ford vans and lorries; International Harvester and Fordson tractors; Austin cars; Leyland and Morris lorries; Guy and Leyland buses; a Latil van converted from a 14-seater bus; Thornycroft JC-type lorries; Scammell 6-wheeled permanently-articulated lorries; and Austin cars). Fleet 1091-98 were various buses ordered by the GW but delivered directly to the Western National bus company; 1099 was a Vauxhall car also sent to Western National. The 1000-series (as did the 1100 series) included some motor vehicles obtained from former cartage agents.

Fleet 1101-3 were three AEC 45hp ex-army lorries that had been bought in 1926 from United Automobile Services. When seven Morris '22' lorries and vans were purchased in June 1928, they were assigned fleet 1100-6, and the AECs were moved back to become 288-90. There they were joined by five ex-army AECs that were bought as late as 1927 (the last obtained by the GW). At least two of these final AECs were buses (fleet 291/3) that went to the Western Welsh bus company. More Morris '22' and '21' vans were purchased in the summer of 1928 (fleet 1120-42). Numbers from 1107 – 1119 were used for (a) ex-agent vehicles; (b) a Karrier road sweeper (1108); (c) a low-deck lorry made by Walkers of Wigan (1109); (d) a Bramco Mercury tractor for the Swindon loco factory (1110); and (e) Guy buses. Fleet 1143-9 were Lancia and Thornycroft buses, with the rest including Fordson tractors, Carette tricycles and other vehicles.

1201-99 were buses registered between September 1926 and June 1928, all of which passed to the new bus companies. 1301-50 were Thornycroft 4/5-ton lorries delivered from December 1926 to March 1927 and 1351-99 were Thornycroft 'PB' lorries delivered between November 1927 and September 1928; 1400-59 were Thornycroft A1-type lorries (including 1400-3 transferred from 1030-3) but 1460-99 were buses on the same Thornycroft chassis, the whole series being supplied between the summers of 1928 and 1930. Some of the buses went directly to the new bus companies. Similarly, 1501-99 were all buses supplied between March 1928 and July 1929, again all eventually passing to private bus companies, some directly. Fleet 1600 was a Guy bus registered on New Year's Day 1929 and more Guys and other bus makes (Gilfold, Thornycroft and Maudslay) were given numbers in the 1600s as well as ex-agent vehicles. At the end of the 1600s a variety of different cars for company use are found. In November 1929 a run of numbers allocated to Thornycroft lorries (types-PB, A1 and J) was begun starting with 1700 which extended to fleet 1882 with a final A8-type 8-wheeled Thornycroft lorry at 1899. Fleet 1900-93 during 1929 were for Associated-Daimler '428' vehicles, with 1994/5 being two AEC 8-wheeled 'Mammoth' lorries. Thornycroft 'A1' lorries were numbered 2000 onwards from November 1929; type-PB were 2100-73 with the remaining numbers unused; 2200-2298 were type-JJ; and 2299 was a 6/8-ton Thornycroft on trial and returned to the makers. The 2300-series contained a variety of tractors, Dennis 2-ton lorries, two Thornycroft JC 10-ton lorries on trial, Guys, Fords and ex-agent vehicles. Fleet 2400-99 were all Thornycroft A1 vans and the 2500-series were Morris vans, excepting 2544-9 that were Morris 6-wheel vehicles.

Second-hand vehicles bought by the GW and those acquired from agents were sent to Slough for numbering, or possibly directly to the district where they were going to work and numbered there. Numbers were assigned *before* repainting. Numbers of new vehicles were allotted before an order was placed rather than on delivery. Sequential numbering of the C&D fleet continued until 1935 when the system was completely re-vamped. The 'tarpaulin-overs' on both horse-drawn and motor vans were numbered but the numbers originally did not coincide with the vehicle fleet number (nor with trailer numbers). Later there was a period when they did, as seen in a number of illustrations in this book. Other pictures may be found in *GWR Goods Services* vol 2A, pp 55/57.

The bodies of all GW motor vehicles had their own numbers, separate from the fleet numbers; body numbers (usually beginning with the prefix 'G') were painted in appropriate places such as on the raves of flatbed lorries. While swapping of bodies went out of favour when the GW ceased to operate buses at the beginning of the 1930s, what did come along was the idea of making fixed bodies 'convertible' so that a flatbed lorry, for example, could have detachable hinged sides that in addition might have hoop sticks for a tilt; or could be converted for cattle haulage by substituting high slatted sides for the normal sides, and providing hoops and tilt cover.

Vehicle numbers prefixed by a letter before 1935

The regular fleet list consisted just of numbers without any letter prefixes and it wasn't until a 1935 renumbering scheme that standard C&D motor vehicles received new numbers prefixed by the letters A, B, C or D. However, some letter-prefixed numbers did exist previously:

(i) The prefix 'S' was used for steam-propelled vehicles. The Yorkshire steam lorry fleet 81 of 1905 became S1 and other early steamers became S2-5 (Appendix 1). Fleet S6-16 were probably the eleven GWR steamrollers, the working locations of which are listed in the fleet list, although no photographs have been found of them bearing 'S' numbers. Four Foden steamers were bought in 1929, and they were assigned the next available numbers S17 to S20. When the early 1930's Road Traffic Acts came into force, the heavy unladen weight of unsprung steam wagons resulted in expensive road taxation, and no more steamers were bought by the GW. Existing steamers retained their S-numbers but when the 1935 re-numbering scheme came into being, the Road Transport Department decided to use the S-prefix to indicate *non-standard* motor vehicles that were not run-of-the-mill C&D stock and were 'special' in some way (see later).

(ii) There was a short period during WW1, and up to the formation of the Road Transport Department in 1922, when letter prefixes were used for new makes of vehicles. The first Thornycrofts bought by the GW (30-cwt vans ordered in 1914, but not all delivered until the end of WW1) were labelled C1-10 (later fleet 501-10). New electric C&D vehicles bought in 1919/20 were labelled E5-14 (with the implication that E1-4 were applied to existing older electric vehicles although only two are known – fleet 82 and fleet 45, of which fleet 45 was withdrawn in 1919). In April 1921 the GW purchased Fords for the first time (1-ton lorries): they were labelled F1-6 (later fleet 325-30). The policy of the new Road Transport Department was to discontinue C, E and F prefixing, and in February 1922 vehicles received normal fleet numbers (it was noted in a committee minute of May 1922 that E13 had not yet been renumbered). We see that F numbers lasted fewer than 10 months.

Ford Model T 1-ton lorry with Bristol registration HT-3451. One of 6 delivered in April 1921 by International Motors. Initial fleet number F5 changed after formation of Road Transport Department in 1922. Electric headlights: side lamps on sides of windscreen. On cabside is a single tax disc below oval window, followed by F5 in shaded gold lettering painted directly on to vehicle (not on a plaque), then 'Load not to exceed/1-0-0', with 'Tare 1-0-0/With all Equipment' in italics. Seriffed lettering along raves. Left-hand drive. No front brakes. Rear wheels of ex-army AEC lorry to right. ***GWR/P J Kelley collection***

The E prefix was revived just before nationalisation for new electric vans.

(iii) The prefix 'T' was used *from the outset* for all trailers drawn by *self-propelled* vehicles (i.e. *not* horse-drawn wagons). Photographs of the 1919 Knox tractor show trailer number T-7. Since three trailers were bought for this tractor it follows that either T-1 to T-4 or T-1 to T-6 had been the running numbers of trailers on (i) the earlier steam-hauled services at Bilston, and between Liverpool and Birkenhead (see Chapters 4 and 6), and (ii) the 4 trailers (called 'lorries' in the purchase orders, see Chapter 4) bought with the two Wallis and Steevens traction engines in 1905. Thereafter new 2- and 4-wheeled tow bar trailers (such as those manufactured by Carrimore, Eagle and so on) were numbered sequentially with a T-prefix and this continued for all the Karrier Cob and Scammell mechanical horse trailers until the 1935 renumbering. It is important to note that when some horse-drawn vehicles such as floats were adapted with special tow bars to be drawn by tractors in the late 1920s/early 1930s, fleet numbers were prefixed by T and 'for use with tractors' was painted on the fascia; floats and other vehicles that remained horse-drawn *never* had T-prefixed numbers. However, the Swindon drawing of 1931 shows that some were adaptable for haulage by both tractor horse or horse by altering the attachments to the splinter bar.

An important illustration from the 1931 Bath & West Show at Torquay regarding the numbering of horse-drawn floats after conversion to haulage by tractor. All horse floats for use with tractors came to be prefixed with letter 'T', but this float, number 1357, shows an intermediate stage where no 'T' has yet been added, even though on the left of the cream-painted plank on the headboard it reads in script 'For use with tractors/Maximum load 4-10-0'. (A similar float also with a windlass (winch), with un-prefixed number 1359, is shown in Kelley, p165.) Both floats have old-pattern hubs, and chains to go around spokes for brakes when parked. Later, and often fitted with old motor vehicle wheels, these converted horse floats were coded Nico C (6-tons) and Nico D (10-tons). The Fordson tractor (YU 5249, fleet 1178) was the first of 18 purchased from Pratts of Sutton, Surrey, on 30 September 1927 (numbers 1178-95). Rear wheels are sprung Muir Hill and have double solid rubber tyres. Rear-view mirror on offside; rolled-up tarpaulin alongside engine. *STEAM Swindon*

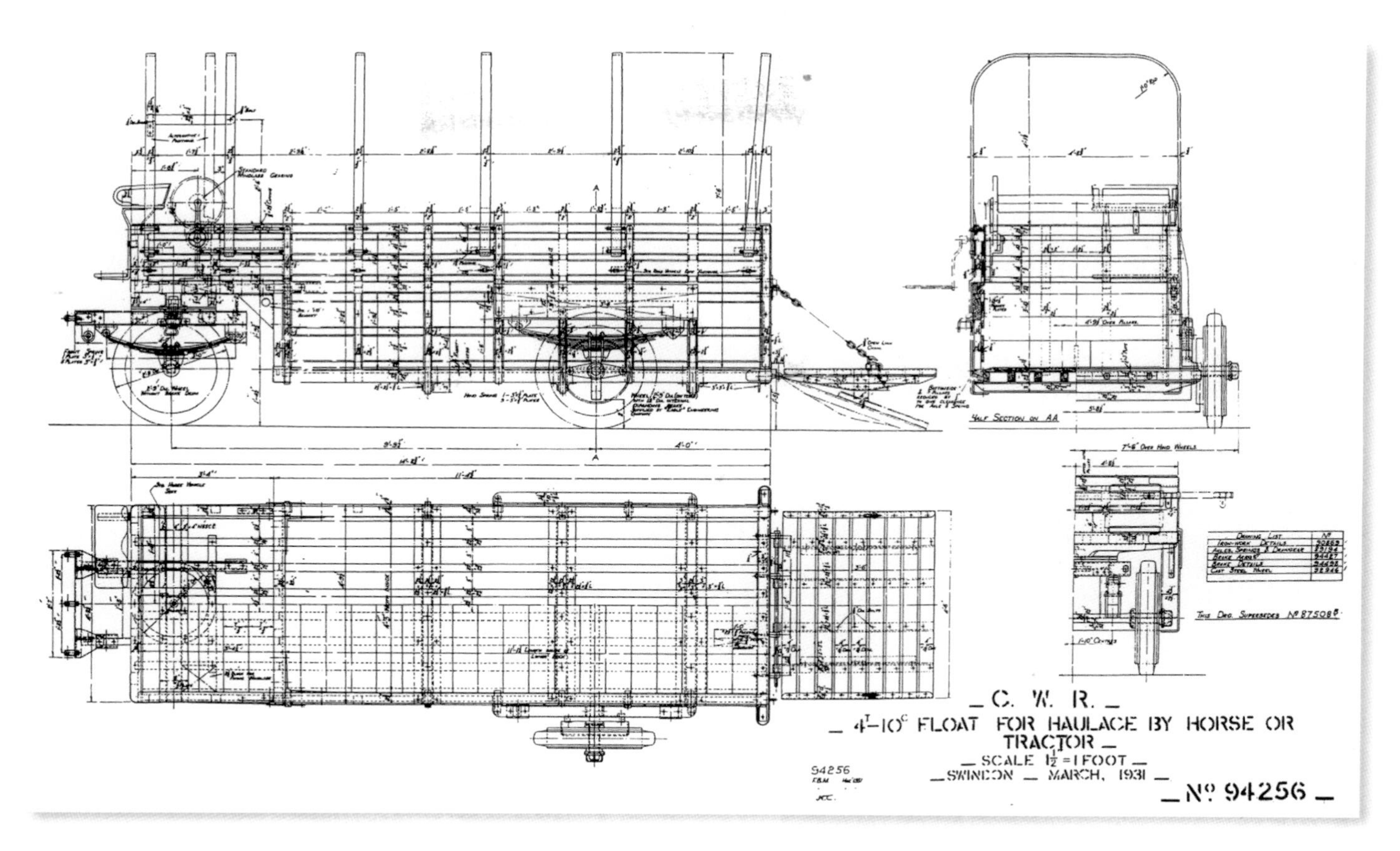

Horse float originally to Diagram E4 now converted to haulage by tractor. Fitted with solid-rubber-tyred wheels from old motor vehicles (rear from ex-army AEC chassis replacing former 4ft 6ins diameter wooden wheels that required a cranked-axle). Brake on rear wheels operated by hand wheel and vertical screw. Splinter bar has fittings for both towbar and shafts. Windlass (winch) at front. Cattle register box above which in script are 'Tare with tilt and hoops' and 'Tare without', neither of which has been painted in (should there be a colour here?).
GWR/D J Hyde collection

All motor vehicles employed by the CME department were given numbers prefixed by

'L'. Those used on the public highway had to pay road tax, have licence plates and had regular fleet numbers as well as L-numbers. But tractors and similar vehicles confined to the works at Swindon, Wolverhampton, Caerphilly and Newton Abbot and elsewhere had no need to be licensed, did not have fleet numbers and were known by their L-numbers. L-numbering continued after the 1935 renumbering scheme. Road-taxed vans and lorries belonging to the CME usually did not have the L-number obviously painted on, although there were exceptions, as illustrated in Chapter 5.

One hundred Thornycroft 'A1' chassis were delivered to the GW in late 1929/early 1930, fleet 2000-99, of which fleet 2000-19 were given Swindon-built van bodies and the rest mostly flat lorry bodies. The first, shown here, UW 9701, was jointly-owned by the LMS and GW. Photographed in June 1940 at Cardiff Newtown (multi-storey stables in right background) when the vehicle conformed to blackout regulations (mask to nearside headlamp), white edges to mudguards (front looks decidedly dodgy). Since these vehicles were 2-tonners, and fortuitously happened to be numbered in the 2000s, when the 1935 re-numbering scheme to include type of vehicle was introduced, re-numbering was not necessary and only a prefix letter was required. However, the letter here is 'A' that applied to flatbed lorries; by rights it should have been 'B'. *GWR/D J Hyde collection*

1935 and afterwards renumbering of GW cartage fleet

In 1935, the numbering system for regular C&D motor vehicles was completely altered so as to indicate both the *type* of vehicle and also its *carrying capacity*. There was a letter prefix followed by a four-digit number. The letter prefix was supposed to indicate in broad terms the type of vehicle: 'A' flatbed lorries with detachable sides; 'B' vans; 'C' 3-wheeled tractors for articulated vehicles; 'D' 4-wheeled tractors having the Scammell coupling. The first digit of four indicated the load – '1' one-ton, '2' two-tons, and so on. The remaining three digits made up the running number of the vehicle. Unlike the C and F prefixing at the end of WW1, the scheme did not distinguish between make of vehicle. The new fleet number was painted on the cabside *with* the prefix letter, but on the chassis *without* the prefix letter.

Before the change, the sequential running numbers for all types of vehicle having all sorts of tonnages had reached the 4000s and greater, so unless the first digit corresponded with the tonnage, most numbers had to be changed. Furthermore, vehicles still running that had fleet numbers below 999 could not just be given a prefix letter in the new scheme. The overall design for renumbering is not completely clear but it is possible to give individual examples either (a) because 'before and after' photographs exist of the same vehicle (same number plate, but different fleet numbers) but this is very rare; or (b) from glossy prints of official photographs kept at the Road Transport/Road Motor Engineer's Department at Slough where pre-1935 (un-prefixed) running numbers of existing vehicles have been crossed out and the new number marked on the print (but without the prefix letter). An example of (a) shows that GK 6138 – a Thornycroft 'JJ' 8-ton lorry – originally fleet 2238 became (A)8036. Regarding (b), Morris 1-ton van 1122 became (B)1010; Fleet 1910, an Associated Daimler 4/5-ton lorry became (A)4223; Fleet 2285, one of the two Thornycroft diesels of 1930, became (A)8085; Fleet 2354, a 1½-ton Ford lorry, became (A)1507. The 30-cwt Thornycroft with a Farmers' Utility body fleet 2444 became (A)2173; Morris 2-ton forward control van of 1932, originally 2800, became (B)2357 and 6-wheel Ford departmental lorry 3181 became 4601.

Woman worker greasing swivel pins of a Thornycroft 'JJ' GK 6138 that was originally fleet 2238 but is now 8036. White-painted mudguards to conform with WW2 blackout regulations. *STEAM Swindon*

Ford 1½-ton lorry of the early 1930s, photographed when new in the forecourt of Bristol Temple Meads station. Livery all-over brown (no cream above waist of cab) but cream panel along raves with 'great western railway' and body number. 'great western railway/f r e davis secretary/paddington' at bottom of cab side. Original fleet number 2354 has been altered to 1507 following 1935 renumbering scheme. *GWR/P J Kelley collection*

Associated Daimler '428' forward control lorry of May 1929, registration GU9318 and original fleet number 1910 that has been altered to 4223 following the 1935 renumbering scheme. 'G.W.R' on cast plate above radiator. Was the Country Lorry vehicle at Shrivenham with pillars and chains for milk traffic? *GWR/P J Kelley collection*

Scammell 3-wheel rigid chassis 30-cwt lorry. Painting date is 4 May 1938 and photograph was taken on 30 May 1938. Assignment of fleet number A4601 is peculiar according to the 1935 re-numbering scheme, since the first digit '4' is supposed to indicate a 4-ton lorry. Bulb for horn inside cab above driver's right hand. Shirt-button consists of an unencircled black 'GWR' on a cream circular disc that itself is encircled by a black line. Toolbox attached to chassis. *GWR/P J Kelley collection*

There are many anomalies in this supposed rationalisation. Fleet 976 (Macfarlane Lang biscuits van) became (B)1827, even though its capacity was 2 tons. Another Macfarlane Lang 2-ton van 2518 retained its fleet number, but with an A prefix rather than the expected B. Sometimes the old fleet number was retained and simply letter-prefixed, as in the case of a Dennis 4-tonner obtained from the Wilts Cooperative Society in the early 1930s and originally allocated fleet 2341 which became B2341 – even though it should have had an A-prefix, and the running number should have commenced with '4'. Repainting took time: in 1940, Thornycroft A1 2-ton van, fleet 2014, GC9159, of December 1929, was still running with an un-prefixed number.

After 1935, newly-built vehicles were given numbers according to the new system which should have lasted for the foreseeable future. However, photographs from Slough show that vehicles with *letter-prefixed numbers have also been altered.* Sometimes the reason seems clear as in the case of Morris 2-ton flatbed of 21 February 1936, painted A3800 when new, being altered to A2638 to reflect its true load capacity. Again, a 2-ton Thornycroft lorry with sides, wrongly painted A3205 when new in June 1936, was corrected later to A2612; a 25/30-cwt van used on the Hill-Evans contract that had been painted A2849 was later altered to A2406. In both cases, as a van, why wasn't B used? The alterations of already-prefixed fleet numbers seem to apply only to A-prefixed vehicles and may have arisen because carrying capacity was rounded up when the scheme was implemented (a 2½-ton capacity was counted as 3-tons), which might have led to overloading, hence the alterations. But what about vehicles whose carrying capacity was less than 1-ton or more than 9 tons? Why was the number of the Hill-Evans van left to start with '2' when it was rated at only 25/30-cwt? The Signal Department van A4055 was altered to (A)2763 in January 1939 and, as far as is known, the 'second alterations' were completed during that year.

Normal control 2-ton Ford chassis of 1935 fitted with Farmers utility body, registration ALN 335. The fleet number of 3135 has been altered to 2592 on this glossy print from the Slough album to reflect its 2-ton capacity. There's also a note saying that the (single) licence holder (on front of body) was subsequently moved forward to the windscreen. *GWR/D J Hyde collection*

Hill-Evans & Co Ltd special contract railhead van, fleet A2849, later altered to A2406 (no letter prefix on original chassis number). Greater London registration. 'GWR PADDINGTON STATION LONDON' at bottom of cab door. 'LONDON STORES/GWR GOODS DEPOT/ALFRED ROAD/PADDINGTON W2' on lower body panel (the name of Paddington New Yard was changed to Alfred Road in 1939). Vehicle has front bumper. *GWR/D J Hyde collection*

Capacities less than 1-ton did not fit the 4-digit 1935 re-numbering scheme. Here is a 15-cwt Commer lorry of late 1939, registration FLL383, with 3-digit fleet number A524, that perhaps could be read as A0524 with '05' meaning ½-ton; '524' without A-prefix on black chassis. Painting date is 9 September 1939, the vehicle being photographed on 7 October 1939. White-edged mudguards to conform to blackout regulations. Spare tyre behind cab. 'great western railway' in cream panels along hinged sides with body number G2780 below panel nearest cab. Cream tailboard with encircled brown GWR roundel; encircled yellow shirt-button on back of cab. Tailboard has no 'holes' that would display rear numberplate and lights, so not intended to be driven with tailboard down. *GWR/P J Kelley collection*

Two-ton Morris 'Equi-Load' van with body extended over the cab roof (so-called 'Luton' van body) for the Signal Department at Neath. Registration EYV758, photographed on 29 December 1938 with fleet number A4055 that was altered to 2763 in 1939 to reflect 2-ton capacity according to the 1935 re-numbering scheme (service vehicles may have had their fleet numbers altered later than C&D vehicles, or had been forgotten about). Electric horn attached to front bumper. Two licence discs on split windscreen that has wipers on passenger side as well as driver's. *GWR/P J Kelley collection*

Vulcan 6V flatbed lorry GYM 5 with fleet number B 5058, even though 'B' was intended for vans. Vulcans were made in Southport. Body G 3159 painted on extreme left cream panel (sometimes body number is found on other vehicles on the extreme right panel after 'Great Western Railway'). End of body is cream, so just before WW2. The type of vehicle used (often with hinged sides) on road trunking duties in the Zonal scheme (see Chapter 10). ***STEAM Swindon***

Two-ton Morris Commercial forward-control chassis fitted with van body. Photographed new on 12 September 1932. Fleet 2800 (later altered to 2357), but no number plate yet. Large brown G W R (no full stops) on cream-painted side, with cream G.W.R. (with full stops) on brown plaque above cab. Electric horn fitted to cross bar in front of radiator. ***Author's collection***

Not only was the B prefix not used where it seemingly ought to have been, but the C and D prefixes were not used consistently in the renumbering scheme. For example, in 1942 a Bedford-Scammell 4-wheeled tractor was numbered C8810 (the series for 3-wheeled tractor mechanical horses), but an apparently similar vehicle photographed at Cardiff Newtown after WW2 is 'correctly' numbered D8945.

When the 1935 scheme came into being, it was decided to use the redundant S-prefix, used originally for steam wagons, to identify *non-standard motor* vehicles (existing steamers retained their numbers). Three- and four-digit S numbers are found. For example, S419 was a Latil tractor fuelled by producer gas dating from 1938 (but a Latil tractor was running in WW2 as just fleet 416); S481 was a Gardner-engined Foden winch tractor operating in 1947. Where 4-digit S numbers appear, the first digit does *not* represent a particular haulage capacity. Thus S1086 was a Leyland 4-wheel winch tractor of 1935; S2530 was given to a 6-ton 4-wheel Morris Commercial; S4600 was an experimental 30-cwt Scammell light lorry having a 10hp air-cooled twin-cylinder engine beneath the body, and driver exit either side; S4623 was a Ford Sussex 6-wheel lorry introduced in December 1938.

Morris forward control chassis fitted with so-called 'Luton' van body that is extended over the roof of the cab and useful for lightweight, but bulky, loads. Registration CYP391 of January 1937. Considered to be a 'special' vehicle, hence the S-prefixed fleet S4000 that has been altered to S3002. Space for advertisement on lower half of body. 'U.W. (not painted in)/SPEED 20 M.P.H./GWR/PADDINGTON STATION/ LONDON'. *Author's collection*

Fordson lorry, registration FGT 465, with GW special cab and fixed sides (body number G2744 painted in panel below the four stowed hoopsticks). 'Mini tilt' behind cab. Painting date (SN30·1·39) is on chassis to right of rear wheel. All-cream tailboard with shirt-button. No light fittings above rear number plate. Photographed in April 1939, by which time fleet A4517 on cab door has been altered in ink to 3008. The revised number 3008 is also just visible properly painted on door in yellow (with no prefix) below A4517. *GWR/P J Kelley collection*

Thornycroft A1 forward control van of 1929 photographed in 1940 still with un-prefixed fleet number. GWR/D J Hyde collection

A summary of all the above is:

Fleet numbers *without* prefix letter: road motors built before 1935, noting exceptions given above for C-, E- and F-prefixed numbers.

Four-digit fleet numbers *with* prefix letter: (a) new vehicles built after 1935 and (b) renumbered road motors built before 1935.

1935 and afterwards renumbering of GW trailers and painting on of Telegraph Codes

As noted above, from the early 1900s motor-hauled trailers were numbered sequentially, without regard to capacity, but always with a 'T' prefix. Policy was to apply the 1935 scheme to indicate carrying capacity to trailers as well as to motors. Furthermore, it was decided to paint on their telegraph codes when renumbering.

Renumbering of trailers had a lower priority than that of C&D vehicles, and took longer, so there was a period in the mid-late 1930s when codes appeared on trailers that were still being numbered according to the old sequential series; later the numbers would be altered to the new scheme. Scammell AL 3-ton flat trailer coded *Dyak F* new in 1936 was originally sequentially numbered T-1059 according to the pre-1935 scheme, but was later changed to T-3304 in the Slough photographic album. Again from 1936, horsebox trailer *Nico H,* originally given sequential number T-1191, was altered to T-9002 in 1937; similarly for T-1021 that became T-7704.

In the renumbering of existing trailers, three-digit numbers were permitted (where the first still indicated load capacity) for what were still serviceable equipment. For example, Eagle 2-wheel trailers of 1926 numbered T-19 and T-36 became T-400 and T-412 respectively, and were later coded *Dyak C/H* (even though the *Dyak C* supposedly could carry only a 2-ton load). *Nico E* 'Harrow Industrial' 3-ton cattle trailer T-395 was altered to T-300.

Horse-drawn vehicles that had been converted for motor haulage now had telegraph codes painted on, such as *Nico C* (converted 4-wheeled 6-ton horse float) and *Nico D* (4-ton). Similarly, *Dido F* was a 6-ton converted 4-wheeled horse trailer and *Dido J* a converted 4-ton horse furniture van. Again, *Vibo D* was a converted 4½-ton horse timber carriage and *Vibo E* (10-ton).

Pictures show that a number of *Dyak* mechanical-horse trailers received code suffixes not to be found in the 1939 code book, such as *Dyak AC/OL/OP/OR/OU*. In fact, there's no *Dyak O* in the code book at all. There is a January 1939 photograph of a Tasker drop frame trailer fitted for carrying glass, that has code *'Dyak.O.L'* painted on and numbered T-1820, that has been renumbered in ink to T-4600, implying that the new code was in place in early 1939. Other new codes must

Two-wheel Eagle (of Warwick) trailer, fleet T36 (renumbered T412 after 1937), photographed at Bampton on 26 October 1926. Two-ton and 4-ton Eagle trailers were later coded Dyak C and Dyak H respectively (no load or code indicated on trailer in 1926, only speed 12mph). Underframe was an equilateral triangle of I-beams with the axle as base, and the hitch and jockey stand at the apex. Three-plank body raised above wheels which have arc-shaped spokes. The new Fordson tractor (fleet 1164, YR2657) was one of nine delivered to the GWR on 12 October 1926. It is fitted with Muir-Hill internally-sprung rear wheels. The livery is grey with two black-painted oil lamps attached at either end of a strap across fuel tank over engine. Tax disc above fleet number on radiator. Fire extinguisher to left of driver. ***GWR/P J Kelley collection***

Scammell Dyak OC trailer altered from T1668 to T4451. ***STEAM Swindon***

Half tilt body for articulated trailer built early in WW2 (white edges to mudguards for blackout regulations). Originally numbered T-2191 (implying 2-tons capacity) but later altered to T-8705 since small writing at right end on bottom plank of front of trailer says 'load not to exceed 6 tons with 3-wheel tractor/8 tons with 4 wheel tractor'. Small lettering at left says 'tyre pressures 95lbs'. The white-painted arc ratchet below the writing can alter the angle of the jockey wheel when parked. Coded Dyak OW ¾ not in 1939 telegraph code book. ***GWR/P J Kelley collection***

Tasker 6-ton trailer of February 1938 fitted with full tilt body and 1934 standard coupling. Originally numbered T801 and erroneously coded Dyak OC (intended for 2-wheel Scammell trailers), vehicle has been not only renumbered to T971 but recoded to Dido R (not in 1939 telegraph code book). No provision for braking from tractor so dickey seat for brakeman. ***GWR/D J Hyde collection***

Brockhouse 15-ton 8-wheel heavy-duty well-deck trailer of June 1936 coded Titan B (not in 1939 telegraph Code Book). Wheels sprung in pairs. Painted in departmental grey, it has a black 1934 standard coupling that sticks forward on which is conspicuously painted 'danger'. 'Great Western Raily' along bottom of well. 'gwr paddington station london' in white on black panel on forecarriage. Divided pairs of rear wheel. Originally numbered T-700, it has been given fleet T-1510, where the first two digits '15' may indicate capacity, that would not accord with the 1935 renumbering scheme. ***Author's collection***

have appeared during or after WW2 (*Dyak AC* dates from 1946).

Perusal of the numbering of mechanical horse trailers built in WW2 that are given in Chapter 6 reveals other incongruities in the numbering system.

A summary of all the above is:

Before 1937, all trailers drawn by tractors and road motors were numbered sequentially and prefixed by 'T'.

After 1937, existing and new trailers were given 4-digit (some 3-digit) numbers prefixed by 'T', the first of which indicated load capacity as in the 1935 scheme for motors.

After 1935, the telegraph code was painted on trailers.

No paperwork seems to have survived about the complete scheme of renumbering motors and trailers so all that is known is provided by the album of glossy pictures kept at Slough on which revised numbers have been inked in. Note that an official print obtained from the GWR studios at Swindon or Paddington (or NRM or STEAM these days) will show the number of the vehicle when the photograph was taken (usually when the vehicle was new), and will not show any subsequent alterations. Photographs of A-prefixed motor numbers taken in the 1935-39 period will not show altered numbers, unless they were part of the Slough album. Similarly for trailers.

More numbering alterations occurred just before nationalisation. The Exeter DGM D. Hawkeswood issued the following cartage circular in 1947:

'To avoid confusion with the number of Motor Vehicles in the 3-ton class, in the near

future all the existing 3-ton *articulated* units will have their present numbers prefixed by

'3' thus altering their present series from 3300 to 33000 and onwards. The 3000 series

will be applicable to 3-ton *rigid* vehicles only. Will you please note that the new numbers

for all 3-ton articulated units will be operative from 21st April 1947 and the following

procedure must be adopted:-

(a) Commencing on and from April 21st all 3-ton articulated units will be automatically known by their new numbers and must be shown on all relevant Returns such as the M.13 and daily cartage statement (7219-3) and all returns appertaining to cartage by their amended GW vehicle number.

(b) The work of prefixing with the figure 3 the existing Articulated Units will be carried out by the RHM Dept and cartage stations where this type of vehicle is allocated must please arrange to notify me immediately when these vehicles have been re-numbered.

Please bring the foregoing specially to the attention of all concerned and arrange

accordingly, advising me of any points on which you are not clear.

For D Hawkeswood'

(This was initialed by Leslie King.)

To add to the mystery of numbering, the District Road Motor Engineer at Bristol, on 10 December 1947, instructed that the 'number 1843 on motor lorry YM 4196 situated at the Fire Station, Swindon, be obliterated and replaced by A2793'. However, 1843 was the fleet number of a 1929 Thornycroft 'A1' with number plate UV3040, and the vehicle bearing YM 4196 was a 1926 Burford 30-cwt lorry, fleet 1006! New work orders often referred to *chassis numbers* of vehicles and this can cause confusion, but that does not seem to be the case in this instance.

Above **Three-ton mechanical horses were numbered in the 3xxx series, but in April 1947 it was decided to prefix them with another '3' to avoid confusion with the numbering of rigid 3-tonners, thus altering their series from 3xxx to 33xxx. Here is an example taken soon after in British Railways days. The trailer no longer has its GW telegraph code.** ***GWR/D J Hyde collection***

Below **According to the April 1947 scheme the additional '3' was supposed to differentiate between 3-ton Scammell mechanical horses and all other 3-ton rigid chassis vehicles. This picture shows that the rule was apparently applied to all 3-wheel Scammells even if having a rigid chassis. BR(W) fire tender, originally dating from the mid-1930s, is numbered 33461W.** ***D J Hyde collection***

CHAPTER NINE

CARTAGE AGENTS

In this chapter we describe those outside firms who performed cartage for the GWR at various times in the company's history. Be aware that occasionally 'cartage agents' were mistakenly called 'goods agents' which is confusing since 'goods agent' was an alternative name for the local *railway* goods manager.

Long before railways and canals came on the scene there was an established network of long-distance and short-distance road services conveying passengers (stage *coaches*) and goods (stage *carriers*), both of which ran to timetables along turnpikes and other good roads. Elsewhere around the country there were local hauliers, but in winter when roads were rutted and impassable, movement of wheeled vehicles was difficult and the use of packhorses was common. Carriers ranged in size from commercial firms that collected and delivered parcels and goods over long distances down to one-man-and-a-boy 'higglers' that took goods from villages to nearby market for sale and brought back goods that had been ordered by villagers.

'Navigations' (navigable rivers) had been used for transport from Roman times, and water transport was extended when canals were excavated in the $18^{th}/19^{th}$ centuries. When appropriate, carriers would use canals for part of a through journey. Similarly, when railways were being built, but yet not completed, carriers used those portions open for traffic to speed up their consignments.

As described in Chapter 1, the Directors of the GWR believed that the principal business of the fledgling broad gauge railway would be passenger traffic, and not much thought was given to freight nor how it would be carted. This attitude gradually changed, particularly in the northern area of the expanding GW under Newcombe's goods management, but even though freight traffic had become significant by the 1850s, the Board of the broad gauge GW continued to choose to use contractors and carriers (later referred to as 'Cartage Agents') to perform goods cartage work rather than provide services itself. The agents were paid a percentage of the GW's charge to customers for conveying goods and parcels, as a commission to cover the agents' expenses and provide a profit. Among terms and conditions to be agreed by cartage agents before being retained by the GWR were that they '......were required to provide suitable vehicles (vans, carts, trolleys, timber carriages), horses and harness; to employ civil, energetic men to the Company's [GWR's] satisfaction for the collection of goods and merchandise within the said district, and for the delivery thereof to and from the said station; and to remove such men, horses or vehicles as may from time to time be objected to by the Company.....'. GW Goods Department officers were frequently reminded that they should make a point of inspecting equipment and employees when visiting stations and take action when the Agent was not a credit to the Company.

When required an agent had to provide a convenient receiving office at the station from which he operated. On the building the words 'Great Western Railway Company — [name] — Agent' had to be painted in a bold manner in a conspicuous place. The same words had to be legibly printed on the sides or fixed covers of all road vehicles used in the Agents' agreements (see Chapter 8).

Two-wheeled single-pony light van belonging to EBeasant, GWR Cartage Agent in Bridgend, called 'Outside Porter'. Driven from inside the van that has small side windows in permanent tilt. ***A G Atkins collection***

Copy
No. 514

I Joseph Taylor Younghusband of
Great Western Buildings, Swan Street, Minories, Londo
hereby agree for myself my executors administrators and
assigns that until the determination by expiry consent or
otherwise of an Agreement between me and the Great Wester
Railway Company dated the fourth day of July One
thousand eight hundred and seventy seven whereby I a
appointed Carting Agent for the said Company I will no
take any Proceedings for or make or assert any claim by
way of set off in account or otherwise howsoever for any
part of the price or value of any of the forty five Van
sold and delivered by me to the said Company and o
which their name has been marked and which are
numbered 3, 4, 5, 6, 7, 8, 9, 10, 11, 12, 13, 14, 15, 16, 17, 18
19, 20, 24, 26, 28, 29, 30, 37, 38, 40, 41, 42, 43, 44, 45, 46, 47
50, 51, 52, 53, 54, 55, 56, 70, 71, 72, 98, 99, and then only
for the value thereof as the same exist at the time of such
determination and subject to deduction set off and retainer
by the said Company of any sums then due or payable
from me to the said Company or for which I may then be
accountable to the said Company under the said Agreeme
or as damages for any breach thereof or otherwise howsoev
And I further agree from time to time so often as
occasion may require to repair and keep in repair each
of the said Vans at my own expense and to return
the same to the said Company in good repair at the
determination of the said Agreement or on demand at
any previous time Provided that in case the permission
given by the said Company to me to use the said Vans
for the purposes of the said Agreement is revoked or
determined as to any of the said Vans then as to
such Van or Vans I am to be at liberty to sue for or
set off the then value of such Van or Vans as if the
said Agreement had been determined but subject to
deduction set off and retainer by the said Company
of any sums then due or payable from me or for which
I may then be accountable as above mentioned In witness

Younghusband legal contract. ***Author's collection***

One of three Bedford normal-control 2-ton vehicles bought from E J & H T Quartly of Dorton Camp, Thame, when their agency was terminated. Fleet 1645/6 had livestock bodies (see Kelley p 104); 1644 did not. This photograph of Fleet 1645 (KX 7759) differs from that of the same vehicle in Kelley p 104: the ventilation flap nearest the cab has been filled in and the 'guard fence' on the side over the back axle (to be swung alongside the rear loading ramp when down) has been removed. On the side of the varnished wooden body is 'General Haulage Contractors' and on the front of the box extension over the cab is 'Phone Long Crendon 23'. Speed 20mph on chassis below door. Still in agent's livery but 'GREAT WESTERN RAILWAY/F R E DAVIS SECRETARY/PADDINGTON' painted below fleet number to left of cab door. *STEAM Swindon*

William Hubbard was GW agent in Aberayron. Livery was black with white lettering. This photo shows his eldest son Idris with his father's private owner wagon in 1938. *Great Western Railway Journal*

As traffic grew in the last quarter of the 19th century, the GW began to expand its own cartage fleet especially in larger towns where there was lots of collection and delivery business ('smalls' traffic). This was not necessarily to the exclusion of agents in all places — in a number of towns, agents worked alongside the GW. For example, according to the 1907 GWR *Towns, Villages, Outlaying Works, etc*, in the cases of Bushbury, Long Knowle, Lower Penn and Tettenhall, all served from Wolverhampton, the Agent handled parcels but GW carts the goods traffic. At these places neither service was free of charge, but whether the customer paid varied from station to station. At Tenbury, the Agent handled goods, and parcels were delivered by porter, and both services were free, as they were for Regent's Wharf served from both Bilston and Ettingshall stations, where GW carts and the GW Agent's boats took goods, while the Agent handled parcels. At Moor in Worcestershire, the Agent handled only fruit and vegetables and their empties. For Cawsand (to and from Plymouth) the mode of conveyance from the station was by 'GWR Agent, steamboat and omnibus' and was not free. The role of buses in parcel and goods C&D at that time should not be underestimated as they would carry items not exceeding 1-cwt: for Catstree in Shropshire, items were taken from Bridgnorth by "GWR Motor Omnibus to 'The Wheel' [a pub] at Worfield, 1 mile from Catstree". At Cerrig-y-Druidion (Denbigh), served by Corwen station, traffic was dealt with by the Agent's traction engine. Sole agents tended to be kept on at remoter stations where C&D goods traffic was not so voluminous or not so regular to justify the use of GW-owned vehicles. Even so, there were places where the customers had to rely on private carriers for C&D from the nearest station, such as (in the 1907 book) Cefn Cribbwr (to and from Kenfig Hill); South and North Cerney (Gloucestershire) via Cirencester; Little Piddle via Dorchester; Snitterfield (Warwickshire) via Stratford-on-Avon; and Woundale (Salop) via Bridgnorth. At other places, no means of conveyance from the nearest GW station is indicated. In the days when the GW had isolated depots in foreign territory, e.g. Leeds, places such as Armley in Yorkshire were served free by the local GW Agent according to the 1907 book. And the GW had its own horse cartage vehicles in such places (Chapter 2). In the case of joint companies, such as the GW & GC line through Ruislip, Gerrards Cross and Denham, Agents were employed by the joint company, but Church Stretton on the Shrewsbury & Hereford line was served free by the Agent appointed by the GW alone.

20

G. W. R.

ROAD MOTOR SERVICES.

PARCELS AND GOODS BY ROAD MOTOR CARS.

Parcels and Goods not exceeding 1 cwt. per package will be conveyed between the Company's Stations and Road Motor Parcel Agencies, or to or from places on the direct route of the cars (provided someone is there to receive such Parcels and Goods). All charges (see page 87) must be prepaid.

LIST OF OFFICIAL AGENTS IN TOWNS AND VILLAGES ON ROAD MOTOR ROUTES IN THIS BOOKLET.

Town or Village.	Road Service starts from Station at	Agents for Parcels, Goods, etc.
Ascot	Windsor	Mr. J. Parkinson, "Horse and Groom" Hotel.
Ashbury	Swindon	Mr. Goddard, "Rose and Crown."
Avebury	Marlborough	Mr. H. Lawes, Red Lion.
Baydon	Swindon	Mr. W. Taylor, "Red Lion."
Burnham	Slough	Mr. Geo. Hebbes, High Street.
Cherhill	Marlborough	Mrs. A. Duck, "Black Horse."
Childrey	Wantage Rd.	Miss G. M. Rowland, Lester House.
Chilton Foliat	Marlborough	Mrs. L. Jarvis, Wheatsheaf Inn.
Coate	Wantage Rd.	Mr. G. Edmonds, "Spotted Cow."
Denchworth	Swindon	Mr. J. Lake, "Star Inn."

21

LIST OF OFFICIAL AGENTS—continued.

Town or Village.	Road Service starts from Station at	Agents for Parcels, Goods, etc.
East Challow	Wantage	Mrs. E. Matthews 3 Council Houses.
East Hanney	Wantage	Mr. E. S Gilbert.
Easton Royal	Marlborough	Mr. S. J. Lovelock.
Farnham Common	Slough	Mr. G. P. Read, G.W.R. Office.
Farnham Road	Slough	Miss A. C. Smith, The Restaurant.
Farnham Royal	Slough	Mr. A. Wheeler, The Stores.
Foxhill	Swindon	Miss O. Rosier, "Shepherd's Rest."
Fyfield	Marlborough	Mr. E. Pile, "Fighting Cocks."
Harwell	Didcot	Mr. Greenaway, Grocer.
Kingston Lisle	Wantage Rd.	Mrs. G. Wells.
Marlborough	Marlborough	Mr. E. H. Roff, 67, London Road.
Milton-Lilbourne	Marlborough	Mr. F. C. Stagg.
Painswick	Stroud	Mr. T. G. Goddard, "Falcon Hotel."
Overton	Marlborough	Mr. A. J. Huntley, "Bell Inn."
Uffington	Wantage Rd.	Mr. W. Norton, Uffington (Berks).
Ramsbury	Marlborough	Mr. J. W. Franklin, "Bell Hotel."
Sonning	Reading	Mrs. A. K. Prior, High Street.
Sparsholt	Wantage Rd.	Mr. G. Stone, "The Star Inn."
Uffington	Swindon	Mr. W. W. Norton.
Wanborough (Upper)	Swindon	Mrs. A. Bray, "Calley Arms."
Wantage	Wantage Rd.	Mr. J. A. Nicholls, Market Place.
West Hanney	Wantage	Mr. W. C. Boar, "Lamb Inn."
Winkfield	Windsor	Mr. E. W. Rice, "Squirrel Hotel."
Winkfield	Windsor	Mr. Chas. Piper, "Fleur de Lys," Lovel Hill.

Our Great Western Railway. Yr.

Thomas Bantock & Co. Agents

HEAD OFFICE:
LOW LEVEL STATION.

PARTNERS: E. G. BANTOCK
M. BANTOCK.

TELEGRAPHIC ADDRESS:
"BANTOCK"
WOLVERHAMPTON.

TELEPHONE 24031/2.

194

At Reading, the 'mode of conveyance' of goods and parcels from the station was by GWR Agent, namely C&G Ayres, who had been carriers since 1825 before the railway arrived. A photograph of the Kings Meadow depot with lots of Ayres open and tilted vehicles and one of their traction engines may be found on p15 of *GWR Goods Services*, part 2A. Thomas Bantock & Co Ltd was another of the earliest GW agents and was by far the longest serving. The firm's involvement went right back to the beginnings of the railway, having been Boatage Agent to the Oxford, Worcester & Wolverhampton Railway and to the GW from 1855 dealing with canal wharf-to-rail transfers. The firm became road cartage agent for the Wolverhampton district in 1858. Their cartage and porterage agency with the GWR was "for the carriage of rail-borne goods by road less than 40 miles along a route taken between places within a 25-mile radius of Wolverhampton Low Level station". In 1860, Bantock owned 51 canal boats (later over 100) working from GW/OWW transfer wharves on the Birmingham Canal Navigations (BCN) which was a network of canals connecting Birmingham, Wolverhampton, and the eastern part of the Black Country and which, at its working peak, contained about 160 miles of navigable waterways. Industries in the area gave rise to a great tonnage of traffic which was transferred to/from rail. The transfer wharves and number of Bantock boats based at them were: at Bromley (Kingswinford, from 1858 to closure in 1958, 5 boats); Hockley (1855-1958, 8); Swan Village (1856-1950, 3); Victoria (Herbert Street, Wolverhampton, 1881-1930, 4); Stourbridge (1858-1956, 5); Shubbery (Walsall Street bridge, Wolverhampton, 1866-1963, 7); Tipton (Factory Basin, 1855-1949, 7); Wednesbury (Leabrook, 6); Pothouse Bridge (near potteries at Bilston, 3 boats); and Stourport (3 boats). Other transfer stations at which Bantock later worked were Bilston Basin (from 1908-1935), Hawne (Halesowen, 1902-1969), Oldbury Basin (1884-1936) and Withymoor (Netherton/Brierly Hill, 1878-1965).

In 1938 the mattress maker Vono of Dudley Port, Tipton, Staffs, bought the mainmast of George V's yacht Britannia, to be used as a flagstaff at their sports ground. It was 102ft long and 20ins in diameter and had been brought by rail from Southampton Town Quay to Great Bridge on a GW Macaw C bogie bolster wagon. The GW carting agent Bantock & Co was responsible for the 2-mile final delivery, using a timber carriage drawn by a Latil tractor. *GWR Magazine*

R T Smith & Co had been operating 'stage-wagon' road services from the Bristol-Gloucester area, to London and to South Wales long before the railways. They were GW agents until 1922 at which time the GW acquired the business. The single-horse van has 'Great Western Railway Co/RT Smith & Co Agents/No236' painted on the tilt, with 'R T Smith & Co/Head Office/Gloucester/No236' painted on the side-planking. ***D J Hyde***

The GW had its own barges working on the BCN, and in 1866 Bantock hired 16 boats from the GW at £15/month.

When the GW was quickly building up its own cartage fleet, the GW purchased equipment from their agents. In 1876, 35 pair-horse vans were bought from Younghusband at Paddington, and in 1878 the GWR bought various horse-drawn road vehicles valued at £150 from Bantock: the GW bought 1 open dray and 1 covered dray at Bewdley; at Brettell Lane 13 open drays, 2 covered carts, 1 open cart and 1 timber carriage; at Cradley Heath 5 open drays; at Dudley 2 open drays, 2 half-covered drays, 3 covered vans, 1 covered cart, 2 open carts, 2 parcel vans, 1 boiler carriage, 1 store dray; at Great Bridge 3 open, and 3 covered, drays; at Kidderminster 18 open drays, 2 covered wagons, 1 parcel van and 1 float; at Lye 2 open drays; at Stourbridge 3 open drays and 2 covered vans; at Stourport 2 open drays and 1 covered van — a total of 76 vehicles. No horses or harnesses were purchased as the GW were to use its own and its own drivers. Despite selling off equipment, Bantocks continued to act as cartage agents at these same depots with more of their own horses and vehicles, as well as at Halesowen, Netherton, Old Hill, Oldbury, Swan Village and West Bromwich.

Bantocks had bought a Ford van in 1910 and 4 Foden steam wagons in 1916. By 1925 they were operating 25 motor vehicles. Their horse-drawn vehicles peaked at about 150 in 1926. In their livery of grey with black lettering, Bantocks remained GW cartage agents beyond nationalisation in 1948 and were finally bought by the Western Region of BR on 13 December 1953. At that time their fleet comprised 140 vehicles in total, of which 80 were Fordsons and the majority of the remainder were Scammell mechanical horses. Over the years they had owned other makes including Guy, Jen-Tug (a light articulated lorry made by Jensen Cars of West Bromwich), Karrier Bantam, Latil 'Haulier' tractors, Morris Commercial, and Sentinel.

Another firm of agents having a long association with the GW was Richard T Smith based in the Bristol/Gloucester area. It had been operating a 'stage-wagon' road service to London and to South Wales long before the railways. When the GW opened to Bristol in 1841, they provided a connecting road service for parcels and freight up to Gloucester and thence down to South Wales as far as Haverford West and Milford Haven. This continued until the South Wales Rly opened throughout to Neyland (New Milford) in 1856. At the same time, they used the GW railway to take goods and parcels from Bristol and Gloucester to their depot in London at the Rose Inn, Smithfield. They were involved in transferring goods between broad and narrow gauges at Gloucester and as a consequence were taken on there as cartage agents. It was the enterprise of such firms that fuelled the expansion of freight traffic on the growing GWR. From the 1850s, they were to become GW agents at 25 places including Aberavon, Brimscombe, Bridgnorth, Bromyard, Brosely, Cinderford, Cirencester, Coalbrookdale, Evesham, Gloucester, Hereford, Ironbridge, Ledbury, Malvern, Newent, Pershore, Pontypool, Ross-on-Wye, Stroud, Swindon, Tetbury and Worcester. This continued until the death in 1922 of the then owner Sir Richard Vassar-Smith, at which time the GW acquired the business, taking over the employees, 25 depots, 122 horses, harness and equipment valued at £2,846, and 228 vehicles valued at £2,988.

On the death in July 1937 of Col G R Powell, the owner of W P Powell & Co (agents at Aberdare, Bridgend, Hirwain, Merthyr, Neath, and Port Talbot since the end of the 19th century), the business was bought by the GW who absorbed 23 motor lorries, 36 horses, 108 horse lorries, together with buildings, equipment, plant and machinery; most of the staff were taken over by the GWR.

Many smaller country carriers became GW agents, such as Lamb at Bridport in 1864; William Payne & Son, from the 1860/70s agents at Bampton (Oxon), Chipping Norton, Eynsham and Witney. Alfred Derry was agent at Bodmin, Cullompton, Dartmouth and Helston; William Derry at Launceston and Plymouth; and James Dobbs at Chepstow, Chester and Lydney Town (where he also provided shunting horses). Abraham Cresswell was appointed agent at Marlow (Bucks) in 1873, but the firm was dismissed in 1881 for "failing to perform duties and render or pay accounts to the GW";

GREAT WESTERN RAILWAY. (763)

APPLICATION FOR ALLOWANCE ON RETIREMENT.

(NON-MEMBER OF PENSION SOCIETY OR ENGINEMEN & FIREMEN'S MUTUAL ASSURANCE SOCIETY).

	Surname	Christian Name	Regd. No.
Name	MOSS	Arthur	82104

Grade and Station: Motor Driver - Worcester Goods

How employed during past 12 months: Motor Driver. 15 cwt Van.

Date of birth and age last birthday: 15.1.80. 66 years.

Completed years of continuous service. If service broken, state circumstances: with agents 21 years. Messrs R. T. Smith & Co., Carting Agents. 23 years. G. W. R. 44

	Actual at Retirement	Standard Rate	Average last 3 years (Standard Rate)
Wages per week	~~94/-~~ 66/- + 28/-	(94/-) 66/=	(63/6) 61/2

If wages have been reduced within ten years prior to retirement, state reason and also average rate for three years preceding reduction: No

Date of retirement: 28.9.46.

*If applicant is permanently incapacitated for further work, state whether he has been examined by a duly qualified Medical Practitioner resident in the District, and with what result: No

Whether eligible for State Pension or Disablement Benefit under N.H.I. Acts (if in receipt of remuneration exceeding £420 p.a. state whether a Voluntary Contributor): State Pension.

G.W.R. EXAMINED WITH REGISTER ACCOUNTANT'S OFFICE

RETIRING ALLOWANCES 6 NOV 1946 COMMITTEE

	£	s. per week	d.
Ex-Gratia Allowance		15	4
State pension deduction		5	0
Nett		10	4

ADDITIONAL ALLOWANCES :—

Inspectors and Foremen's Special Pension Fund: Not a Member

Salaried Staff Supplemental Pension Fund: Not a Member

To take effect from 29th day of September 1946.

Special Remarks :— During his period of employment with the Company Moss has performed his duties in a satisfactory manner and has continued to carry on in his employment with us after attaining his sixty-fifth birthday consequent upon our staff requirements.

Prior to entering the service of the G.W.R., Company he was employed from 1902 (21 years) by Messrs. R.T. Smith & Co., Carting Agents, who were taken over by the Company on 1.1.1923.

P.B. 9/11/46

For C. H. ADEY. Divisional Officer. For DAVID BLEE Head of Department.

17th September, 1946. 3rd October 1946

For Staff and Establishment Office use. ADVISED 23 OCT 1946

For H. ADAMS CLARKE Chief Staff and Establishment Officer.

*NOTE.—If the applicant is under 65 years of age, this application must be accompanied by a Medical Certificate.

1,500 L.C. 1946 (17) S

Retirement allowance, Arthur Moss. ***Author's collection***

Cresswell's successor was Porter & Son. The various cartage agents at Devizes are reported in Priddle & Hyde. The Wantage Tramway was, perhaps, an unusual example of a GW cartage agent.

When the expanding GW took over railways that had their own cartage agents they were retained, providing their performance was satisfactory. A well-known example relates to cartage on the Bristol & Exeter Rly. Those who drummed up business from the traders and the public to persuade them to send their goods on roads and canals (and subsequently railways) were called 'canvassers' and it was a canal canvasser, J C Wall, who became agent for parcels and goods on the B&E in 1855. In 1870 he became General Traffic Manager, and later General Manager, of that railway even though at the same time he retained ownership of his private cartage company. When the B&E and GW amalgamated in 1876, the firm of J C Wall was retained and they remained agents until 1903. Stations served by the firm included: Abbotsbury, Avonmouth, Bampton (Devon), Bath, Bridgwater, Bristol, Calne, Camborne, Chippenham, Dulverton, Exeter, Falmouth, Highworth, Hungerford, Ivybridge, Launceston, Liskeard, Malmesbury, Martock, Melksham, Penryn, Penzance, Redruth, St Austell, St Ives, Shepton Mallet, Taunton, Teignmouth, Tiverton, Truro, Wells, and Weston-super-Mare.

After 1903 various new agents were appointed in place of J C Wall, such as the firm of Rendell and Lean at Camborne, Falmouth, Liskeard, Penryn, Penzance, St Austell, St Ives and Truro. In 1904, the GW completed new stables for six horses at Hayle at a cost of £467/12/8d on the termination of the arrangement under which J G Done had performed the cartage work. One light horse lorry was purchased from Payne & Son of Dawlish in April 1904 for £12. A five-stall stable was built in the goods yard at Shipton in 1906, an adjacent timber stable being purchased from Mr Clifford for a store for provender and straw. S C Burt became agent at Calne, Chippenham, Highworth, Malmesbury and Melksham after J C Wall, but in 1925 the firm was taken over by the GW owing to Burt's "Financial Embarrassment"; all the horses and equipment (valued at £400) came to the GW. The cartage agent at Tiverton and Tiverton Junction appointed after J C Wall was not satisfactory and was dismissed.

In 1908, a number of horse-drawn vehicles were purchased for £490 from Messrs Derry in the West Country. In 1912 horse vehicles were purchased from S H Corfield: 3 vans at Weston-super-Mare for £165; 1 van (£55) and 1 light lorry (£43) at Bridgwater; 1 van (Highbridge and Burnham), 1 van (Martock), 1 cart (Clevedon), and 1 van (Langport), all at £55 each. In the same year various horse vehicles were bought from H & G Simons for £414, viz: one 1-horse lorry, four 1-horse vans and one glass trolley, all at Oxford; and one timber carriage at Yeovil. A W White & Co were GW agents at Bournemouth, Gosport, Portsmouth and Southampton; in 1917 these agencies were terminated "in consequence of rearrangements necessitated by continuance of war". Whites were also agents at Winchester where they remained in GW service until 1932 (see page 72).

At the Grouping, the GW often continued with the agents of absorbed companies, as at Dowlais (ex-TVR) where the Jenkins family had held the agency since the 1870s. When Dowlais cartage was diverted to the GW at Merthyr in the early 1930s a £200 gratuity was paid to the Jenkins firm and the estimated saving was £800/year. When the cartage agencies of absorbed companies were found not up to standard, they were terminated; at Ely Cardiff (ex-TVR), an arm of the A L Green firm of carriers was dismissed as being unsatisfactory and the GW itself took over in

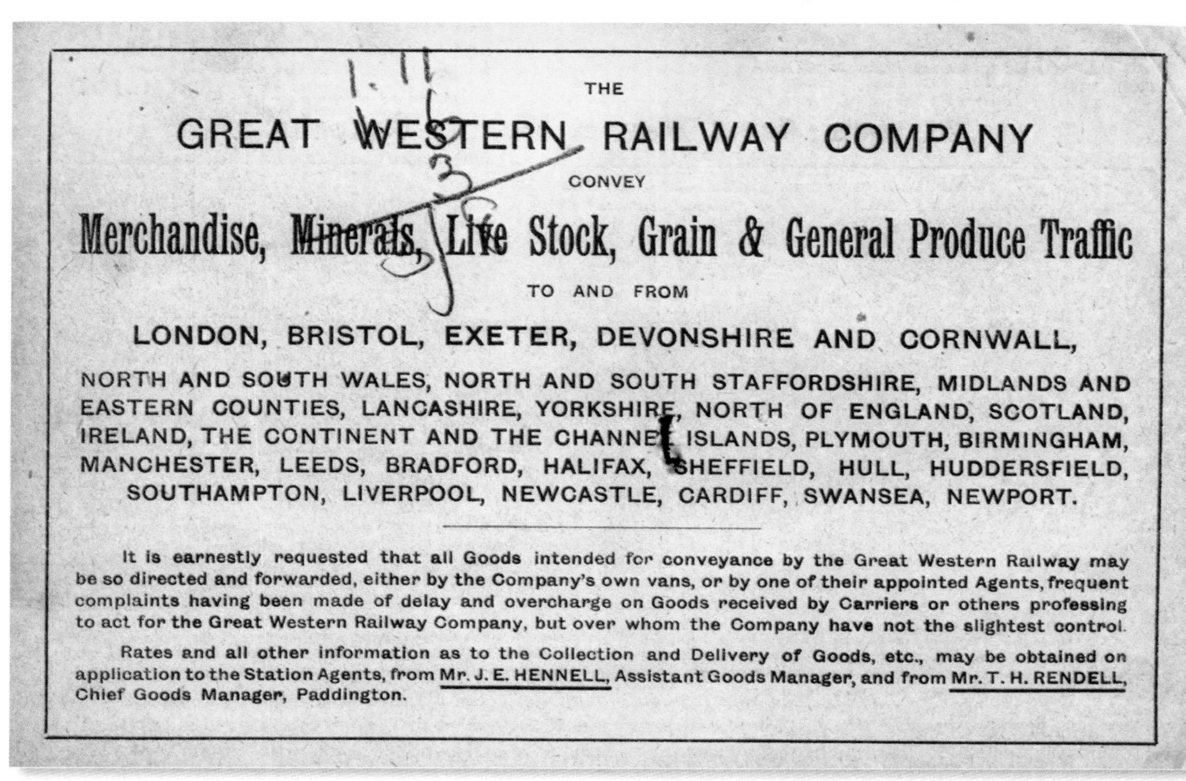
THE

GREAT WESTERN RAILWAY COMPANY

CONVEY

Merchandise, Minerals, Live Stock, Grain & General Produce Traffic

TO AND FROM

LONDON, BRISTOL, EXETER, DEVONSHIRE AND CORNWALL,

NORTH AND SOUTH WALES, NORTH AND SOUTH STAFFORDSHIRE, MIDLANDS AND EASTERN COUNTIES, LANCASHIRE, YORKSHIRE, NORTH OF ENGLAND, SCOTLAND, IRELAND, THE CONTINENT AND THE CHANNEL ISLANDS, PLYMOUTH, BIRMINGHAM, MANCHESTER, LEEDS, BRADFORD, HALIFAX, SHEFFIELD, HULL, HUDDERSFIELD, SOUTHAMPTON, LIVERPOOL, NEWCASTLE, CARDIFF, SWANSEA, NEWPORT.

It is earnestly requested that all Goods intended for conveyance by the Great Western Railway may be so directed and forwarded, either by the Company's own vans, or by one of their appointed Agents, frequent complaints having been made of delay and overcharge on Goods received by Carriers or others professing to act for the Great Western Railway Company, but over whom the Company have not the slightest control.

Rates and all other information as to the Collection and Delivery of Goods, etc., may be obtained on application to the Station Agents, from Mr. J. E. HENNELL, Assistant Goods Manager, and from Mr. T. H. RENDELL, Chief Goods Manager, Paddington.

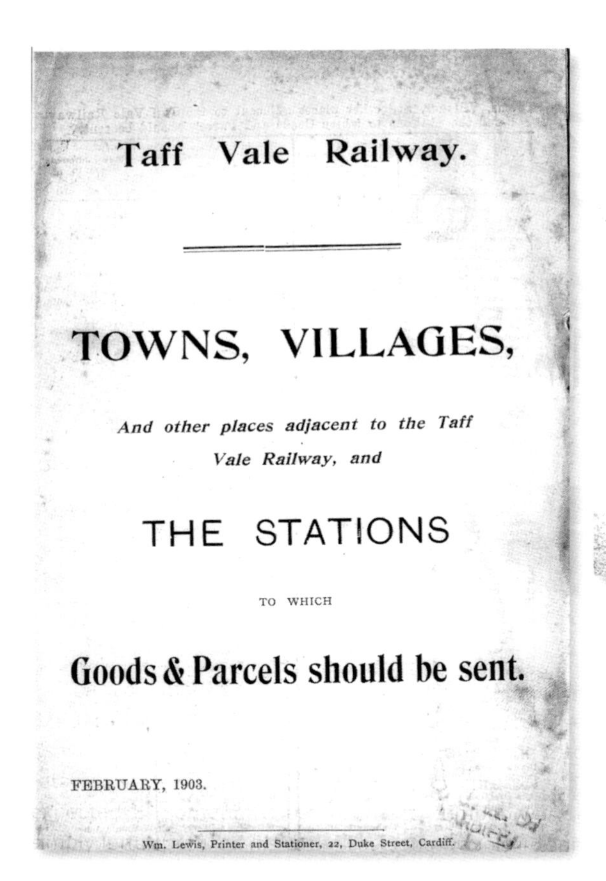

Taff Vale Railway.

TOWNS, VILLAGES,

And other places adjacent to the Taff Vale Railway, and

THE STATIONS

TO WHICH

Goods & Parcels should be sent.

FEBRUARY, 1903.

Wm. Lewis, Printer and Stationer, 22, Duke Street, Cardiff.

GOODS DELIVERY AGENTS.

Rotunda Buildings, Cardiff (National Telephone 393) ...	MR. H. GREEN.
Cardiff Docks (National Telephone 389)	MR. W. HAYNES.
Aberdare ...	MR. H. GREEN.
Abercynon ...	MR. H. GREEN.
Cardiff (Queen Street) (National Telephone 388) ...	MR. H. GREEN.
Ferndale ...	MR. H. GREEN.
Hafod ...	MR. H. GREEN.
Merthyr ...	MR. H. GREEN.
Porth (National Telephone 5) ...	MR. H. GREEN.
Penarth ...	MR. H. GREEN.
Penarth Dock...	MR. H. GREEN.
Penrhiwceiber ...	MR. H. GREEN.
Pontypridd (National Telephone 23) ...	MR. H. GREEN.
Trealaw ...	MR. H. GREEN.
Treforest ...	MR. H. GREEN.
Treherbert ...	MR. H. GREEN.
Treorchy ...	MR. H. GREEN.
Wattstown ...	MR. H. GREEN.
Ystrad ...	MR. H. GREEN.
Mountain Ash ...	L. & N.W. Co.
Cowbridge ...	MR. J. GEORGE
Sully and Biglis ...	MR. ROBERTSON.

1923. Rationalisation of cartage provision occurred when absorbed companies had stations in the same town as the GWR, and this led to agencies having to be dispensed with, however well they may have been performing. Ashwin & Co had been agents at Stratford-on-Avon since 1883, but in 1922 were given three months' notice of termination on the merging of the stations belonging to the GW and the Stratford-on-Avon & Midland Jct Railways; at Cirencester after the Grouping, the MSWJ agent (E G Cox) was dispensed with in 1925 with an estimated saving of £223/year; his lorry valued at £85 was purchased by the GW.

In 1922 the Davies firm, agents at Maesteg, were given £600 in compensation for their working loss caused by the 3-month-long miners' strike of 1921. When the Swansea Harbour Trust asked the GW to take ownership of their docks in 1923 (see *GWR Docks & Marine*), Powesland & Mason's contract for the supply of nine docks locomotives was included. P&M were also the SHT's cartage agents and they requested the GW to take over those assets as well, including 61 horses, and that took effect from 1 January 1924.

RHYMNEY RAILWAY.

Towns, Villages,

And other Places adjacent

TO THE

Rhymney Railway,

AND

THE STATIONS

TO WHICH

Goods and Parcels should be sent.

Also list of some of the places to which the Rhymney Co. carry traffic from Cardiff in connection with other Railway Companies.

NOTE.—In this book "G.F.T.L." means "Goods in Full Truck Loads," and "C. & D." means "Collected and Delivered."

OCTOBER, 1906.

REES' ELECTRIC PRESS, PLYMOUTH STREET, CARDIFF.

R.R. Co.'s Agents for the Collection and Delivery of Goods and Parcels.

Stations.	Carting Agents.
Cardiff: Goods Dept., Nat. Tel. 655; Parcels & Passenger ,, ,, ,, 1199	L. & N. W. Co., Nat. Tel. 85 (Goods and Parcels).
Caerphilly ...	L. & N. W. Co. (Goods). Mr. H. Hicks (Parcels).
Abertridwr, Senghenydd ...	,, W. Jones (Goods).
Llanbradach ...	,, Enos Williams ,,
Ystrad Mynach, Hengoed and Maesycwmmer ...	,, W. G. Seaborne ,,
Dowlais ...	,, W. P. Powell ,,
Pengam ...	,, D. Phillips ,,
Bargoed and Aber Bargoed ...	,, Jno. Thomas ,, ; ,, Joseph Dury (Parcels).
Brithdir...	,, William Lewis (Goods).
Tir Phil and New Tredegar P.O. Tel. 8 ...	,, T. Saunders (Goods and Parcels), P.O. Tel. 19.
Pontlottyn ...	,, Jno. Morgan (Goods).
Rhymney, P.O. Tel. 23 ...	L. & N. W. Co. ,,
Aberfan for Merthyr Vale ...	Mr. W. Worthing ,,

G. W. R. (763)

57

APPLICATION FOR ALLOWANCE ON RETIREMENT.

(NON-MEMBER OF PENSION SOCIETY OR ENGINEMEN & FIREMEN'S MUTUAL ASSURANCE SOCIETY.)

	Surname	Christian Name	Regd. No.
Name	PONTING	Thomas William	87910

Grade and Station	Checker, Llanelly (Goods)
How employed during past 12 months	Checker, Llanelly (Goods)
Date of birth and age last birthday	12th September, 1881. 64 65 years
Completed years of continuous service. If service broken, state circumstances	16 years with G.W.R. 21 years with late Carting Agents, Messrs. D. Davies & Sons - total 37 years, in all. Entered Carting Agent's Service April 1909 (92/-) (60/10)

	Actual at Retirement	Standard Rate	Average last 3 years (Standard Rate)
Wages per week	64/- +28/-	64/-	55/- to 64/- p.w. 30-7-45 58/-

If wages have been reduced within ten years prior to retirement, state reason and also average rate for three years preceding reduction	No
Date of retirement	28th September, 1946 (Saturday)
* If applicant is permanently incapacitated for further work, state whether he has been examined by a duly qualified Medical Practitioner resident in the District, and with what result	No.
Whether eligible for State Pension or Disablement Benefit under N.H.I. Acts (if in receipt of remuneration exceeding £250 p.a. state whether a Voluntary Contributor).	Yes.

G. W. R. EXAMINED WITH REGISTER ACCOUNTANT'S OFFICE

	£	s. per week	d.
Ex-Gratia Allowance		13	6
State pension deduction		5	0
Nett		8	6

RETIRING ALLOWANCES 6 NOV 1946 COMMITTEE

ADDITIONAL ALLOWANCES :—

Salaried Staff Supplemental Pension Fund — Not a Member

Inspectors and Foremen's Special Pension Fund — Not a Member For C. R. DASHWOOD

To take effect from 29th day of September 1946

Special Remarks :—

P.B. 9/11/46

R. A. Ryan District Officer. For DAVID BLEE Head of Department.

For General Manager's Office use. 14 OCT 1946 ADVISED

6th September 1946.

For H. ADAMS CLARKE General Manager. Chief Staff and Establishment Officer

* NOTE.—If the applicant is under 65 years of age, this application must be accompanied by a Medical Certificate.

1,000—Est. 906—1-46—(17)—S

Retirement allowance, Thomas Ponting. *Author's collection*

Leyland permanently-articulated lorry, fleet 1086, with Shropshire registration UX 1406, taken over from Agent Jones of Oswestry in February 1930. Given body number G 1062 painted to right of 'Great Western Railway' on cream panel on trailer. Brown 'G.W.R.' on cream panel at front of cab. *STEAM Swindon*

When reliable motor vehicles became common after WW1, more and more cartage agents were dispensed with, particularly following the rapid expansion of the Country Lorry service into areas previously covered by agents (Chapter 10). Between 1923 and 1933 the company took over the collection and delivery work previously performed by agents at 149 stations. Even so, in 1926, as an auxiliary to the Railhead system whereby the GW undertook throughout-conveyance of traffic to villages remote from the railway by payment of a flat rate for delivery, independent country carriers were employed in those places where the traffic was too small to justify the introduction of the railway's own lorries.

Some examples of locations where agents were dispensed with and, where known, the names of agents at those places at different times, are given below:

1925 Cullompton (William Derry); Exeter (J C Wall 1847-1903); Hayle (F A Trott); High Wycombe (W V Baines & Son from 1862); Lawrence Hill (T H Corfield); Pwllheli; Teignmouth (J C Wall to 1903); Torquay; and Wellington (Somerset) (M Early, Parcels Agent from 1914).

1926/7 Aberbargoed; Aberystwyth (Jones Bros); Bargoed (D Thomas); Beaconsfield (J Nutt); Cheddar (Wright); Gerrards Cross (J Nutt); Ledbury (Gale, Parcels Agent); Midsomer Norton (Mrs Wheeler); Pengam (Morgan); Radstock (Mrs Wheeler); and Senghenydd (J Nicholson).

1928 Ashburton (W Nicholls); Guernsey; Jersey; Pontlottyn; Rhymney; and Welshpool.

1929 contracts terminated at 26 stations

1930 contracts terminated at 13 stations

1931 contracts terminated at 29 stations

1932 Bradford-on-Avon; Henley-on-Thames (T R Toomer & Co); New Tredegar; Tirphil; Trowbridge (F B Norris); and Winchester (A W White & Co).

1933 Llanbradach (diverted to GW cartage at Caerphilly); St Columb Road (P T Holyn); and Wilton.

In 1932, of the 735 GW stations with cartage facilities, agents still did the job at 270.

CHAPTER TEN

C&D CONCENTRATION SCHEMES

Country Lorry Services

The chief mileage traffic at country stations was grain and flour for merchants, 'artificial manure' (fertilisers), lime, seeds and feeding stuffs for farmers, coal and building materials. Much of this traffic was put on rail at docks or private sidings. Farmers and merchants themselves had traditionally carted these goods to and from their local railway stations, but a change took place after WW1 since farmers went in for more grass (dairy) farming as being cheaper and less risky than arable farming. Emphasis went over to the production of milk, butter, cheese and meat. In the 1920s, the home production of butter was only a quarter of home consumption; cheese, one fifth; bacon and hams just over a half; and wheat, one fifth. With more land laid down to pasture rather than crops, this meant that:

(i) farmers became more dependent on outside supplies of animal feeds, particularly in the winter, so that mileage traffic to country stations increased considerably; and

(ii) fewer horses were available for cartage, so that farmers found it more economical to engage others to do the job.

This coincided with the growth in numbers of small private road hauliers equipped with motor vehicles who were not only willing to do carting from and to local railway stations, but who were prepared to transport from docks or mills direct to farms, thus bypassing the railway altogether. It was clear to the GW that the traditional system at rural stations needed modernising and it led to what became known as the 'Country Lorry Service' in which railway-owned motor lorries radiated from a base station for distances of up to 20 or more miles, covering an extended rural area, supplying farmsteads, villages, etc with the daily needs of the community, the lorries returning to the station with the produce of the district for transport by rail to distant markets. The service additionally gave farmers the freedom to purchase goods from non-local merchants and the ability to sell further afield.

The work done by the Teme Valley Yorkshire steam wagon of 1904 based at Henwick (Chapter 4) can be argued to be the first GW country lorry service. A few years later, GW buses running in West Wales began to be overloaded with goods as well as passengers. To relieve the situation, goods motor vehicles running to a timetable were introduced between Llandyssul and New Quay (Cardiganshire) and between Haverfordwest and St Davids (Pembrokeshire) in May 1907, thus beginning other embryonic country lorry services. But the real growth of the system took place in the interwar period with the availability of reliable motor lorries. At the end of 1925 there were nine Country Lorry services in operation which were at: Llandyssul/New Quay (by then with an ex-army AEC 3½-ton lorry); Haverfordwest/St Davids (1907), and Mathry Road/St Davids (1924) – both with Burford 1½-tonners; Montgomery (1924), Yeovil (1924) and Frome (1925) – all with AEC 3½-tonners; Kingsbridge/Salcombe (Thornycroft 1½-ton); Ellesmere (AEC 3½-ton); Pwllheli/Lleyn Peninsular (various vehicles used), the last three services opening in 1925.

Thereafter the Country Lorry scheme expanded very quickly. The readiness of the GW to handle station-to-station traffic was forcefully advertised and local shop keepers and country tradespeople as well as farmers were happy to leave cartage to the railway, so that the service became a maid-of-all-work. In 1926 it was instituted at eleven stations: Llansantffraid, Abergavenny, Radstock, Helston, St Clears/Laugharne/Pendine, Oswestry, Tipton, St Austell, Chippenham, Hungerford, and Taunton. In 1927, at a further 26 places: Bridport, Warminster, Cheddar, Badminton, Slough, Leamington, Maidenhead, Henllan, Castle Cary, Aberystwyth, Hagley, Dorchester, Highbridge, Salisbury, Westbury, Swindon, Colwall, Tiverton, Albrighton, Crudgington, Bewdley, Devizes, Wootton Bassett, Cullompton,

Above and right A Country Lorry based at Albrighton on the Wolverhampton-Wellington (Salop) line, delivering seed potatoes to a local farm in February 1928, with tarpaulin put on cab roof during unloading. The enamelled plate on the side of the lorry declares 'G.W.R./Country Lorry Service/this lorry will COLLECT and DELIVER FROM and TO/all parts of the DISTRICT/APPLY TO goods agent'. The vehicle is an ex-London General Omnibus Company AEC 45hp ex-army 3½-ton lorry, originally a flatbed with 'great western railway' in a cream panel along the side raves (was at Ebbw Jct 1919-23). Now pictured with 2-plank sides having three stanchions that fix into brackets that had later been attached over the cream panel area, the middle bracket obliterating part of 'western' above rear wheel. Near the top of these stanchions are brackets for hoopsticks. Fleet number 685 in brown on a cream plaque on cabside, and in white on black chassis where are also indistinct unladen-, front axle- and back axle-weights. This design of cab had no side windows. Registration LX9733. Solid tyres, double at rear. Canvas 'door' and acetylene headlights. *GWR/D J Hyde collection*

Bridgwater and Pershore. As an example, the service for outlying districts around Aberystwyth using a Thornycroft 30-cwt vehicle carried all sorts of goods within the area covered by Rhydyfelin, Llanfarian, Figure Four, Chancery, Blaenplwyf, Llanddeinol, Llanrhystyd, Llanon, Capel Bangor, Goginan, Pontyrwyd, Talybont, Taliesin and Treddol. Some places were served by Country Lorries from different stations, such as Bourton in Shropshire from both Much Wenlock and Presthope; Cruwys Morchard (from Cadeleigh and Tiverton); Harbertonford (from Kingswear and Totnes); Tibberton (Gloucester and Newent); Wellington (Hereford) from both Hereford and Leominster stations; and Whitton (Kington and Tenbury Wells).

In 1928 services were introduced at the following 29 depots: Ashburton, Baschurch, Bedwyn, Bridgnorth, Bromyard, Clevedon,

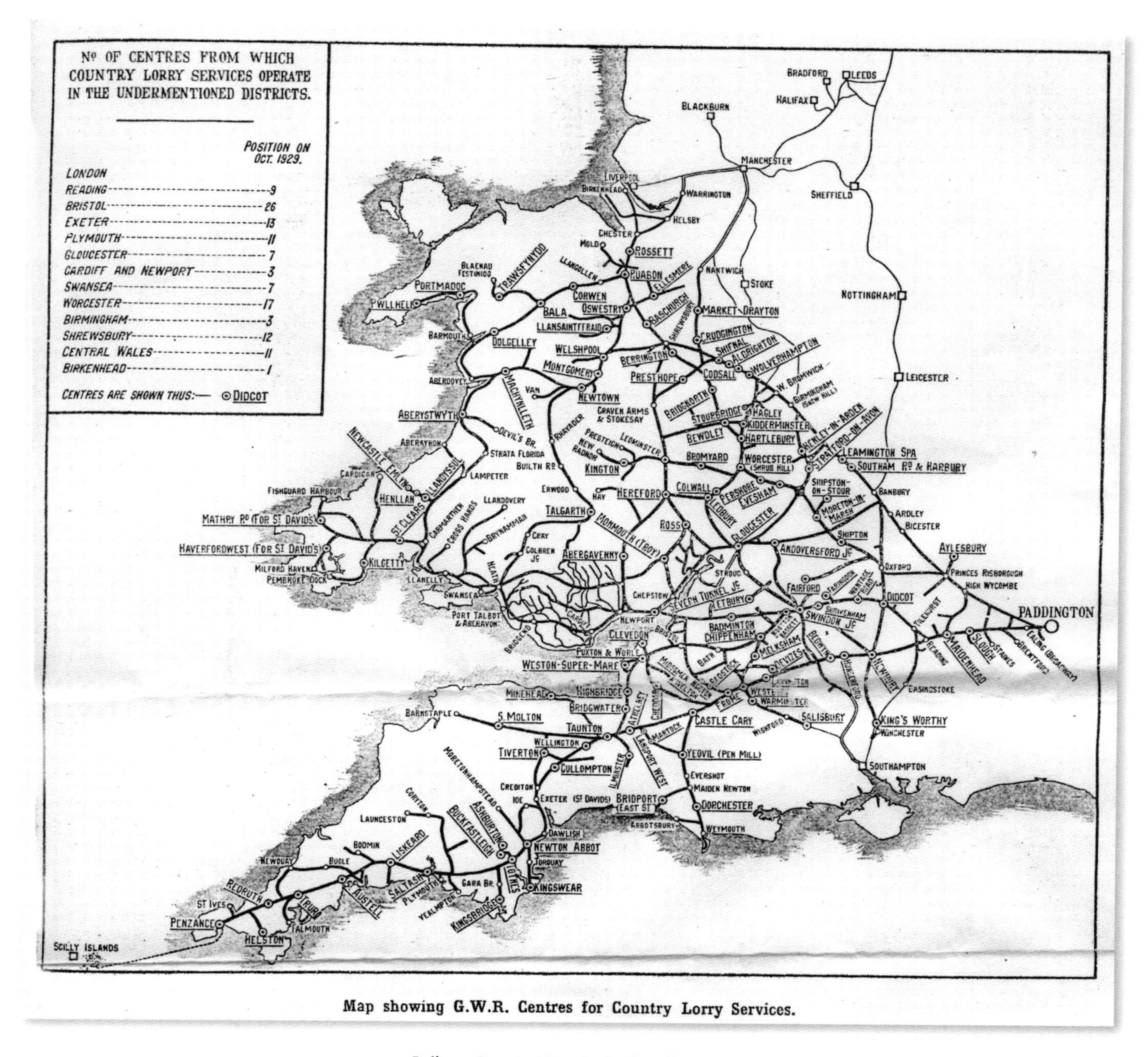

Map showing G.W.R. Centres for Country Lorry Services.

Railway Gazette Map. ***Author's collection***

Corwen, Didcot, Evesham, Faringdon, Ilminster, King's Worthy, Lavington, Ledbury, Martock, Melksham, Monmouth, Newton Abbot, Penzance, Presthope, Severn Tunnel Junction, Shifnal, Shrivenham, Southam Road, Trawsfynydd, Wantage Road, Wellington (Somerset), Welshpool and Weston-Super-Mare. At Melksham, a Fordson tractor and trailer did the job. The service at Trawsfynydd opened in April 1928, but was transferred to Dolgelly that October. The GW was so proud of its achievement that it proclaimed in 1927 that the Country Lorry service was being augmented by an average of one every fortnight, and in 1928 by one every nine days! The 100th service was brought into operation at Codshall (Staffordshire) in 1929, by which time 150 motors were in use all over the system on Country Lorry services. In 1932, the total number of Country Lorry services had grown to 142 and reached 170 in 1936. The services began to be advertised in the GW public passenger timetables. Between 1937 and 1939, new services were introduced at Brecon, Cleobury Mortimer, Dinmore, Dorrington, Hayle, Kidwelly, Llandrillo, Minsterley, Newnham Bridge, Pontrilas, Saundersfoot, Shepton Mallet, and Steventon. At the outbreak of WW2, there were 184 Country Lorry services in operation.

The Country Lorry service delivering and collecting goods from a farm near Lechlade in January 1935. Two-ton Thornycroft 'Handy' lorry and 2-wheeled Eagle trailer having chain surrounds. Fleet 3009, registration ALN409. 'g.w.r./paddington station/london' at bottom of cabside. Electric lights. ***GWR/D J Hyde collection***

GREAT WESTERN RAILWAY.

GOODS AND PARCELS LORRY SERVICES.

DULVERTON and DISTRICT.

Weight not exceeding	*See Note below Scale "A." Up to 3 miles.	Scale "B." Over 3 and up to 5 miles.	Scale "C." Over 5 and up to 7 miles.	Scale "D." Over 7 and up to 9 miles.	*Scale "E." Over 9 and up to 12 miles.	Scale "F." Over 12 and up to 15 miles.	Scale "G." Over 15 and up to 20 miles.
	s. d.	s. d.	s. d.	s. d.	s. d.	s. d.	s. d.
7 lbs. ..	0 6	0 6	0 6	0 6	0 7	0 7	0 7
11 " ..	0 6	0 6	0 6	0 6	0 7	0 7	0 8
14 " ..	0 6	0 6	0 6	0 6	0 7	0 7	0 9
28 " ..	0 6	0 6	0 6	0 6	0 9	0 9	0 10
56 " ..	0 6	0 6	0 8	0 8	0 11	0 11	1 0
84 " ..	0 7	0 7	0 10	1 0	1 2	1 3	1 4
1 cwt. ..	0 8	0 8	1 0	1 3	1 6	1 7	1 9
2 " ..	1 0	1 0	1 9	2 0	2 6	2 9	3 0
3 " ..	1 2	1 6	2 6	2 9	3 3	4 0	4 6
4 " ..	1 5	2 0	3 3	3 6	4 0	5 0	6 0
5 " ..	1 8	2 6	4 0	4 3	4 9	6 3	7 6
6 " ..	1 11	3 0	4 9	5 0	5 6	7 6	9 0
7 " ..	2 2	3 6	5 6	5 9	6 3	8 9	10 6
8 " ..	2 5	4 0	6 3	6 6	7 0	10 0	12 0
9 " ..	2 8	4 6	7 0	7 0	7 9	11 3	13 0
10 " ..	2 11	5 0	7 6	7 6	8 6	12 6	14 0
11 " ..	3 1	5 3	7 9	8 0	9 3	13 3	15 0
12 " ..	3 3	5 6	8 0	8 6	10 0	14 0	16 0
13 " ..	3 5	5 9	8 3	9 0	10 9	14 9	17 0
14 " ..	3 7	6 0	8 6	10 0	11 6	15 6	18 0
15 " ..	3 9	6 3	8 9	10 6	12 3	16 3	19 0
16 " ..	3 11	6 6	9 0	11 0	13 0	17 0	20 0
17 " ..	4 1	6 9	9 3	11 6	13 6	17 9	21 0
18 " ..	4 3	7 0	9 6	12 0	14 0	18 6	22 0
19 " ..	4 5	7 3	9 9	12 3	14 6	19 3	23 0
20 " ..	4 6	7 6	10 0	12 6	15 0	20 0	24 0

* SPECIALLY REDUCED RATES IN FORCE BETWEEN DULVERTON STATION & DULVERTON VILLAGE

For full loads (minimum 2 or 4 tons per lorry load) special rates will be charged as follows :—

Distance.	2-ton Loads. per ton. s. d.	4-ton Loads. per ton. s. d.
Up to 1 mile	2 6	2 6
Over 1 mile and not exceeding 2 miles	3 0	2 6
" 2 " " 3 "	3 6	2 6
" 3 " " 4 "	4 6	3 6
" 4 " " 5 "	5 6	3 6
" 5 " " 6 "	6 3	4 6
" 6 " " 7 "	7 0	5 0
" 7 " " 8 "	7 9	5 6
" 8 " " 9 "	8 6	6 0
" 9 " " 10 "	9 3	6 6
" 10 " " 11 "	10 0	7 0
" 11 " " 12 "	10 6	7 6
" 12 " " 15 "	12 6	9 0
" 15 " " 20 "	15 6	11 6

In the case of Goods train traffic conveyed to or from Dulverton Station at rates including collection or delivery, the above charges will be reduced by the appropriate amount included in the rail rate for cartage.

Special journeys are not undertaken for less than reasonable lorry loads, and the scale for small consignments only applies where sufficient general traffic is available to justify the running of the lorry.

Special rates will be quoted on application for exceptionally heavy consignments of traffic.

Through rates can also be quoted on application, i.e. combined road and rail rates between certain stations and the principal villages in the district for grain, oilcake, etc., traffic.

The above rates do not apply to articles of exceptional bulk in relation to weight, such as agricultural implements, bales of feathers, light furniture, or to traffic such as coal, bricks, etc., involving considerable handling. Particulars of charges on application.

For General Notices and Regulations relating to the Company's Road Motor Cars, see separate bills or announcement in Company's Time Table; or apply to **Mr. R. H. Nicholls**, Paddington Station; **Mr. A. E. Hicks**, Exeter; or nearest Station Master, in regard to passenger train traffic; or **Mr.** [illegible] Paddington Station; **Mr. C. J. Challenger**, Exeter; or nearest Goods Agent, in regard to goods train traffic.

JAMES MILNE General Manager.

As years passed it was necessary to augment the strength at certain existing centres. For example, at Helston, a service which was started with one ex-army AEC lorry in May 1926, and one more in 1927, required six vehicles by March 1932. In contrast, at a few places where the Country Lorry service had been introduced, it did not prove successful or was better subsumed into railhead services (see later). Hence services were withdrawn at Malvern Link in 1933; at Hagley, at Himley, and at Wombourn (from Wolverhampton) in 1936. Country Lorries spread their work over different areas on different days of the week: at Taunton, one round covered the Quantock Hills on Mondays, Wednesdays and Fridays, and the Blackdown Hills on Tuesdays, Thursdays and Saturdays.

After WW2, with the beginning of the Zonal Scheme (see opposite) we find that the total number of locations at which services were offered had reduced to 153. Places no longer having Country Lorries in 1946 were: Andoversford, Axbridge, Bewdley, Blaenau Ffestiniog, Calne, Cheltenham, Chepstow, Chirk, Craven Arms, Dartmouth, Didcot, Dorchester, Ellesmere, Hallatrow, Henwick, Hereford, Kingswear, Lavington, Llantwit Major, Machynlleth, Marlborough, Mathry Road, Newnham Bridge, Peplow, Puxton & Worle, Ruabon, St Germans, Shrivenham, Somerton, South Molton, Stourbridge,

Morris 6-ton forward-control double-decker milk churn lorry, fleet 2902, new in 1932. Body number G 1494 painted on extreme right of cream panel on rave. Double rear tyres. Safety guards (under-run protection) along the lower side. No rear mudguard. Petrol tank looks very muddy compared with the rest of the vehicle. A picture of an unloaded similar vehicle, fleet 2904, with a pivoted beam device for lifting/lowering churns fitted at the rear is in Stevens-Stratten and Aldridge, p 36. ***GWR/D J Hyde collection***

This return to arrive at Road Transport Superintendent's Office, Paddington, not later than Tuesday morning in each week.

Car No. 1650

G.W.R.

SILVERTON (DEVON) Station.

G.W. 8

STATEMENT OF TRAFFIC CONVEYED BY COUNTRY LORRY SERVICE.

Week ending August 15th 1934

(802)

Date	Outboundary Traffic, *i.e.*, Country Cartage										Particulars of Traffic conveyed at "through" rates, *i.e.*, combined Rail and Road rates (Dels Grain)					Within boundary Traffic, *i.e.*, Town Collection and Delivery										
	Weight				Cartage Charge			Rebate on C. & D. Traffic			Weight		Road Motor Proportion (OBak raised)			Traffic at rates including Collection and Delivery					Traffic charged at S. to S. rates					
	Outwards		Return													Weight		Rebate			Weight		Cartage Charge			
Miles	T.	C.	T.	C.	£	s.	d.	£	s.	d.	T.	C.	£	s.	d.	T.	C.	£	s.	d.	T.	C.	£	s.	d.
Goods Traffic																Where working										
Mon. 40											4	10				Silverton										
Tues. 43		2				1	6				6	18				" + Stoke Canon										
Wed. 73	2	1				3	6									Cadeleigh ½ day Exeter ½ day										
Thurs. ...																Exeter all day										
Fri. 41		5				1	1				4	11				Silverton										
Sat. 36											5	15			4d	"										
Total 189	2	8				6	1				21	14			4d											
Parcels Traffic	Number		Number								Number					Number					Number					
Mon. ...	10					1	1																			
Tues. ...	2					1	-																			
Wed. ...																										
Thurs. ...																										
Fri. ...																										
Sat. ...																										

Statement of Traffic by Country Lorry. ***Author's collection***

COMBINED ROAD
AND
RAIL SERVICES

Collection & Delivery of General Merchandise in **REMOTE AREAS**

Road Motor services operate from the principal country stations, bringing the majority of outlying shops, farms and private houses within easy access of the railway.

Consult your local Goods Agent on all matters relating to freight transport

GWR · LMS · LNER · SR

Opened in 1929 at Craven Arms and at Leominster, the Country Lorry services were joint with the LMS. In fact, following the GW's lead, Country Lorries were operated by the other members of the 'Big Four' and in WW2 a combined poster was issued using sketches based on GW pictures.

As Country Lorries wore out, they were replaced by 'renewals' in the accounts. Even with the difficulties of supplies of materials during WW2, in 1942/43 livestock bodies were made for a Ford 4/6-ton chassis and a Thornycroft 5/6-ton 'Sturdy' chassis No 4643, the latter including a cab. Other vehicles used in the Country Lorry service are described in Chapter 11.

Country Lorry services at rural stations could bring in large amounts of traffic to rail. In one three-month period in 1936, 5,000 tons was carried by rail just within countryside stations around Bristol. At harvest time lorries and drivers, loaders and clerical staff were transferred temporarily to get the work done (rather like the extra staff transferred temporarily to Weymouth for Channel Islands traffic, as described in *GW Docks & Marine*). In 1946 for example over 6,000 tons of fruit was carted in the Vale of Evesham.

Other vehicles used in the Country Lorry service are described in Chapter 11.

Thornycroft 'JJ' country lorry, fleet A 2214, GK6114 of 1931, photographed in the late 1930s delivering bales of wool for grading at Messrs Beavan's tannery in Holt (Wilts). The dilapidated vehicle has a body with hinged sides but provision for five hoopsticks. ***GWR/D J Hyde collection***

LOADING UP FRUIT AND VEGETABLES AT PERSHORE FOR CONVEYANCE BY GOODS AND PASSENGER SERVICES.

Loading up fruit and vegetables at Pershore in Worcestershire in 1946 for travel by rail. *GWR Magazine*

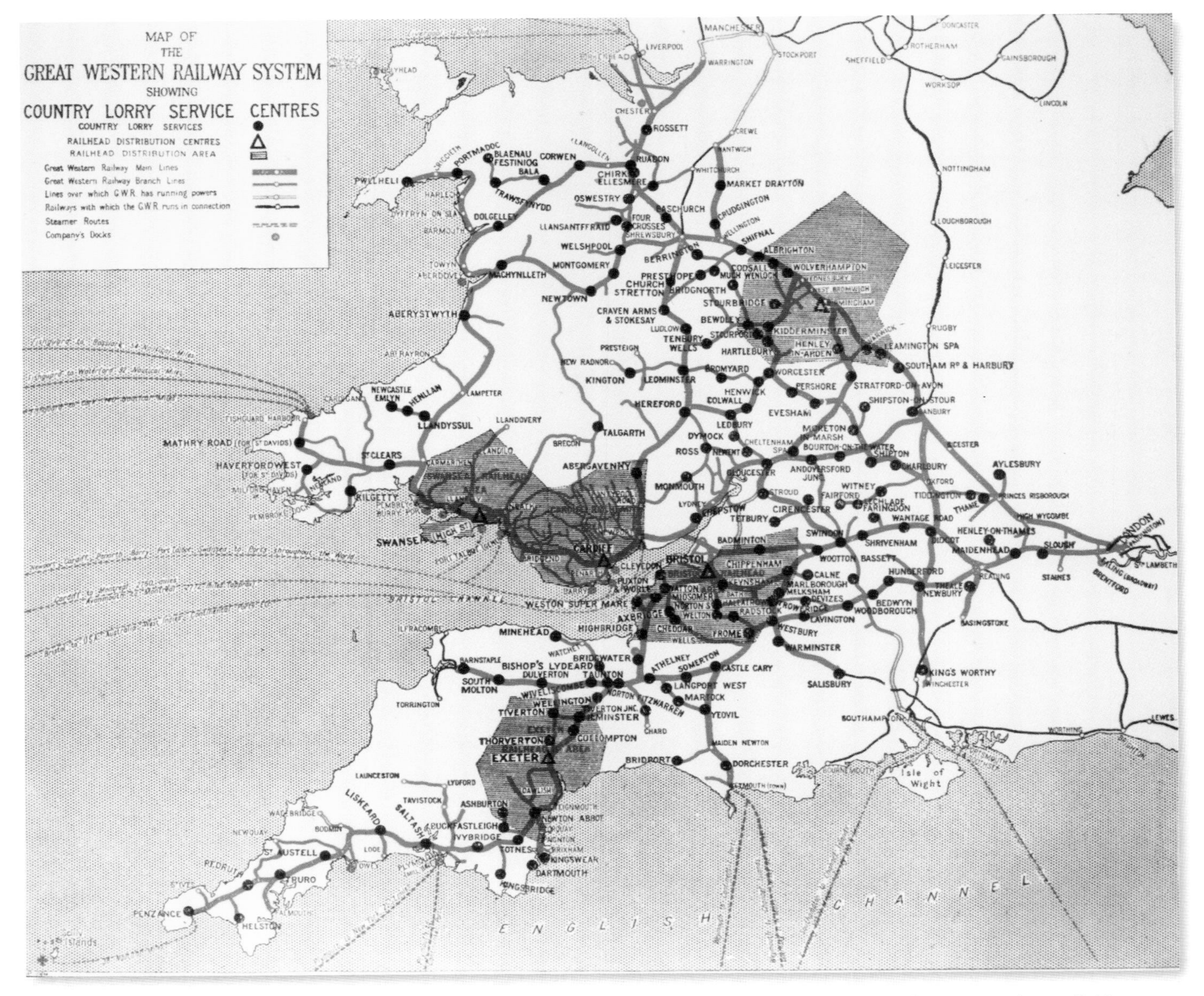

Railhead Distribution

The introduction by the GWR of fast overnight long-distance vacuum freight trains in the early years of the 20th century speeded up the transport of goods traffic between the main towns (see *GWR Goods Train Working*). However, despite the quickening up of the train journey, cartage at both ends was still by horse-drawn delivery vehicles, with a limit of no more than about 3 miles from the arrival goods depot. Traffic for places beyond the limit of horse cartage, but within the hinterland of the delivery depot, had to be taken onwards by local goods train to the station nearest to the destination before again being delivered by horse within local limits. Traffic for places off the main lines was taken by cross-country rail routes or by branch lines, again to be delivered locally. The limited range of horse-drawn cartage caused lots of extra handling, and time delays. And all the same sort of thing applied in reverse for goods being collected before embarking on a fast long-distance rail journey.

Matters all changed however after WW1 when reliable motor lorries became available so that the range of C&D cartage could be extended. The extended limits encompassed places to which, before WW1, goods had been taken forward by a series of local trains to the station closest to the recipient. The use of motor vehicles meant that some goods could now be delivered (and collected) all the way by road from and to a main depot. Furthermore, the time taken was most often less than the former series of rail journeys (that is, a motor vehicle might be able to deliver and collect goods in some remote location, and get back to the depot, before the next timetabled branch goods train was scheduled). Hence a variety of so-called 'concentration schemes' came into being across the GW system in the 1920s where more and more use was made of motor vehicles for parts of the journey from the sending town to the receiving town. This further improved the provision of a next-day delivery service in 'smalls' traffic, and avoided the transhipment of goods from one railway wagon to another *en route*. Thus depot costs were saved, transit times shortened, and fewer railway wagons were required and, with less handling, the likelihood of damage to goods was reduced. Distribution of goods thus became concentrated at fewer places (so-called 'Railheads'), each of which covered by road a much greater cartage area than before. It is of interest to note that Pickfords had 'canal heads' in the early 1800s to which traffic was conveyed in bulk by boat to be delivered locally by road wagons.

In 1926, Railheads were opened at Abergavenny, Helston, Hungerford, Llansantffraid (ex-Cambrian Rlys), Oswestry, Radstock, St Austell, St Clears, Shipton, and Taunton. In 1929, C&D traffic for seven surrounding stations was concentrated at Bridgend, and traffic formerly dealt with at Devonport and Sutton Harbour was concentrated at Plymouth. But the new scheme was not just the use of motor vehicles for longer-distance cartage, since it also involved simplified methods of charging whereby it was made available at a flat rate per ton, irrespective of distance. The service was open to the general public as well as firms.

Although Railheads were introduced by the GW for operational purposes, it was realised that the scheme was good for distribution of goods such as tobacco, groceries, chemists' sundries, confectionery and so on from large manufacturers who required deliveries to numerous towns and villages at guaranteed dates and times, yet who also wanted to bypass the complexity of the traditional railway system of charging based on distance. Previously traffic in small lots from numerous consignees would have been sent by rail as separate packages to a goods depot in a large town, from where the goods would have been sent forward by rail to local stations, many of which were on remote branches. Under the new arrangements, products from manufacturers all over the country were loaded in bulk to a given large goods depot (the Railhead again) for distribution by GW road vehicles, rather than by local rail services. Delivery was made to the door of the customer at least a day earlier than was possible by a train-only/horse transport service, since rail transhipment and multiple handling were avoided.

In addition to the above services, an increasing number of firms entered into contracts for special bulk rail rates and railhead services as an alternative to using their own (or a private long distance carrier's) road vehicles from factory to customer. Contracts of this sort that affected six Railheads and the exclusive use of eight lorries were negotiated in 1926. The first of these general railhead services was inaugurated at Cardiff in March 1927. The GW took responsibility for unpacking and sorting the bulk loads that arrived from the manufacturer, and did all the paperwork for deliveries and returned empties. In addition, the GW would arrange that its carmen unpack the goods and place them on the shelves if required. Gradually additional firms became attracted to the idea, and by 1933 no less than 200 were involved, including motor tyre manufacturers. The fleet of railhead road vehicles operating from Cardiff's Newtown goods depot at that time comprised 12 motor vans, each of which made a daily run averaging about seventy miles delivering large numbers of multiple package consignments to businesses in the valleys above Cardiff. As many as 80 calls per day were made by some of the drivers engaged on the railhead work.

SCALE OF CHARGES FOR SMALL CONSIGNMENTS
UP TO AND INCLUDING 1 TON
applicable to the following Stations.

Abergavenny
Aberystwyth
Albrighton
Andoversford
Ashburton
Athelney
Axbridge
†Aylesbury
Badminton
Bala
Banbury
Baschurch
Bedwyn
Berrington S.V.
Bewdley
Bishop's Lydeard
Blaenau Festiniog
Bourton-on-Water
Bridgnorth
||Bridgwater
Bridport
Bromyard
Buckfastleigh
Calne
Castle Cary
Charlbury
Cheddar
Cheltenham
Chepstow
Chippenham
Chirk
Church Stretton
Cirencester
Clevedon
Codsall
Colwall
§Corwen
Craven Arms
Crudgington
Cullompton
*Dartmouth
Devizes
Didcot
Dolgelley
Dorchester
Dulverton
Dymock
Ellesmere
§Evesham
Fairford
Faringdon
Four Crosses
Frome
§Gloucester
Hallatrow
Hartlebury
Henley-in-Arden
Henley-on-Thames
Henwick
§Hereford
||Highbridge
Hungerford
Ilminster
Ivybridge
Keynsham
Kidderminster
Kilgetty
Kingswear
King's Worthy
Kington
Langport West
Lavington
Leamington
Lechlade
Ledbury
Leominster
Liskeard
Llansantffraid
Ludlow
Machynlleth
Maidenhead
§Market Drayton
Marlborough
Martock
Melksham
||Midsomer Norton
Minehead
Monmouth
Moreton-in-Marsh
Much Wenlock
Newbury
Newent
Newton Abbot
Newtown
Norton Fitzwarren
Oswestry
Pershore
Portmadoc
Presthope
Puxton & Worle
Pwllheli
||Radstock
Redruth
Ross
Rossett
Ruabon
‡St. Clears
Salisbury
Saltash
Shifnal
Shipston-on-Stour
Shipton
Shrivenham
Slough
Somerton (Som.
Southam Road
South Molton
Stourbridge
Stourport
§Stratford-on-Avon
Swindon
Talgarth
Taunton
§Tenbury Wells
Tetbury
Thame
Thorverton
Tiddington
Tiverton
Tiverton Junction
Totnes
Trawsfynydd
Truro
Wantage Road
Warminster
Warwick
Wellington, Som.
§Welshpool
Westbury, Wilts.
Weston-super-Mare
Witney
Wiveliscombe
Wolverhampton to Bridgnorth
Woodborough
Wootton Bassett
§Worcester
Yatton
Yeovil

NOTE.—* The rates for the cartage of traffic in the Dartmouth District are increased by an amount of 2/4 per ton, representing the Ferry charge between Kingswear and Dartmouth.
† The scales for distances over 10 miles do not apply in the case of the Aylesbury service; the 7 to 9 miles scale, however, applies to the 10 miles zone.
‡ Special Rates to Laugharne and Pendine, *see page* 8.
§ The scale for distances over 12 miles does not apply in the case of these Services.
|| Special 1-Ton Rates apply, *see page* 5.

Weight not exceeding	Up to 3 miles	Over 3 and up to 5 miles	Over 5 and up to 7 miles	Over 7 and up to 9 miles	Over 9 and up to 12 miles	Over 12 and up to 15 miles	Over 15 and up to 20 miles
	s. d.	s. d.	s. d.	s. d.	s. d.	s. d.	s. d.
7 lbs.	0 6	0 6	0 6	0 6	0 7	0 7	0 7
11 ,,	0 6	0 6	0 6	0 6	0 7	0 7	0 8
14 ,,	0 6	0 6	0 6	0 6	0 7	0 7	0 9
28 ,,	0 6	0 6	0 6	0 6	0 9	0 9	0 10
56 ,,	0 6	0 6	0 8	0 8	0 11	0 11	1 0
84 ,,	0 7	0 7	0 10	1 0	1 2	1 3	1 4
1 cwt.	0 8	0 8	1 0	1 3	1 6	1 7	1 9
2 ,,	1 0	1 0	1 9	2 0	2 6	2 9	3 0
3 ,,	1 2	1 6	2 6	2 9	3 3	4 0	4 6
4 ,,	1 5	2 0	3 3	3 6	4 0	5 0	6 0
5 ,,	1 8	2 6	4 0	4 3	4 9	6 3	7 6
6 ,,	1 11	3 0	4 9	5 0	5 6	7 6	9 0
7 ,,	2 2	3 6	5 6	5 9	6 3	8 9	10 6
8 ,,	2 5	4 0	6 3	6 6	7 0	10 0	12 0
9 ,,	2 8	4 6	7 0	7 0	7 9	11 3	13 0
10 ,,	2 11	5 0	7 6	7 6	8 6	12 6	14 0
11 ,,	3 1	5 3	7 9	8 0	9 3	13 3	15 0
12 ,,	3 3	5 6	8 0	8 6	10 0	14 0	16 0
13 ,,	3 5	5 9	8 3	9 0	10 9	14 9	17 0
14 ,,	3 7	6 0	8 6	10 0	11 6	15 6	18 0
15 ,,	3 9	6 3	8 9	10 6	12 3	16 3	19 0
16 ,,	3 11	6 6	9 0	11 0	13 0	17 0	20 0
17 ,,	4 1	6 9	9 3	11 6	13 6	17 9	21 0
18 ,,	4 3	7 0	9 6	12 0	14 0	18 6	22 0
19 ,,	4 5	7 3	9 9	12 3	14 6	19 3	23 0
20 ,,	4 6	7 6	10 0	12 6	15 0	20 0	24 0

The way goods depots were run was changed to suit the new service as the business grew. For example, prior to 1932, at Cardiff Newtown, inwards traffic was dealt with at the eastern end, and outwards at the western (see *GWR Goods Services*, vol 2B). Later the western building was used almost exclusively for handling warehouse, railhead and other special traffics.

Railhead distribution services were extended to Bristol and Exeter in 1929, to Swansea in 1930 and to Birmingham in 1932, this time jointly with the LMS. In the January 1932 *GWR Magazine* we read that 'one of the most enterprising firms in the country' arranged with the GW to distribute their produce within a radius of 70 miles from Bristol. Eventually goods were being distributed in this manner for over 200 firms from 24 centres on the system including additional Railhead depots in Newport and Reading. Needless to say, effective railhead distribution was linked to efficient warehousing at goods depots. The service was speedier than conveyance by normal means, but was reserved for those firms prepared to pay for it on agreed terms. Firms involved in Railhead schemes wanting deliveries in country areas were able to use the Country Lorry service (see above).

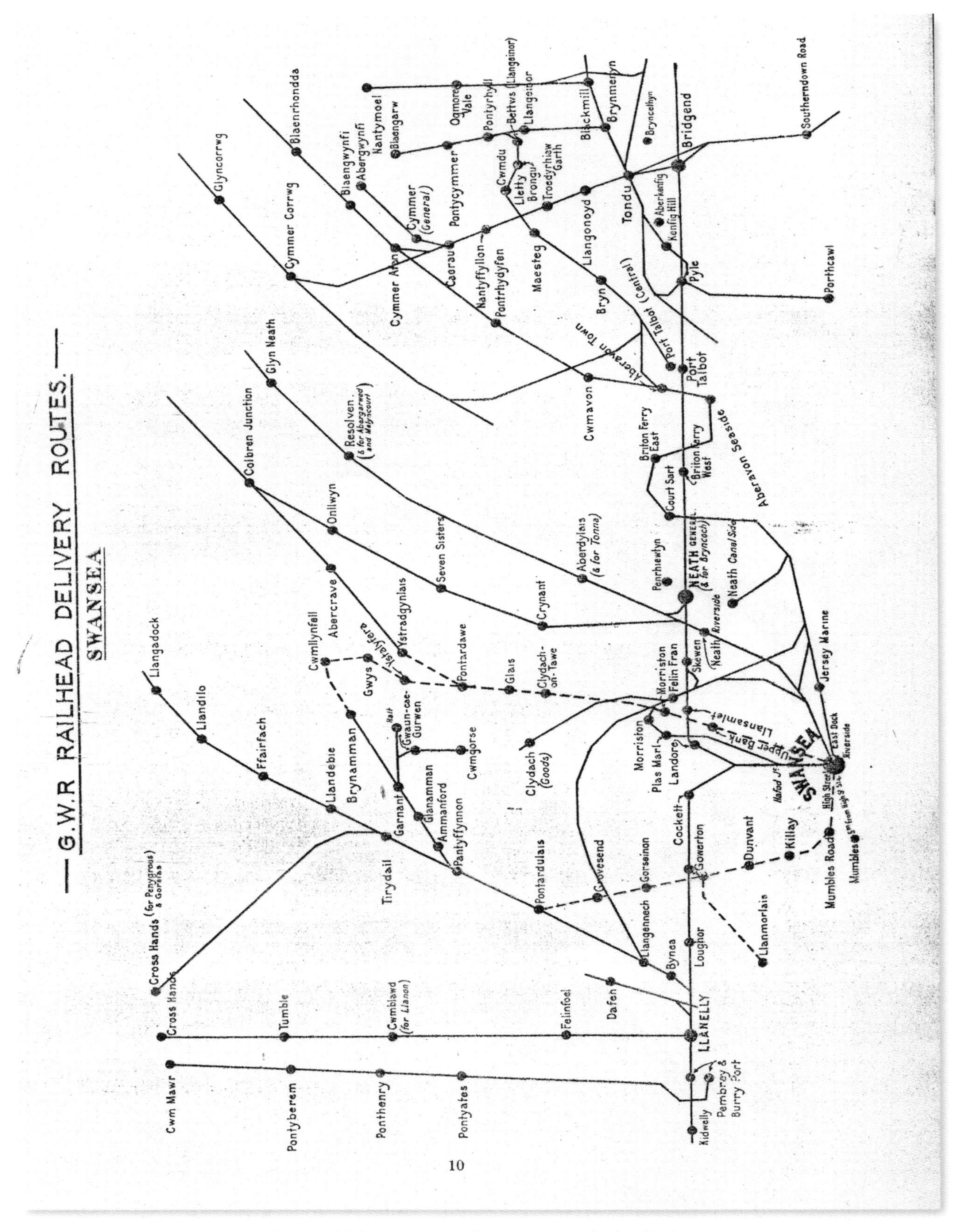

Above and following pages **Delivery routes.** ***Author's collection***

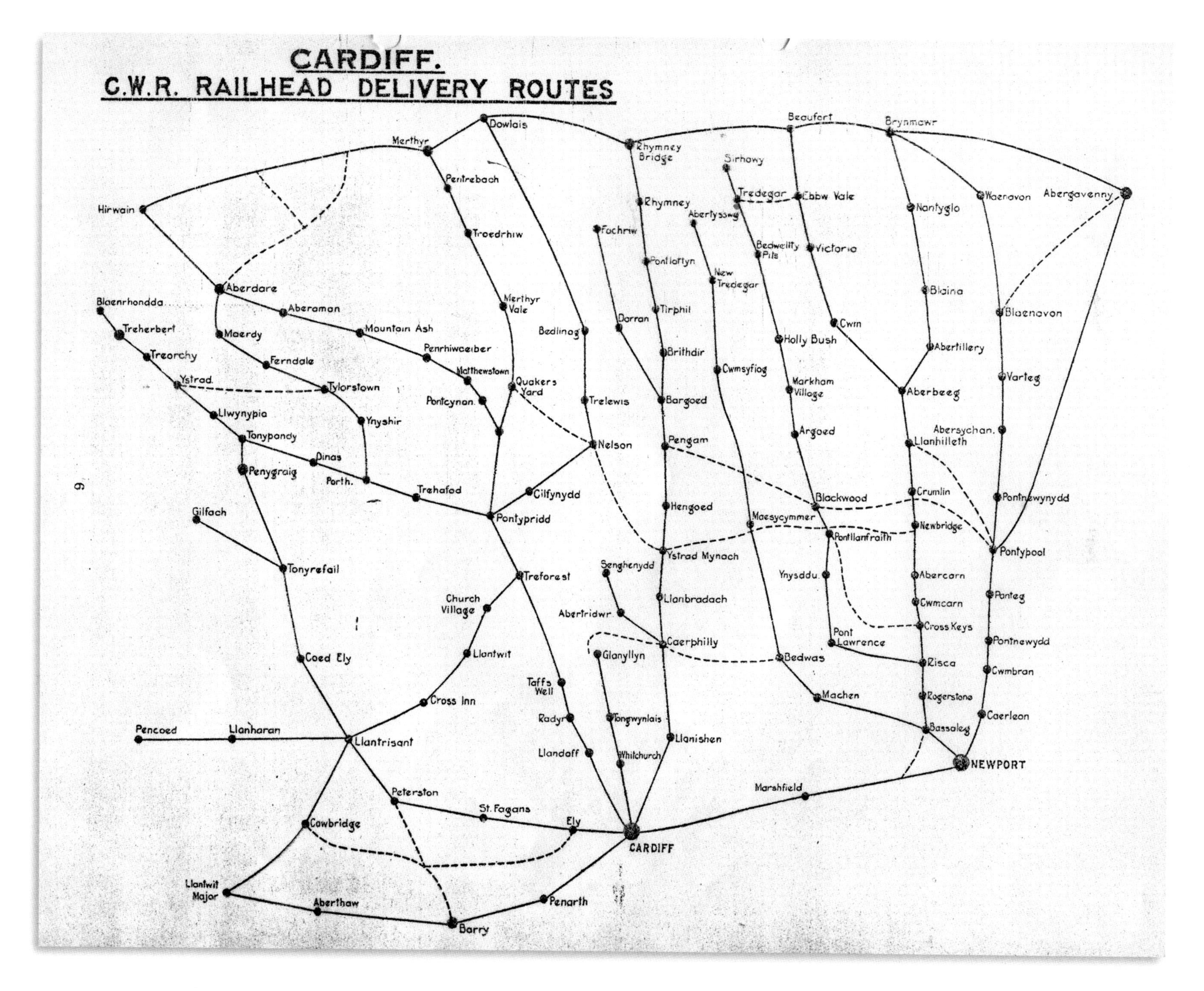
CARDIFF.
C.W.R. RAILHEAD DELIVERY ROUTES
Dowlais
Merthyr
Beaufort
Brynmawr
Rhymney Bridge
Sirhowy
Hirwain
Pentrebach
Tredegar
Ebbw Vale
Waenavon
Abergavenny
Rhymney
Nantyglo
Abertyssweg
Fochriw
Troedrhiw
Bedwellty Pits
Victoria
Pontlottyn
New Tredegar
Aberdare
Blaina
Blaenrhondda
Aberaman
Merthyr Vale
Tirphil
Blaenavon
Treherbert
Maerdy
Bedlinog
Darran
Cwm
Holly Bush
Mountain Ash
Brithdir
Abertillery
Treorchy
Penrhiwceiber
Ferndale
Cwmsyfiog
Matthewstown
Markham Village
Varteg
Ystrad.
Quakers Yard
Tylorstown
Aberbeeg
Pontcynon.
Trelewis
Bargoed
Llwynypia
Ynyshir
Argoed
Abersychan.
Llanhilleth
Tonypandy
Pengam
Nelson
Dinas
Penygraig
Porth.
Blackwood
Crumlin
Trehafod
Cilfynydd
Pontnewynydd
Hengoed
Gilfach
Pontypridd
Maesycymmer
Newbridge
Pontllanfraith
Ystrad Mynach
Pontypool
Tonyrefail
Senghenydd
Treforest
Ynysddu.
Abercarn
Church Village
Llanbradach
Ponteg
Abertridwr.
Cwmcarn
Cross Keys
Pont Lawrence
Caerphilly
Pontnewydd
Coed Ely
Llantwit
Glanyllyn
Bedwas
Risca
Cwmbran
Taffs Well
Cross Inn
Machen
Rogerstone
Caerleon
Radyr
Tongwynlais
Pencoed
Llanharan
Bassaleg
Llanishen
Llantrisant
Llandaff
Whitchurch
NEWPORT
Peterston
Marshfield
St. Fagans
Cowbridge
Ely
CARDIFF
Llantwit Major
Aberthaw
Penarth
Barry
6

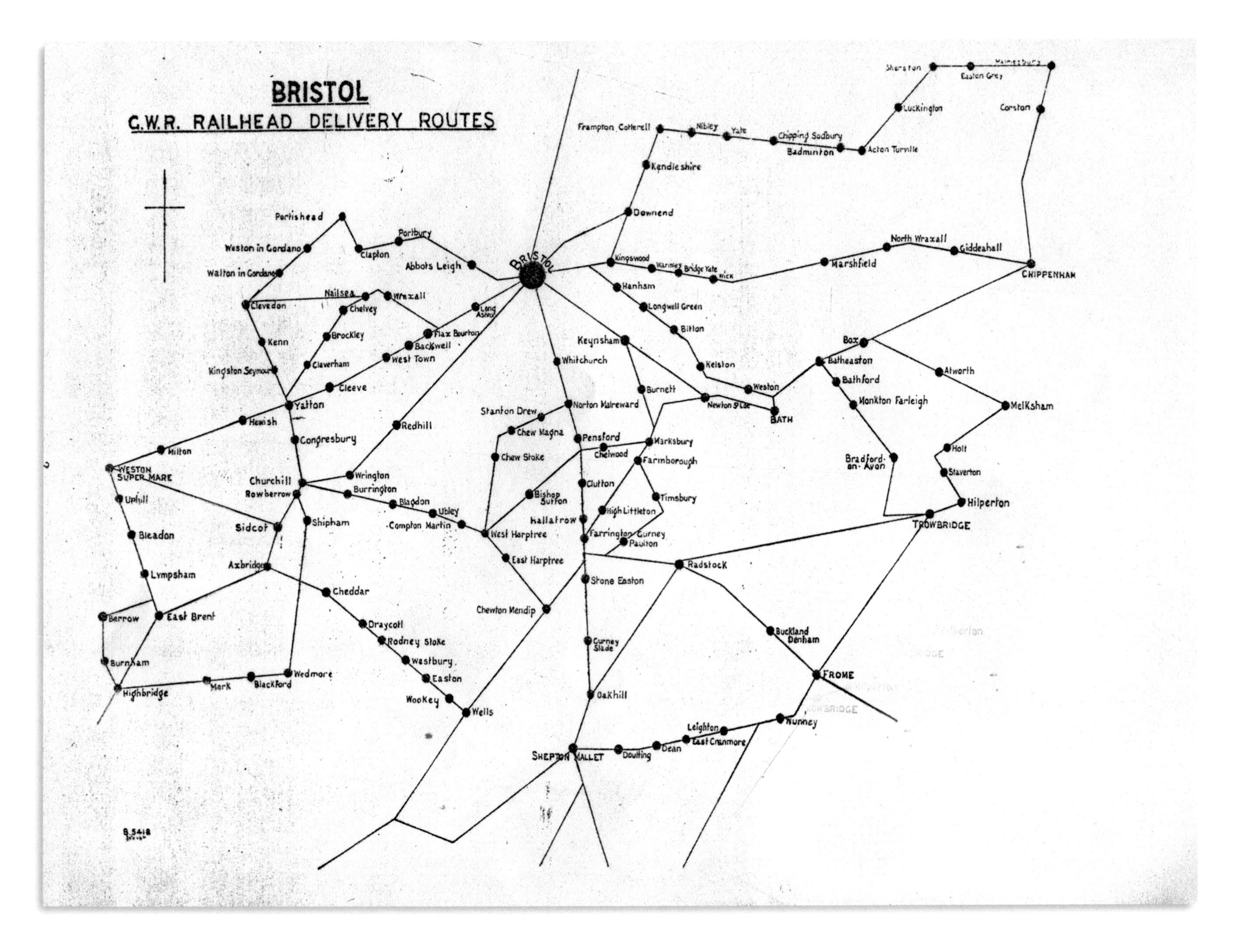
BRISTOL
G.W.R. RAILHEAD DELIVERY ROUTES
Sherston
Easton Grey
Luckington
Corston
Frampton Cotterell
Nibley
Yate
Chipping Sodbury
Badminton
Acton Turville
Kendleshire
Downend
Portishead
Portbury
Weston in Gordano
Clapton
Walton in Gordano
Abbots Leigh
BRISTOL
Kingswood
Warmley
Bridge Yate
Wick
Marshfield
North Wraxall
Giddeahall
CHIPPENHAM
Hanham
Longwell Green
Bitton
Kelston
Weston
BATH
Newton St Loe
Box
Batheaston
Bathford
Monkton Farleigh
Atworth
Melksham
Holt
Staverton
Hilperton
TROWBRIDGE
Bradford-on-Avon
Nailsea
Wraxall
Clevedon
Chelvey
Long Ashton
Brockley
Flax Bourton
Backwell
West Town
Kenn
Claverham
Kingston Seymour
Cleeve
Yatton
Hewish
Redhill
Congresbury
Milton
WESTON SUPER MARE
Uphill
Churchill
Rowberrow
Wrington
Burrington
Blagdon
Ubley
Compton Martin
Sidcot
Shipham
Bleadon
Lympsham
Axbridge
Cheddar
Berrow
East Brent
Burnham
Highbridge
Mark
Blackford
Wedmore
Draycott
Rodney Stoke
Westbury
Easton
Wookey
Wells
Keynsham
Whitchurch
Burnett
Norton Malreward
Stanton Drew
Chew Magna
Chew Stoke
Pensford
Chelwood
Marksbury
Farmborough
Clutton
Bishop Sutton
Timsbury
High Littleton
Hallatrow
West Harptree
Farrington Gurney
Paulton
East Harptree
Radstock
Stone Easton
Chewton Mendip
Buckland Denham
Gurney Slade
FROME
Oakhill
Leighton
East Cranmore
Nunney
Dean
Doulting
SHEPTON MALLET
B.5418

New Distribution Depot for Messrs. Cadbury at Exeter.

In pursuance of their policy in recent years of affording special rail-connected accommodation and distributing facilities for the use of important traders whose traffic is regularly passing over the Company's system in large quantities, the Company have just provided a depot for Messrs. Cadbury, of Bournville, on a site adjoining the down main line at the north end of St. Davids station, Exeter.

The depot is served on the one side by a rail connection from the down main line. The other side fronts, and has direct access to, the main Cowley Road. An excellent idea of the pleasing appearance of the building is afforded by the accompanying illustrations. The structure is of red brick, roofed with red Roman pattern tiles, and was erected by Messrs. Wilkins, Torquay, under the supervision of the Great Western Railway Company's divisional engineer, and in accordance with designs prepared by Messrs. Cadbury's architects.

The rail side of Messrs. Cadbury's new depot at Exeter, showing the unloading deck.

The other side of the depot, which adjoins the main road.

The building, which embodies the results of several years' experience in depot operation by Messrs. Cadbury, measures about 75-ft. by 60-ft. The ground floor, designed for use as a stock room, has an area of about 500 sq. yards at platform level, with direct access on the one side to a covered jetty serving the rail, and on the other to a covered platform where road vehicles are berthed.

The storage space on this floor has a hard granolithic surface, but the central trolleying way connected with the rail and road jetties is paved with hard wood blocks.

The offices, waiting room, and other accommodation, are situated on the Cowley Road side of an upper floor, and behind these are two show rooms, where the firm's commodities are on exhibition for their customers.

The building is electrically lighted throughout, and heated by a low-pressure hot-water system capable of maintaining a temperature of 60 degrees F. in the stock-room, and 65 in the offices, when the outside air is 32 degrees F. The system is operated and controlled from a boiler in a half-basement under the building.

Zonal Collection and Delivery

Up to and during WW2, 'smalls' traffic was dealt with using the various Railhead concentration schemes outlined above where road vehicles played a significant part in carrying goods for part (or even all) of the journey. As a result, the GW boasted a one-day C&D service between principal towns, with approximately 70 percent of all small consignments reaching their destinations the day after they were sent. Even so, the company realised that this was not going to be good enough for the post-war era, and in 1944 the GWR began to plan a new scheme, which would ultimately ensure faster next-day deliveries to *all* parts of its territory. The fundamental principle of the new service (known as the *Zonal Collection & Delivery* system) was that every small consignment was loaded from one originating centre to one destination centre, with no transhipment or delay. Leslie King (Assistant to G J Challenger and then D Hawkeswood, District Goods Managers at Exeter) told the author that the scheme was seen from the outset as a prelude to branch line closures.

In the new system, territory served by the GW was divided up into zones which varied in size according to population density and geography (it is interesting that the official documentation used an old GW map dating from 1929 on which to mark the zones). The aim was to assemble sufficient traffic at a small number of stations to enable direct wagon-loads to be dispatched to other zones. This meant that in non-industrial areas traffic had to be drawn in from much further afield. Within each area was a goods depot (the *Zonal Railhead*), chosen for its central locality and having good main line services. Complementary to every Railhead were one or more subsidiary *Sub-Railheads*, strategically selected so that the whole zone could be linked up by motor vehicles. The necessary volume of rail traffic at sub-railheads was obtained by arranging for each of them to serve an area previously covered by three or four railway stations (known as *absorbed depots*). Goods that could not be made up into full wagon-loads at the sub-railhead were sent forward to the Zonal Railhead by road or, where suitable services existed, by *passenger* train. Zonal railheads and sub-railheads were linked by timetabled motor vehicles, which meant that perishable and urgent traffic could be taken all the way by road on the same day.

The 1944 review created 36 zones, the first of which was established in December 1945 and covered 180 square miles in the neighbourhood of Birmingham, running from Erdington and Great Bridge in the north to Lapworth in the south. The smalls traffic which had previously been handled at twenty stations and three subsidiary depots (see Railhead maps earlier in this chapter) was now concentrated at five stations, viz: Cradley Heath, Lye, Tyseley, Wednesbury and West Bromwich. Birmingham was chosen to pioneer the scheme because:

(i) The Railhead Distribution transfer lorries that had been running pre-war between Hockley and 14 surrounding stations had shown what could be achieved by 'trunk motoring';

(ii) the area was compact so that the system was easily developed;

(iii) there was a large volume of traffic in the area; and

(iv) the railway accommodation available at key points was easily adaptable for the needs of Zonal operations.

The success of the Birmingham experiment after only a few months of operation caused the time schedule for other areas to be speeded up. Many of the planned Zonal Railheads were established in the summer and autumn of 1946 (Cardiff, Pontypridd, Port Talbot, Worcester, Redruth, Reading, Leamington, Wolverhampton, Swindon, St. Austell, Newport, Plymouth, Trowbridge), with Bristol and Slough coming into play on 1 January 1947. These 16 zonal railheads had 47 sub-railheads. The Shrewsbury and Swindon zones were the largest, each covering an area of 1,000 square miles. Swindon formerly had forty-five stations handling small consignments, whereas in the zonal scheme just six railheads took over all this work. By 1 November 1947, every planned GWR domestic scheme had been introduced, except where structural alterations to buildings for the new system were still taking place. (All invoicing and accountancy at Birmingham was centralised at Hockley, but as the main offices there had not yet been rebuilt following the blitz, the introduction of that phase had to be delayed.) In the first year of full operation in 1947, there was a reduction of over 130,000 tons of rail transhipment from one wagon to another – even though the total C&D tonnage had increased by over 312,000 tons compared with 1946. By the end of 1947, nearly 300 station trucks had been eliminated which enabled branch line and some main line services to be retimed.

New cartage vehicles were required for the additional road mileage involved in the improved service (110,000 miles per annum in the case of Birmingham alone, for which 25 extra vehicles were introduced). An essential feature was the provision of maintenance facilities for cartage vehicles. In the case of the Worcester zone, for example, the main repair depot was in Worcester itself, supplemented by servicing points at Littleton & Badsey, and Kidderminster. These three garages dealt with about 140 vehicles spread throughout the zone, employing the well-established routines of the Road Motor Engineer's department (Chapter 7).

When the Zonal Scheme was finally in place, the only points forwarding and receiving smalls traffic on the GW were the 36 zonal railheads and 112 sub-railheads, as against 1,100 goods stations before the introduction of zoning. Photographs of the redundant depot at Lawrence Hill (Bristol) and redundant horse lorries after the introduction of the Zonal Scheme will be found on p 218/9 in *GWR Goods Services*. Most of the pre-war Railhead Distribution services for particular traffic (tobacco, biscuits, wines and spirits, bacon, etc) were readily incorporated into the zonal scheme. Traders forwarding smalls from private sidings benefited, without losing special rates, by reorganising their dispatch arrangements.

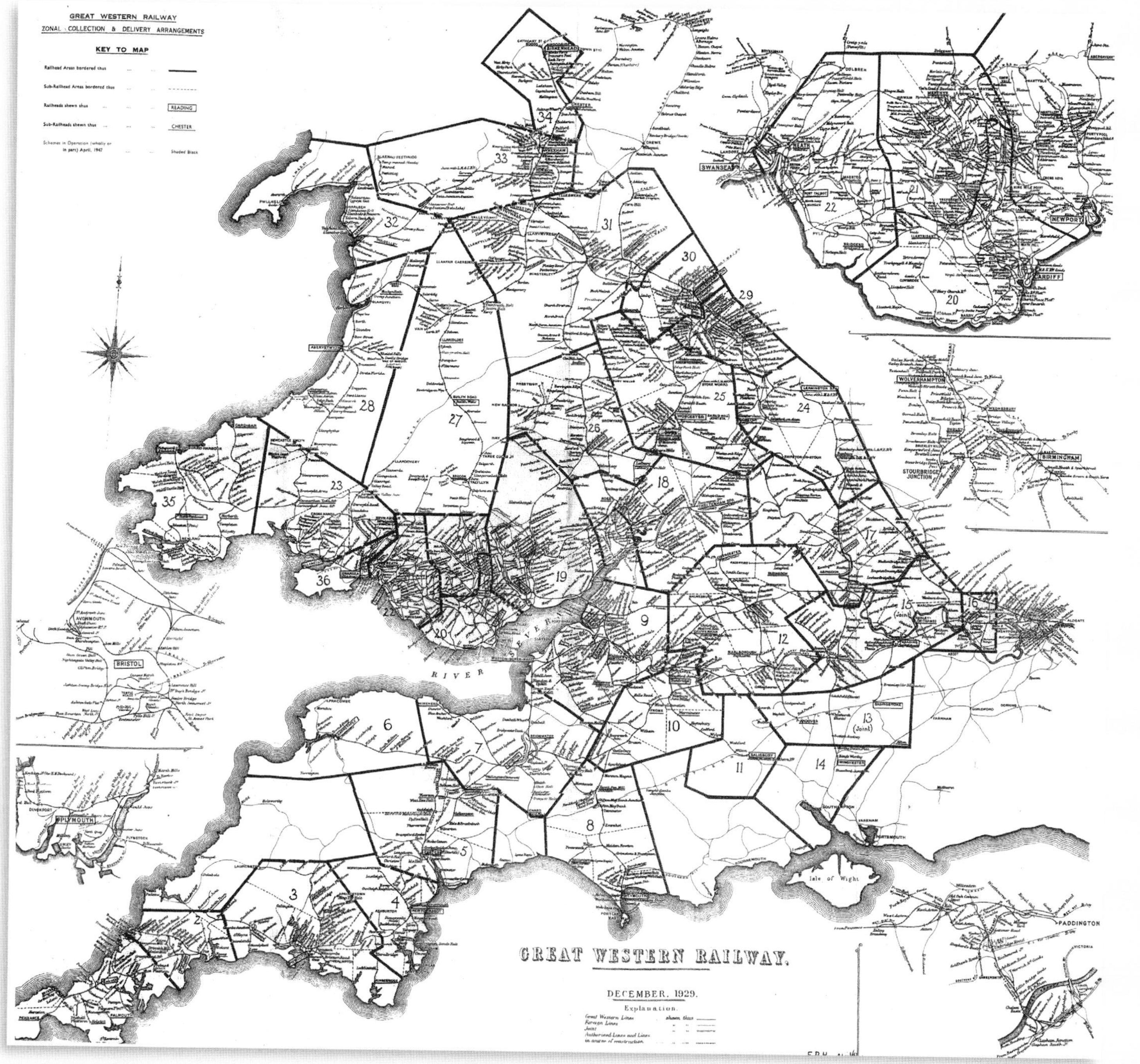

Zonal map. *Author's collection*

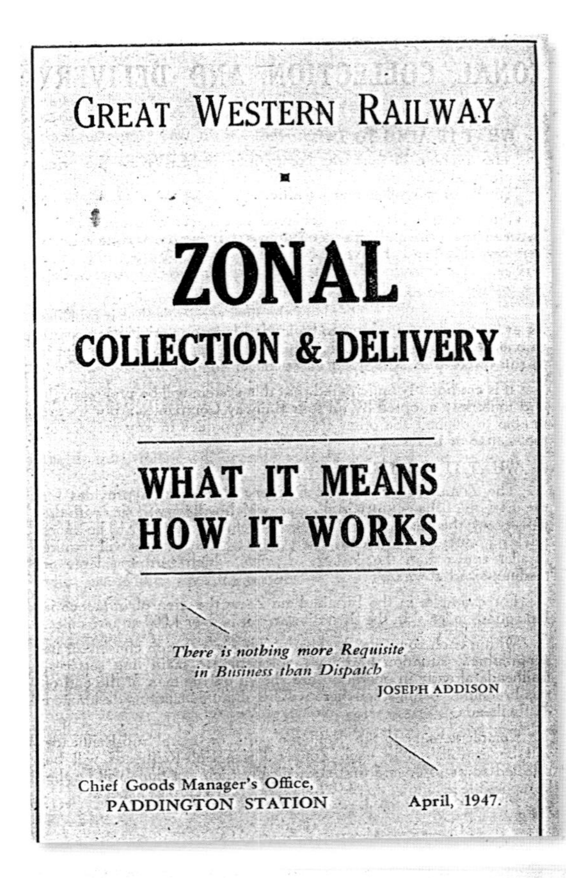

GREAT WESTERN RAILWAY

ZONAL

COLLECTION & DELIVERY

WHAT IT MEANS
HOW IT WORKS

There is nothing more Requisite in Business than Dispatch
JOSEPH ADDISON

Chief Goods Manager's Office,
PADDINGTON STATION

April, 1947.

ZONAL COLLECTION AND DELIVERY

1. **WHAT IT AIMS TO DO.**

The keynote of post-war competition is SERVICE—the prime aim of Zonal Collection and Delivery is to give a next day's delivery to "smalls or miscellaneous" traffic.

Pre-war, this ideal was achieved in respect of traffic passing between the principal cities and towns. It is true Country Lorry Services, Railhead Delivery Schemes, Green Arrow and other services were introduced as steps towards improving more widely the service for "smalls."

The fundamental principle of the new service is that it provides for every small consignment to be loaded from one originating centre to one destination centre, eliminating transhipment, and the aim is to run direct trucks between all such centres nightly.

It is confidently anticipated that this system will be progressively and uniformly adopted by all four Railway Companies; but we are unable to commit the other Railway Companies in any respect on the matter at this stage.

2. **WHAT IT MEANS.**

The Zonal Collection and Delivery Organisation provides for the division of the country into areas, which will vary in size with the density of the district, and its geographical features. The more thickly populated or industrialised parts of the country will require smaller zones than the country districts which surround large or medium-sized towns.

For example, in the Birmingham Zone the area of influence is 160 square miles. In the Swindon area it is over 1,000 square miles.

Within each zone is a Railhead. This is a station chosen for its geographical situation and its relationship to main line services. Railheads already in operation are shewn on the map at the end of this brochure. Altogether there will be about 36 stations designated as Railheads.

Complementary to the Railhead, one or more Sub-Railheads will be established in each Zone. These Sub-Railheads will be selected so as to ensure that strategically their positions will be the best possible in linking up the whole zone from a cartage aspect.

Page 2

The cartage of "smalls" traffic for a zone will thus be concentrated at the Railhead, and at the Sub-Railheads. Generally speaking no other stations will handle "smalls," except for "Carted by Public" consignments. This means that under each Sub-Railhead will be concentrated the miscellaneous traffic of two or more small stations, which are known as "Absorbed" depots.

3. **HOW IT WORKS.**

(a) OUTWARDS.

Let us take the forwarding side first.

A Sub-Railhead will perform daily the collection of traffic in the areas at present served by its "Absorbed" depots. Upon arrival of the direct collection vehicles at the Sub-Railhead from the various absorbed areas, traffic will be loaded either (i) into truck, or (ii) on a Trunk Motor.

By reason of the greater assembly of traffic at a Sub-Railhead, it will be possible to make many more direct wagons than previously from that station to other Sub-Railheads or Railheads. The first principle, therefore, is to ensure direct wagon loading from Sub-Railhead or Railhead to equivalent destination stations.

For that portion of the traffic which cannot be loaded direct, the Trunk Motors will operate on scheduled services between the Sub-Railheads and the Railhead. The number of trips will depend on the amount of traffic to be conveyed.

At the Railhead, traffic from the Sub-Railhead trunk motors will be assembled with the direct tonnage collected at the Railhead and loaded in direct wagons to other Sub-Railheads or Railheads. The greater assemblage of traffic will enable many more direct wagons to be made thus expediting transits.

(b) INWARDS.

In the reverse direction; if a consignment cannot reach a Sub-Railhead by direct truck, it will have been loaded by truck to the Railhead, in which case it will be transferred to the Sub-Railhead by the trunk motor.

Upon arrival at a Sub-Railhead, traffic will be loaded on the direct delivery vehicle serving a particular area, and the traffic will not touch an "Absorbed" station, unless invoiced "To be called for," when it will be left at the "Absorbed" station by a motor.

THIS ORGANISATION IS ENTIRELY DEPENDENT UPON THE CORRECTNESS OF THE LOADING OF TRAFFIC, AND THE FORWARDING OF AS MANY DIRECT WAGONS AS POSSIBLE.

Page 3

(c) AUXILIARY SERVICES.

As necessary, certain Railheads will be linked by scheduled road motor services, e.g., Cardiff and Pontypridd, Birmingham (Hockley) and Wolverhampton. In this way a further expedition of transit is effected.

Where it is possible to utilise passenger or early morning freight services which will give an arrival before noon at destination, such facilities are used between Railheads and Sub-Railheads or between one Railhead and another, thus reducing the quantum of trunk motoring.

(d) CLERICAL.

The procedure at present for the clerical work is for all inwards invoices to be addressed:—

"Railhead or Sub-Railhead for 'Absorbed' station" charged at the "Absorbed" station rates.

On the outwards side, the procedure is governed by the size of the "absorbed" station, and whether it operated as a "Weight Only" station or not. Each case has to be dealt with on its merits and will be subject to separate instructions in this respect.

4. **THE ORGANISATION.**

The outline of the scheme, as it has been developed so far is:—

Area No.	Railhead	Suggested Sub-Railheads	Road Distance from Railhead to Sub-Railhead Miles
28	Aberystwyth	Aberayron	16
		Machynlleth	18
32	Barmouth	Dolgelly	10
		Portmadoc	25
6	Barnstaple	South Molton	12
13	Basingstoke (Jt.)	Andover	20
		Alton	12
34	Birkenhead	Chester	15
29	Birmingham	Cradley Heath	10
		Lye	10
		Tyseley	4¾
		Wednesbury	7½
		West Bromwich	4½

Page 4

Above and opposite **Zonal Handbook.** ***Author's collection***

Area No.	Railhead	Suggested Sub-Railheads	Road Distance from Railhead to Sub-Railhead Miles
9	Bristol	Bath	12
		Hallatrow	12
		Wells	21
		Weston-Super-Mare	21
27	Builth Wells	Brecon	15
		Llanidloes	24
20	Cardiff	Barry	8
		Caerphilly	8
		Llantrisant	11
8	Weymouth	Bridport	20
		Dorchester	8
		Yeovil	29½
5	Exeter	Cullompton	13
		Tiverton	14
18	Gloucester	Cheltenham Spa	9
		Ross	16
		Stroud	10
35	Haverfordwest	Cardigan	25
		Fishguard & G.	15
		Milford Haven	7
		Narberth	10
		Pembroke Dock	10
26	Hereford	Kington	20
		Ledbury	14
		Leominster	13
		Ludlow	24
24	Leamington	Banbury	18
		Stratford-on-Avon	11
23	Llanelly	Ammanford	15
		Carmarthen	19
		Llandyssul	36
19	Newport	Abergavenny	20
		Abertillery	17½
		Ebbw Vale	21
		Pontypool	9
4	Newton Abbot	Paignton	10
		Teignmouth	6½

Page 5

Area No.	Railhead	Suggested Sub-Railheads	Road Distance from Railhead to Sub-Railhead Miles
17	Oxford	Abingdon	6
		Bicester	14
		Chipping Norton	19
		Didcot	10
		Thame	14
		Witney	12
3	Plymouth	Ivybridge	11
		Kingsbridge	20
		Liskeard	19
		Tavistock	15
21	Pontypridd	Aberdare	10
		Merthyr	12
		Tonypandy	6
22	Port Talbot	Bridgend	12
		Neath	6
15	Reading (Jt.)	Camberley	15
		Henley-on-Thames	8
		High Wycombe	21
		Maidenhead	12
		Newbury	17
		Wallingford	19
		Wokingham	7
1	Redruth	Falmouth	11
		Helston	10
		Penzance	17
		St. Ives	15
		Truro	9
2	St. Austell	Bodmin	11½
		Fowey	9
		Newquay	15½
11	Salisbury	..	—
31	Shrewsbury	Craven Arms	20
		Market Drayton	19
		Oswestry	18
		Wellington (Salop)	12
		Welshpool	19
16	Slough	..	—
36	Swansea	..	—

Page 6

Area No.	Railhead	Suggested Sub-Railheads	Road Distance from Railhead to Sub-Railhead Miles
12	Swindon	Chippenham	20
		Cirencester	15
		Devizes	20
		Faringdon	12
		Hungerford	17½
		Marlborough	13
7	Taunton	Bridgwater	11
		Langport West	13
		Minehead	24
		Watchet	16½
10	Trowbridge	Castle Cary	24
		Frome	9
		Melksham	5
		Warminster	9
14	Winchester	..	—
30	Wolverhampton	Bridgnorth	14
		Dudley	6
25	Worcester	Kidderminster	15
		Malvern Link	6
33	Wrexham	Corwen	21
		Ruabon	5

To enable many of the Railheads and Sub-Railheads to deal efficiently with the greater volumes of traffic, structural alterations and extensions will be necessary. The opportunity is also being taken of introducing new methods of working at these stations to facilitate the handling of "smalls" traffic.

5. **THE PUBLIC AND ZONAL.**

This scheme was designed first and foremost for the betterment of the service to the public and it is essential they should be made fully conversant with its organisation, and how they can secure the maximum benefits from it.

It will be the personal responsibility of each Representative and of every employee coming into contact with the public, to apprise himself of the up-to-date information of the schemes as they are progressively introduced, so that at any time a factual and detailed picture of the organisation can be presented to the public.

The majority of the large business firms have, during the War, organised their despatch arrangements so as to hand to the Railway Companies either direct loads for particular destinations, (usually

Page 7

attained by holding back despatches until sufficient has been accumulated to justify through loading) OR loads for transhipment at certain of the recognised centres.

Traders should be encouraged, by knowledge of the services available, to despatch daily on a Zonal basis. Provided firms are fully conversant with the geographical outline of the scheme, they will in many instances be able to organise their despatch so as to provide direct loads daily either to Sub-Railheads or Railheads, so avoiding despatch to a Transfer Centre.

Every time a consignment is loaded for transfer, there is immediately created the possibility of delay.

The scope and potentialities of this scheme must be impressed upon Transport Managers and other executives responsible for the transport organisation.

Traders forwarding "smalls" by truck from Private Sidings should be shewn that they can obtain the benefit of the Zonal service, without losing the advantage of the rates associated with private sidings. By re-organising their despatch arrangements to conform to the Zonal outline they should, at least, be able to load trucks of "smalls" to many of the Railheads, better still to the distant Sub-Railhead where the volume of traffic for a particular area permits. Loading to a transfer centre should be avoided wherever Zonal schemes exist.

6. **SELLING POINTS :—**

(i) No extra charge will be made to the public for the service.

(ii) It provides much more efficient service to traders for "smalls," i.e., next morning delivery for the bulk of such traffic.

(iii) It eliminates or curtails the number of transhipments, thus reducing the journey time of traffic.

(iv) It lessens the possibility of claims by damage and losses, through more direct loadings.

(v) It will progressively provide a service for non-railborne traffic arising within a zone.

The superior services, which Zonal Collection and Delivery affords, should be the means of attracting to rail a considerable volume of traffic, which might otherwise be lost to other forms of transport on account of service, and it is SERVICE which the Railway representative has to sell.

Page 8

5,000 (9) 4/47.

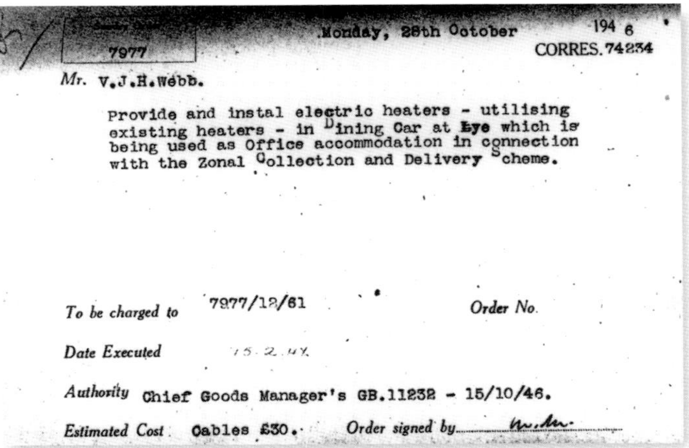

Monday, 28th October 194 6

7977 CORRES. 74234

Mr. V.J.H.Webb.

Provide and instal electric heaters - utilising existing heaters - in Dining Car at Eye which is being used as Office accommodation in connection with the Zonal Collection and Delivery Scheme.

To be charged to 7977/12/61 Order No.

Date Executed 15.2.47.

Authority Chief Goods Manager's GB.11232 - 15/10/46.

Estimated Cost Cables £30. Order signed by

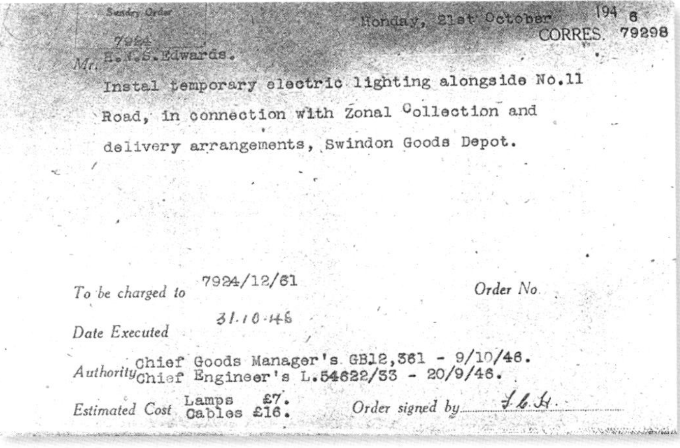

Monday, 21st October 194 6

7924 CORRES. 79298

Mr. H.W.S.Edwards.

Instal temporary electric lighting alongside No.11 Road, in connection with Zonal Collection and delivery arrangements, Swindon Goods Depot.

To be charged to 7924/12/61 Order No.

Date Executed 31.10.46

Authority Chief Goods Manager's GB12,361 - 9/10/46. Chief Engineer's L.54622/33 - 20/9/46.

Estimated Cost Lamps £7. Cables £16. Order signed by

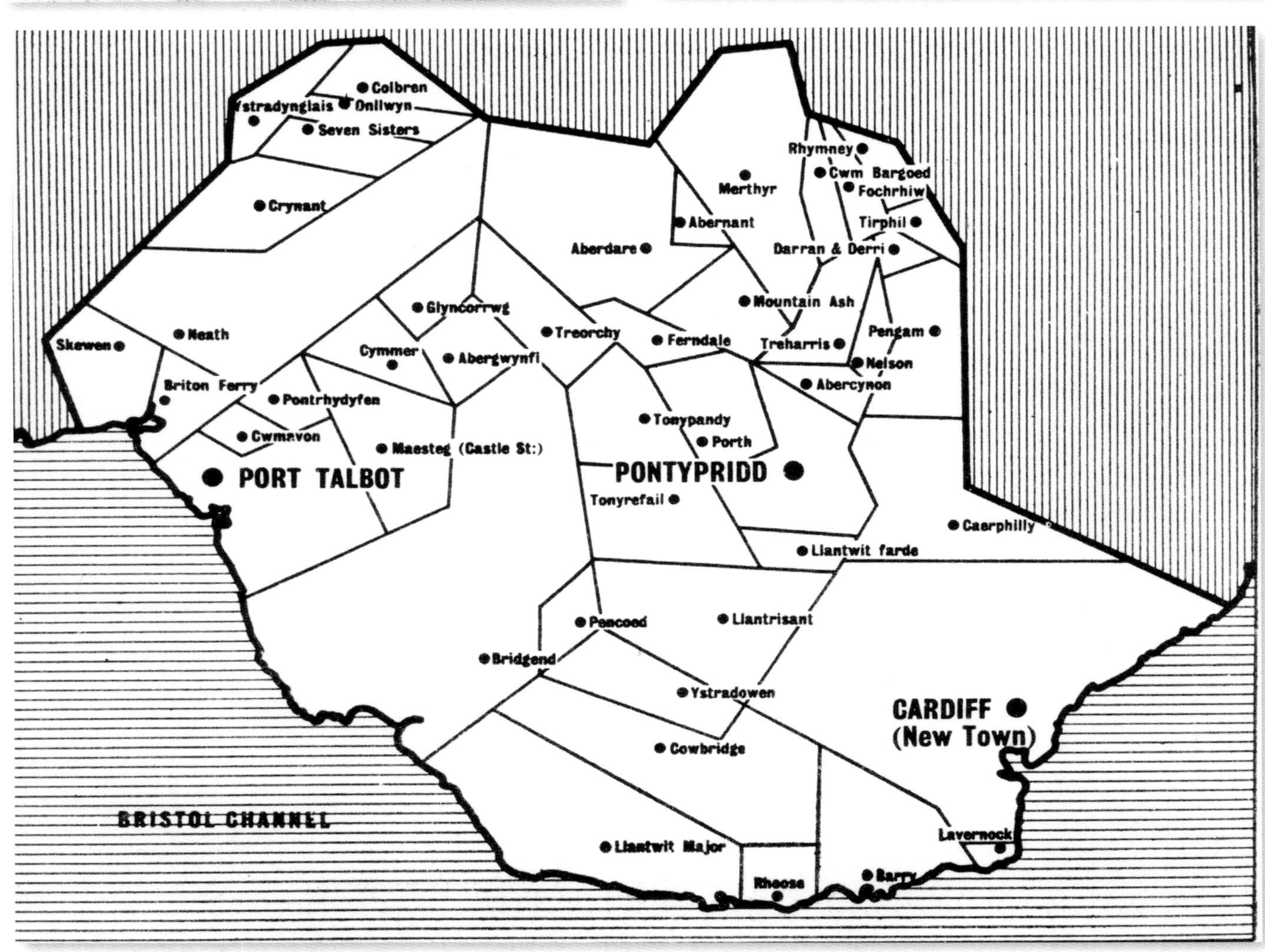

Above and opposite **South-East Wales zonal maps.** ***Author's collection***

The three maps taken from *Next Station* (Barman) illustrate the evolution of the zones in South East Wales (Cardiff, Pontypridd & Port Talbot), from the original methods of very local collection and delivery by horse transport, through the late 1920s' scheme of concentration using road motors, to the post-WW2 zonal system. Before 1927 consignments were carried to or from 156 stations by rail; afterwards traffic was gradually concentrated at 46 stations from which goods would be collected and sent out by road; and in 1946 the 46 delivery areas were amalgamated into 11 delivery areas grouped in three zones with railheads at Cardiff, Pontypridd and Port Talbot.

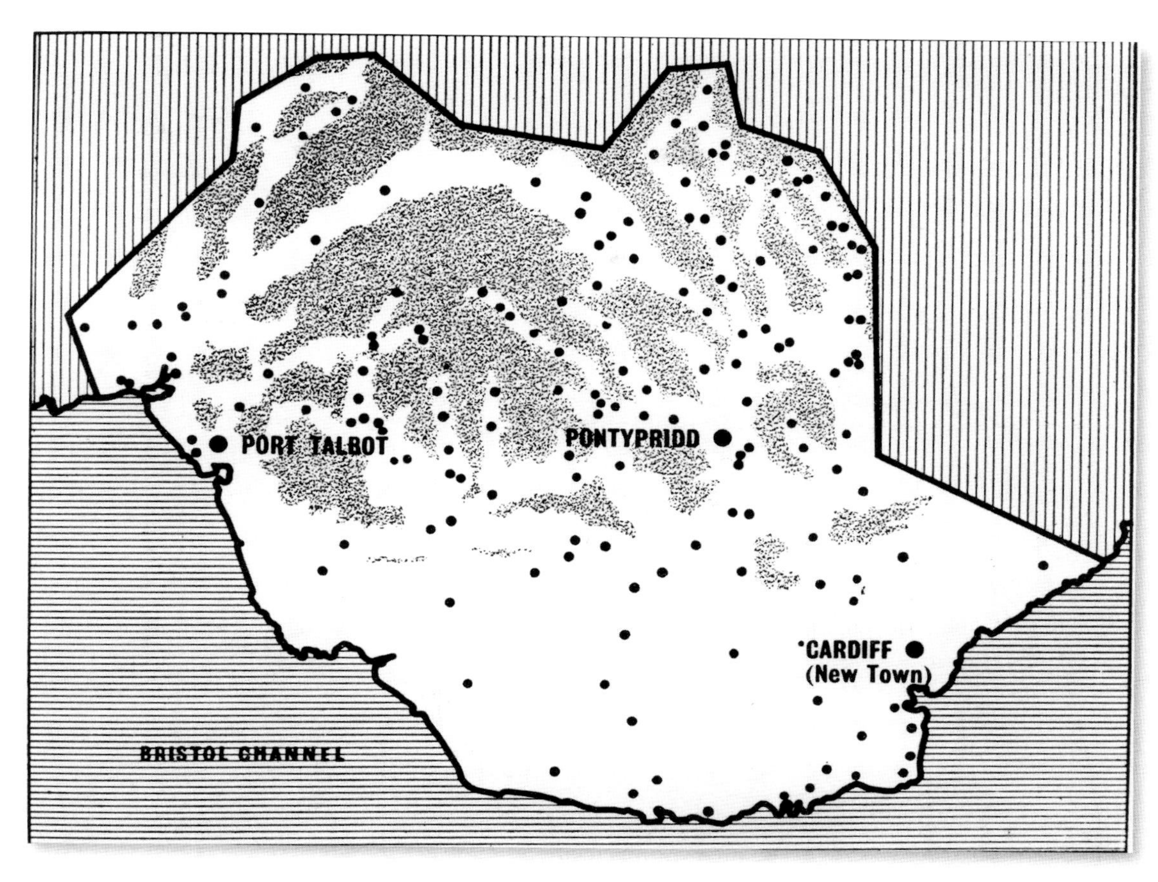
PORT TALBOT
PONTYPRIDD
CARDIFF
(New Town)
BRISTOL CHANNEL

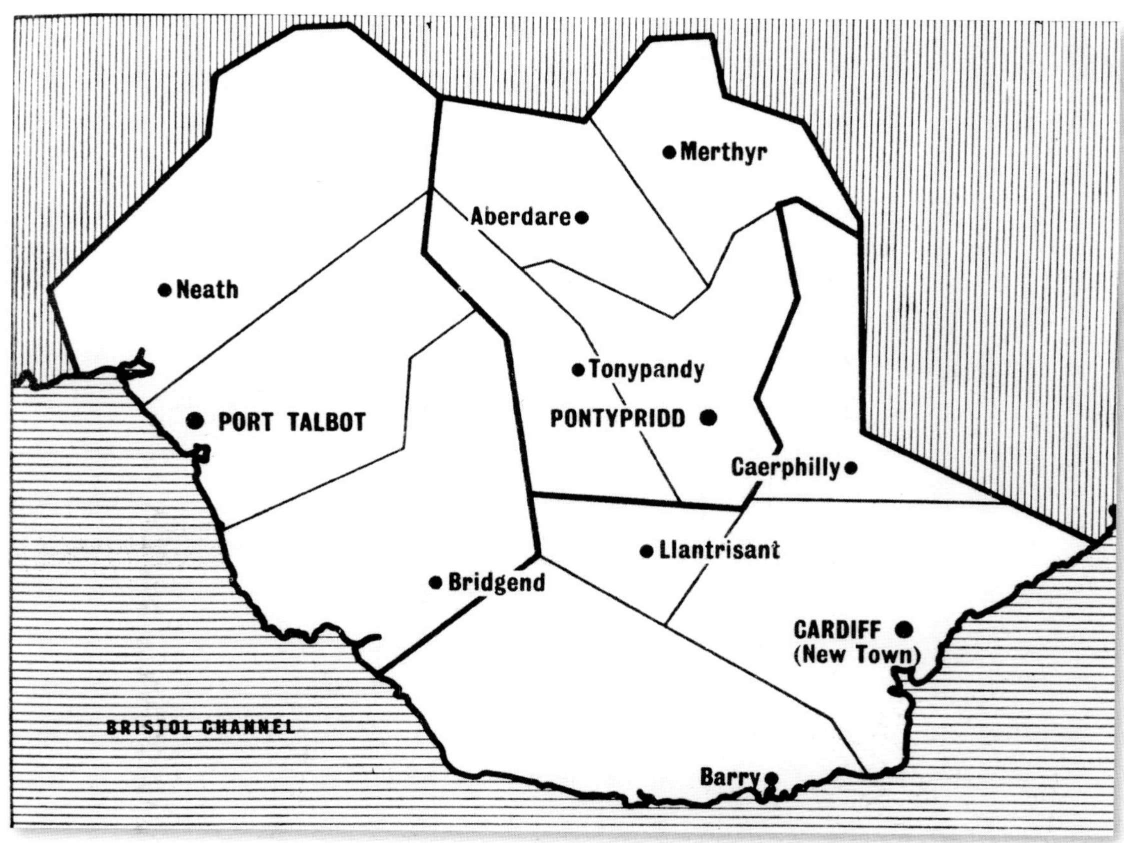
Merthyr
Aberdare
Neath
Tonypandy
PORT TALBOT
PONTYPRIDD
Caerphilly
Llantrisant
Bridgend
CARDIFF
(New Town)
BRISTOL CHANNEL
Barry

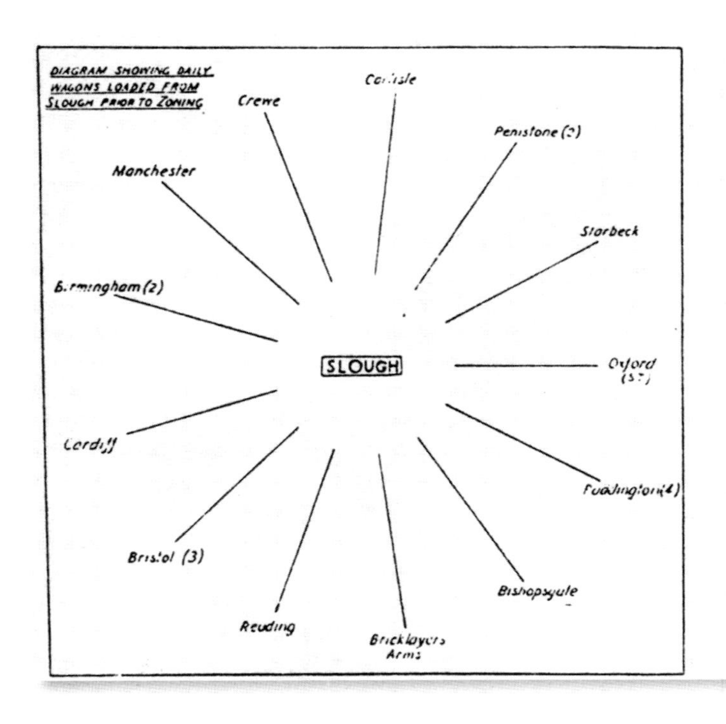

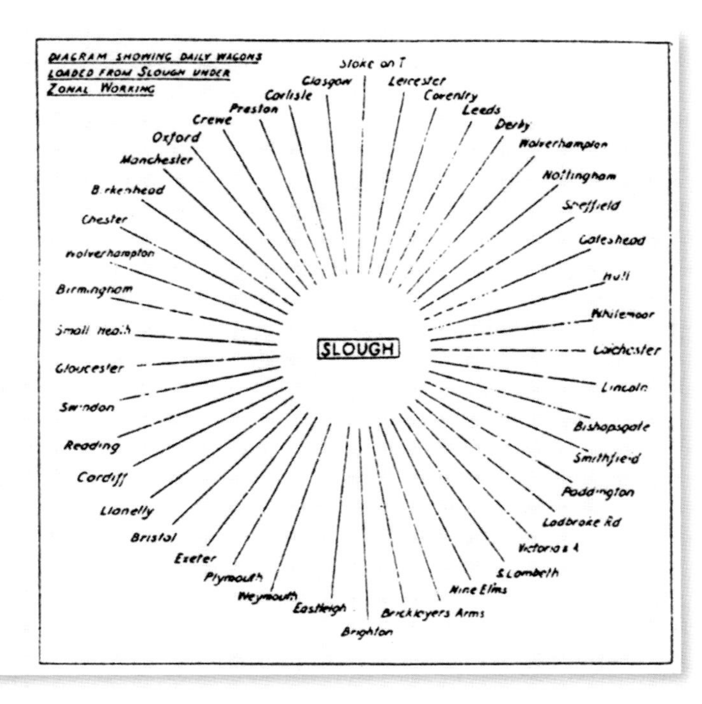

Above **'Radial' maps Slough zonal.** ***Author's collection***

PRIVATE and not for Publication.

GREAT WESTERN RAILWAY.

CHIEF GOODS MANAGER'S OFFICE,
PADDINGTON STATION, W.2.
12th August, 1946.

Circular No. P.W.P. 25.

ZONAL COLLECTION AND DELIVERY OF "SMALLS" TRAFFIC.
BIRMINGHAM ZONE LOADING INSTRUCTIONS.

On and from Monday, 2nd SEPTEMBER, 1946, WEDNESBURY will be instituted as a Sub-Depot to operate under the influence of Birmingham Main Concentration Point, and from this date will cease to be an absorbed station under West Bromwich.

In addition, the existing Sub-Depot of Tyseley will be extended to include the area previously served by Earlswood Lakes. With the commencement of the amended working, Earlswood Lakes will cease to deal with "Smalls" traffic (including Returned Empties).

Returned Empties for addresses in Birmingham and Tyseley must continue to be loaded to Small Heath. (This does not apply to returned empties for Hall Green, Knowle & Dorridge, Shirley and Solihull.)

The traffic referred to above must, on and from Friday, 30th August, 1946, be loaded, invoiced and charged in accordance with the following instructions :—

"Smalls" traffic (including returned empties) at present invoiced to	On and from 30th August, 1946, invoice to be headed as shewn below, but the rates applicable to the station in Col. 1 to be charged.	"Smalls" traffic (including returned empties) to be loaded and labelled to Best loading point, i.e. Sub-Depot.	Alternative loading point to be used if traffic for stn. shewn in Col. 3 is insufficient for direct loading.
1	2	3	4
Wednesbury	Wednesbury	Wednesbury	Birmingham (Hockley)
Earlswood Lakes	Tyseley for Earlswood Lakes	Tyseley	"

Consignments of 1 ton and over (or consignments including returned empties requiring the use of a whole wagon) **for one consignee** must be loaded, labelled and invoiced to the individual stations shewn in Column 1.

Consignments of less than 1 ton must be combined to make direct wagons of 1 ton or over to the Sub-Depots shewn in Column 3.

If the total traffic for any Sub-Depot is less than 1 ton in weight, it must be combined with traffic for Hockley and loaded to that point.

Composite wagons of "Smalls" traffic must not be loaded to the Main Concentration point, Sub-Depots or other stations in this zone, but in the event of a wagon being loaded direct to any of the stations in Column 3, and there is a residue of traffic for the remainder of the zone which does not justify a direct wagon to Hockley (i.e. less than 1 ton in weight), the whole of the traffic should be loaded and labelled to the Sub-Depot to which the direct wagon is being loaded.

If the whole of the traffic for the zone is less than 1 ton in weight, it should be loaded to the appropriate transfer point in accordance with Circular No. 1225 (Reprint) " Instructions in connection with the forwarding of Tranship Traffic."

These instructions are also applicable to "Smalls" traffic consigned "to wait order" or for cartage by public.

Whenever possible, endeavours should be made to separate traffic for the zone loaded to Hockley from traffic loaded to that depot for transhipment.

With the operation of this scheme, Nominated Loading to stations within the Zone will cease to operate.

The instructions given in Circular No. 1225, the book of Miscellaneous Instructions governing the conveyance of Merchandise and Livestock, and the Towns and Villages Book, must be read in conjunction with the foregoing.

The necessary amendments to Circular No. R.1704, " Concentration of Traffic and Accounts Work," March, 1935, covering the above instructions will be sent you in due course.

DAVID BLEE,
Chief Goods Manager.

(4,000–8–46—4557)

Above and following pages **Zonal flyers.** ***Author's collection***

PRIVATE and not for Publication.

GREAT WESTERN RAILWAY.

CHIEF GOODS MANAGER'S OFFICE,
PADDINGTON STATION, W.2.
August, 1946.

Circular No. P.W.P.22.

ZONAL COLLECTION AND DELIVERY OF "SMALLS" TRAFFIC.

PORT TALBOT ZONE LOADING INSTRUCTIONS.

In connection with my Circular P.W.P.10, 12/7/46, relating to the introduction of a zonal collection and delivery scheme based on Port Talbot, arrangements have been made for a further Sub-Depot instituted at Bridgend to be embodied within the scheme on and from Monday, 2nd September, 1946.

The zone will then comprise the areas at present served from the following stations :—

PORT TALBOT
- Abergwynfi
- Bryn
- Bryndu
- Caerau
- Cwmavon
- Cwmdu
- Cymmer
- Cymmer Afan
- Glyncorrwg
- Lletty Brongu
- Llangynwyd
- Maesteg (Castle St.)
- Pontrhydyfen
- Troedyrhiew Garth

BRIDGEND
- Blackmill
- Blaengarw
- Brynmenyn
- Kenfig Hill
- Llangeinor
- Nantymoel
- Ogmore Vale
- Pencoed
- Pontycymmer
- Pontyrhyll
- Porthcawl
- Pyle
- Tondu

NEATH
- Abercrave
- Aberdylais
- Briton Ferry
- Cilfrew
- Colbren
- Crynant
- Glyn Neath
- Jersey Marine
- Llansamlet
- Neath Abbey
- Neath (Cadowton)
- Onllwyn
- Resolven
- Seven Sisters
- Skewen
- Ystradgynlais

Port Talbot will be the **Main Concentration Point** of the zone which will be sub-divided into areas under the control of Sub-Depots operating at Neath and Bridgend.

All stations in the zone other than the Main Concentration Point and the Sub-Depots mentioned above will cease to deal with "Smalls" traffic (including returned empties).

Such traffic, passing to stations within the Port Talbot and Neath areas on and from Friday, 30th August, 1946, must continue to be loaded, invoiced and charged in accordance with the instructions set out in my Circular P.W.P.10, 12/7/46, and the undermentioned additional instructions will apply to stations within the Bridgend Sub-Depot area :—

"Smalls" traffic (including returned empties) at present invoiced to	On and from 30th August, 1946, invoice to be headed as shown below but the rates applicable to the station in Col. 1 to be charged.	"Smalls" traffic (including returned empties) to be loaded and labelled to — Best loading point., i.e. Sub-Depot.	Alternative loading point to be used if traffic for stn. shown in Col. 3 is insufficient for direct loading.
1	2	3	4
BRIDGEND	Bridgend	Bridgend	Port Talbot
Bridgend for Blackmill (at Blackmill rates)	,, for Blackmill	,,	,, ,,
Bridgend for Blaengarw (at Blaengarw rates)	,, ,, Blaengarw	,,	,, ,,
Bridgend for Brynmenyn (at Brynmenyn rates)	,, ,, Brynmenyn	,,	,, ,,
Bridgend for Kenfig Hill (at Kenfig Hill rates)	,, ,, Kenfig Hill	,,	,, ,,
Bridgend for Llangeinor (at Llangeinor rates)	,, ,, Llangeinor	,,	,, ,,
Bridgend for Nantymoel (at Nantymoel rates)	,, ,, Nantymoel	,,	,, ,,
Bridgend for Ogmore Vale (at Ogmore Vale rates)	,, ,, Ogmore Vale	,,	,, ,,
Bridgend for Pontycymmer (at Pontycymmer rates)	,, ,, Pontycymmer	,,	,, ,,

PRIVATE and not for Publication.

GREAT WESTERN RAILWAY.

CHIEF GOODS MANAGER'S OFFICE,
PADDINGTON STATION, W.2.
12th September, 1946.

Circular No. P.W.P. 33.

ZONAL COLLECTION AND DELIVERY OF "SMALLS" TRAFFIC.

READING ZONE LOADING INSTRUCTIONS.

On and from 1st OCTOBER, 1946, a zonal collection and delivery scheme in connection with "SMALLS" traffic (including **returned empties**) based on READING will come into operation.

The zone will comprise the areas at present served from the following stations :—

READING
- Aldermaston
- Midgham
- Mortimer
- Pangbourne
- Theale
- Tilehurst

NEWBURY
- Burghclere
- Compton
- Hamstead Norris
- Hermitage
- Highclere
- Thatcham
- Boxford
- East Garston
- Great Shefford
- Lambourn
- Welford Park
- Woodhay

HENLEY-ON-THAMES
- Shiplake
- Twyford
- Wargrave

WALLINGFORD
- Cholsey & Moulsford
- Goring & Streatley
- Watlington

MAIDENHEAD
- Bourne End
- Cookham
- Marlow
- Taplow

Reading will be the **Main Concentration Point** of the zone, which will be sub-divided into areas under the control of **Sub-Depots** to be instituted at Henley-on-Thames, Maidenhead, Newbury and Wallingford.

All stations in the zone other than the Main Concentration Point and the Sub-Depots mentioned above will cease to deal with "Smalls" traffic (including returned empties).

Such traffic must, on and from Saturday, 28th SEPTEMBER, 1946, be loaded, invoiced and charged, in accordance with the following instructions :—

"Smalls" traffic (including returned empties) at present invoiced to	On and from 28th September, 1946, invoice to be headed as shewn below, but the rates applicable to the station in Col. 1 to be charged.	"Smalls" traffic (including returned empties) to be loaded and labelled to — Best loading point, i.e. Sub-Depot.	Alternative loading point to be used if traffic for station shewn in Col. 3 is insufficient for direct loading.
1	2	3	4
READING	READING	**READING**	
Aldermaston	Reading for Aldermaston	Reading	—
Midgham	,, ,, Midgham	,,	—
Mortimer	,, ,, Mortimer	,,	—
Pangbourne	,, ,, Pangbourne	,,	—
Theale	,, ,, Theale	,,	—
Tilehurst	,, ,, Tilehurst	,,	—
HENLEY-ON-THAMES	HENLEY-ON-THAMES	**HENLEY-ON-THAMES**	READING
Henley-on-T. for Shiplake (C. & D. "Smalls" only at Shiplake Rates)	Henley-on-T. for Shiplake	Henley-on-T.	Reading
Shiplake (S. to S. "Smalls" only)	,, ,, Shiplake	,,	,,
Twyford	,, ,, Twyford	,,	,,
Wargrave	,, ,, Wargrave	,,	,,
MAIDENHEAD	MAIDENHEAD	**MAIDEN-HEAD**	READING
Maidenhead for Taplow (at Taplow rates)	Maidenhead for Taplow	Maidenhead	Reading
Bourne End	,, ,, Bourne End	,,	,,
Cookham	,, ,, Cookham	,,	,,
Marlow	,, ,, Marlow	,,	,,

PRIVATE and not for publication.

GREAT WESTERN RAILWAY.

CHIEF GOODS MANAGER'S OFFICE,
PADDINGTON STATION, W.2.
12th September, 1946.

Circular No. P.W.P.27.

ZONAL COLLECTION AND DELIVERY OF "SMALLS" TRAFFIC.
LEAMINGTON ZONE LOADING INSTRUCTIONS.

On and from 1st OCTOBER, 1946, a zonal collection and delivery scheme in connection with "SMALLS" traffic (including **returned empties**) based on LEAMINGTON will come into operation.

The zone will comprise the areas at present served from the following stations :—

LEAMINGTON SPA	BANBURY	STRATFORD-ON-AVON (including Wilmcote)
Claverdon	Adderbury	Bearley
Hatton	Aynho for Deddington	Danzey for Tanworth
Southam Road & Harbury	Bloxham	Henley-in-Arden
	Cropredy	Long Marston
	Fenny Compton	Milcote
	Fritwell & Somerton	Shipston-on-Stour
	Heyford	
	Kings Sutton	

Leamington will be the **Main Concentration Point** of the zone, which will be sub-divided into areas under the control of **Sub-Depots** to be instituted at Banbury and Stratford-on-Avon.

All stations in the zone other than the Main Concentration Point and Sub-Depots mentioned above will cease to deal with "smalls" traffic (including returned empties).

Such traffic must, on and from Saturday, 28th SEPTEMBER, 1946, be loaded, invoiced and charged in accordance with the following instructions :—

"Smalls" traffic (including returned empties) at present invoiced to	On and from 28th September, 1946, invoice to be headed as shewn below, but the rates applicable to the stations in Col. 1 to be charged.	"Smalls" traffic (including returned empties) to be loaded and labelled to: Best loading point, i.e. Sub-Depot.	Alternative loading point to be used if traffic for stn. shewn in Col. 3 is insufficient for direct loading.
1	2	3	4
LEAMINGTON	LEAMINGTON	**LEAMINGTON**	—
Claverdon	Leamington for Claverdon	,,	—
Hatton	,, ,, Hatton	,,	—
Southam Road & Harbury	,, ,, Southam Road & Harbury	,,	—
BANBURY	BANBURY	**BANBURY**	LEAMINGTON
Aynho for Deddington	Banbury for Aynho for Deddington	,,	,,
Adderbury	Banbury for Adderbury	,,	,,
Bloxham	,, ,, Bloxham	,,	,,
Cropredy	,, ,, Cropredy	,,	,,
Fenny Compton	,, ,, Fenny Compton	,,	,,
Fritwell & Somerton	,, ,, Fritwell & Somerton	,,	,,
Heyford	,, ,, Heyford	,,	,,
Kings Sutton	,, ,, Kings Sutton	,,	,,
STRATFORD-ON-AVON (including Wilmcote)	STRATFORD-ON-AVON	**STRATFORD-ON-AVON**	LEAMINGTON
Bearley	Stratford-on-A. for Bearley	,,	,,
Danzey for Tanworth	,, ,, Danzey for T.	,,	,,
Henley-in-Arden	,, ,, Henley-in-A.	,,	,,
Long Marston	,, ,, Long Marston	,,	,,
Milcote	,, ,, Milcote	,,	,,
Shipston-on-Stour	,, ,, Shipston-on-Stour	,,	,,

PRIVATE and not for publication.

GREAT WESTERN RAILWAY.

CHIEF GOODS MANAGER'S OFFICE,
PADDINGTON STATION, W.2.
12th September, 1946.

Circular No. P.W.P. 30.

ZONAL COLLECTION AND DELIVERY OF "SMALLS" TRAFFIC.

ST. AUSTELL ZONE LOADING INSTRUCTIONS.

On and from 1st OCTOBER, 1946, a zonal collection and delivery scheme in connection with "SMALLS" traffic (including **returned empties**) based on ST. AUSTELL will come into operation.

The zone will comprise the areas at present served from the following stations :—

ST. AUSTELL	NEWQUAY	FOWEY	BODMIN
Bugie	St. Columb Road	Lostwithiel	Bodmin Road
Drinnick Mill			
Grampound Road			
Luxulyan			
Par			
Roche			

St. Austell will be the **Main Concentration Point** of the zone, which will be sub-divided into areas under the control of **Sub-Depots** to be instituted at Newquay, Fowey and Bodmin.

All stations in the zone other than the Main Concentration Point and Sub-Depots mentioned above will cease to deal with "Smalls" traffic (including returned empties).

Such traffic must, on and from Saturday, 28th SEPTEMBER, 1946, be loaded, invoiced and charged in accordance with the following instructions :—

"Smalls" traffic (including returned empties) at present invoiced to	On and from 28th September, 1946, invoice to be headed as shewn below, but the rates applicable to the stations in Column 1 to be charged.	"Smalls" traffic (including returned empties) to be loaded and labelled to: Best loading point, i.e. Sub-Depot.	Alternative loading point to be used if traffic for station shewn in Column 3 is insufficient for direct loading.
1	2	3	4
ST. AUSTELL	ST. AUSTELL	**ST. AUSTELL**	—
Bugle	St. Austell for Bugle	St. Austell	—
Drinnick Mill	,, ,, Drinnick Mill	,,	—
Grampound Road	,, ,, Grampound Rd.	,,	—
Luxulyan	,, ,, Luxulyan	,,	—
Par	,, ,, Par	,,	—
Roche	,, ,, Roche	,,	—

1	2	3	4
NEWQUAY	NEWQUAY	**NEWQUAY**	ST. AUSTELL
St. Columb Road	Newquay for St. Columb Rd.	Newquay	St. Austell
FOWEY	FOWEY	**FOWEY**	ST. AUSTELL
Lostwithiel	Fowey for Lostwithiel	Fowey	St. Austell
BODMIN	BODMIN	**BODMIN**	ST. AUSTELL
Bodmin Rd.	Bodmin for Bodmin Rd.	Bodmin	St. Austell

The following stations are to be now regarded as "Starred" Stations (Scale "A"), and instructions to this effect will be issued through the General Circular :—

Bodmin Road
Bugle
Drinnick Mill
Grampound Road
Luxulyan
Roche

PRIVATE and not for Publication.

GREAT WESTERN RAILWAY.

CHIEF GOODS MANAGER'S OFFICE,
PADDINGTON STATION, W.2.
September 12th, 1946.

Circular No. P.W.P.36.

ZONAL COLLECTION AND DELIVERY OF "SMALLS" TRAFFIC.

WOLVERHAMPTON ZONE LOADING INSTRUCTIONS.

On and from OCTOBER 1st, 1946, a zonal collection and delivery scheme in connection with "SMALLS" traffic (including **returned empties**) based on WOLVERHAMPTON will come into operation.

The Zone will comprise the areas at present served from the following stations :—

WOLVERHAMPTON	BRIDGNORTH
Codsall	Eardington
Himley	Hampton Loade
Tettenhall	Highley
Wombourn	Ironbridge & Broseley
Albrighton	Linley
Cosford	
Shifnal	

Wolverhampton will be the **Main Concentration Point** of the zone which will be sub-divided into areas under the control of **Sub-Depots** to be instituted at Bridgnorth and Dudley, the latter being instituted at a later date.

All stations in the zone other than the Main Concentration Point and the Sub-Depots mentioned above will cease to deal with "Smalls" traffic (including returned empties).

Such traffic must, on and from Saturday, September 28th, be loaded, invoiced and charged in accordance with the following instructions :—

"Smalls" traffic (including returned empties) at present invoiced to	On and from September 28th, 1946, invoice to be headed as shewn below but the rates applicable to the station in Col. 1 to be charged.	"Smalls" traffic (including returned empties) to be loaded and labelled to — Best loading point, i.e. Sub-Depot.	Alternative loading point to be used if traffic for stn. shewn in Col. 3 is insufficient for direct loading.
1	2	3	4
WOLVERHAMPTON	Wolverhampton	WOLVERHAMPTON	—
Codsall	Wolverhampton for Codsall	,,	—
Himley	,, ,, Himley	,,	—
Tettenhall	,, ,, Tettenhall	,,	—
Wombourn	,, ,, Wombourn	,,	—
Albrighton	Albrighton	,,	—
Cosford (previously dealt with through Albrighton)	Cosford (at Cosford rates)	,,	—
Shifnal	Shifnal	,,	—
BRIDGNORTH	Bridgnorth	BRIDGNORTH	Wolverhampton
Eardington	Bridgnorth for Eardington	,,	,,
Hampton Loade	,, ,, Hampton Loade	,,	,,
Highley	,, ,, Highley	,,	,,
Ironbridge & Broseley	,, ,, Ironbridge & Broseley	,,	,,
Linley	,, ,, Linley	,,	,,

The following stations are to be now regarded as "Starred" stations (Scale "A") and instructions to this effect will be issued through the General Circular :—

Cosford
Eardington
Hampton Loade
Highley
Himley
Linley

Consignments of 1 ton and over (or consignments including returned empties requiring the use of a whole wagon) **for one consignee** must be loaded, labelled, and invoiced in accordance with existing instructions.

PRIVATE and not for Publication.

GREAT WESTERN RAILWAY.

CHIEF GOODS MANAGER'S OFFICE,
PADDINGTON STATION, W.2.
12th December, 1946.

Circular No. P.W.P. 58.

ZONAL COLLECTION AND DELIVERY OF "SMALLS" TRAFFIC.

BRISTOL ZONE LOADING INSTRUCTIONS.

On and from 1st JANUARY, 1947, a zonal collection and delivery scheme in connection with "SMALLS" traffic (including **returned empties**) based on BRISTOL will come into operation.

The zone will comprise the areas at present served from the following stations :—

BRISTOL		HALLATROW
Avonmouth Dock	Nailsea & Backwell	Camerton
Avonmouth Town	Patchway	Clutton
Blagdon	Pill	Pensford
Burrington	Pilning	
Chipping Sodbury	Portbury	WESTON-SUPER-MARE
Clevedon	Portishead	Puxton & Worle
Coalpit Heath	Saltford	Sandford & Banwell
Congresbury	Severn Beach	
Filton Junction	Shirehampton	
Flax Bourton	Winterbourne	
Henbury	Wrington	
Keynsham	Yatton	
Langford		

Bristol will be the **Railhead** of the zone, which will be sub-divided into areas under the control of **Sub-Railheads** to be instituted at Hallatrow and Weston-super-Mare.

All stations in the zone other than the Railhead and the Sub-Railheads mentioned above will cease to deal with "Smalls" traffic (including returned empties).

Such traffic must, on and from Monday, 30th December, 1946, be loaded, invoiced and charged in accordance with the following instructions :—

"Smalls" traffic (including returned empties) at present invoiced to	On and from 30th December, 1946, invoice to be headed as shewn below, but the rates applicable to the station in Col. 1 to be charged.	"Smalls" traffic (including returned empties) to be loaded and labelled to — Best loading point, i.e., Sub-Railhead.	Alternative loading point to be used if traffic for station shewn in Col. 3 is insufficient for direct loading.
1	2	3	4
BRISTOL	BRISTOL	BRISTOL	—
Bristol for Avonmouth Town (exc. Nat. Smelting Co.'s tfc.) (C. & D. "Smalls" only at Avonmouth Town rates.)	Bristol for Avonmouth Town	Bristol	—
Bristol for Brislington (C. & D. "Smalls" at Brislington rates.)	,, ,, Brislington	,,	—
Brislington (S.S. "Smalls")	,, ,, ,,	,,	
Shirehampton (at present invoiced to Bristol at Shirehampton rates)	,, ,, Shirehampton	,,	—
Avonmouth Town (S.S. "Smalls" only)	,, ,, Avonmouth Town	,,	—
Chipping Sodbury	,, ,, Chipping Sodbury	,,	—
Coalpit Heath	,, ,, Coalpit Heath	,,	—
Filton Junction	,, ,, Filton Junction	,,	—
Filton Junction for Henbury (at Henbury rates)	,, ,, Henbury	,,	—
Filton Junction for Patchway (at Patchway rates)	,, ,, Patchway	,,	—
Filton Junction for Pilning (at Pilning rates)	,, ,, Pilning	,,	—
Flax Bourton	,, ,, Flax Bourton	,,	—
Keynsham & Somerdale	,, ,, Keynsham & Somerdale	,,	—

G.W.R. Zonal Goods Organisation—1

Vehicles ready to leave Tyseley sub-railhead, in the Birmingham zone, on their morning rounds

Vulcan 5/6-ton lorries, a type of vehicle found suitable for the operation of trunk services in certain districts

Routing consignments with the aid of a wall chart showing railheads and sub-railheads in their correct geographical relationship

Goods shed at Dudley altered to provide additional berthing space for zonal scheme road vehicles, and other improvements

October 24, 1947 THE RAILWAY GAZETTE 465

A teething trouble in the early days of the scheme was that firms who had been sending regular traffic to a station that was now absorbed into a sub-railhead, kept sending paperwork to that station instead of the railhead – a misunderstanding also made by some GW staff – but it was all ironed out quickly. Prompt arrival of invoices was crucial and a 'transit of invoices' scheme was begun in January 1947, whereby invoices were conveyed in special canvas wallets by nominated night passenger trains between 13 sorting centres, known as *District Concentration Offices*. Accuracy of loading was fundamental to zonal working and this was carefully looked over by those in charge. Before WW2, peaks in tranship traffic at large depots used to be solved by employing casual labour. But carrying supernumerary staff was no longer possible after WW2, so the reduction in tranships resulting from zonal working was very important.

Needless to say, the zonal scheme could not possibly have succeeded without efficient cartage. Three distinct services were provided by the GW cartage fleet in the Zonal scheme, namely *trunk motoring*; *link motoring*; and direct C&D cartage work at the railheads and sub-railheads. Trunk haulage was for low tonnages of goods insufficient to make up full railway truck loads between railheads and sub-railheads. Link haulage was the same, but between those railheads that were not too far apart. Nearly 100 vehicles were employed on these services. Generally speaking, 2/3-ton and 5/6-ton rigid motors (sometimes with 2- and 4-wheel trailers), and 8-ton articulated units and trailers, were employed on trunk motoring. All the old cartage rounds of the defunct independent goods stations, now grouped into a zone, had to be taken on by the cartage fleets based at the railheads and sub-railheads. Entirely new rounds had to be designed for areas where previously the local station did not perform cartage and where the public themselves had been expected to collect their goods. There were at least 335 non-carting stations across the GW system that were absorbed into zonal systems. Parcels traffic was included in these rearrangements. Should the general public choose to send off or receive smalls traffic from an 'absorbed depot', a cartage vehicle would call on one of its rounds – otherwise all traffic and clerical work was dealt with at the sub-railhead.

As an example of routing under the Zonal scheme compared with pre-war practice, consider sending a consignment from Windsor to Llantrisant. Formerly it would have been sent from Windsor to Paddington, thence to Cardiff and thence to Llantrisant, all by rail. This involved a day lost in transit at Paddington and Cardiff. But under the Zonal method, the consignment would be taken by road from Windsor to Slough railhead, thence to Llantrisant sub-railhead or to Cardiff railhead on the night of the day on which it was collected, and then by trunk motor to Llantrisant to arrive the next morning.

The concentration of operations at 148 railheads and sub-railheads meant that depots originally constructed to deal with traffic

In addition to all the regular local cattle markets and horse fairs, there were annual regional and national agricultural shows. In the period covered by this book, permanent showgrounds did not exist and regional shows were held at different places on GW territory. Also national shows (particularly the prestigious Royal Agricultural Show) were sometimes held in a part of the country served by the GWR. Shows held regularly on GW territory, with the locations for some years between the wars, are listed in Chapter 21 of *GWR Goods Train Working*.

Agricultural shows involved much more than the typical country market fair. There was a heavy concentration of a large variety of farming goods as well as livestock. Before the opening of a big agricultural show, much preliminary work was necessary, such as a survey of the proposed site and a study of the facilities (drainage, lighting, loading docks, water supply) available for dealing with the cattle and other exhibits. A train would take a small team from the Chief Goods Manager's office at Paddington to inspect the site and facilities.

Sometimes the location of the show was right next to railway sidings, as at the Royal Show held at Chester in 1925 (where the showground was adjacent to the GW's Saltney goods yard), but most often road transport was required to convey livestock and deadstock between railway and showground. Up until WW2 at least, and for some years after, little of the traffic from distant places would have come all the way by road. In consequence, many special trains would be put on. For the Royal Show at Cardiff in 1919, 21 special trains involving 600 rail vehicles brought stock and implements, with another 100 vehicles of livestock arriving attached to passenger trains and in addition 600 packages of poultry brought by passenger train; a similar amount of outwards traffic was involved. *GW Goods Train Working* has details of the running of special trains for agricultural shows, and the arrangements for transporting all traffic by road from and to the 'concentration point' (the set of sidings or loading docks chosen as being nearest/most convenient to the show ground itself). Over 2,100 wagon-loads of material for show stands and exhibits were received at Cardiff in 1919; nearly 1,700 tons of equipment was conveyed to Windsor for the Centenary Royal Show in 1939.

Although by the end of the 1920s, haulage of floats and livestock vehicles to and from agricultural show grounds was almost exclusively being performed by GW Fordson tractors (both wheeled and crawler), there was still at least some haulage by railway horses. The Oxfordshire Show of 1927 became the first occasion when motor traction was used exclusively, and in 1930 all the cartage work at the shows held at Liskeard, Reading, Shrewsbury and Torquay was carried out by motor traction. In 1934, a Fordson industrial tractor was bought for £193/2/6 from Pratt's of Sutton for show traffic. More on this will be found in Chapters 6 and 8.

Other facilities for Farmers

Insurance of Livestock.

A scheme for the insurance of livestock against death or injury during loading and unloading operations and transit by Goods Trains is operated by the Railway Companies in Great Britain. Brief particulars of Premiums are given below:—

	Premium:	*Insurable Maximum Value:*
Horses and Ponies	8d. per head	£50 per head
Cattle	4d. ,, ,,	£25 ,, ,,
Calves	1d. ,, ,,	£2 ,, ,,
Sheep and Lambs	½d. ,, ,,	£3 ,, ,,
Pigs—		
Bacon	1½d. ,, ,,	£6 ,, ,,
Porkers	1d. ,, ,,	£3 ,, ,,

Minimum Premium, 2d. per consignment.

Sugar Beet Transport.

Special equipment, suitable for the handling and conveyance of Sugar Beet from farm to factory by road and rail, is at the disposal of farmers during the season. Favourable rates to meet all requirements.

Farm Removals.

Special arrangements are in operation for the removal of livestock, implements and household effects. Packing and unpacking by experts, speedy conveyance, insurance at exceptionally low rates, and 33⅓% reduction in fares to new residence, are features of this service.

Full particulars of the above services are obtainable from Chief Goods Manager, Paddington Station, London, W.2, or the local G.W. Agent.

Paddington Station, London, W.2

JAMES MILNE, *General Manager.*

It is well known that railway cattle wagons had to be cleaned out and disinfected after use. The disinfection regulations drawn up by the Ministry of Agriculture were revised in 1926, and railway cattle wagons were thereafter disinfected with a 'white cyllin' solution of increased strength under a new schedule adopted by all the companies, rather than white-lime. (An attempt by the Government to impose disinfection of railway wagons which had conveyed hides and skins was successfully resisted at the time by the railways on the score of expense and impracticability.) Before 1926, it would seem that cattle-carrying *road* vehicles did *not* have to be disinfected. However, because the railways were often accused of being responsible for the spread of foot-and-mouth disease (even though they did disinfect their rail cattle trucks whereas road hauliers did not), the Ministry issued an order enjoining *all* carriers of cattle to have to disinfect all vehicles, road and rail alike.

CHAPTER TWELVE

SPECIAL CARTAGE FACILITIES

In the days of horse-drawn vehicles, heavy or difficult loads travelling by rail required teams of animals to move items to/from stations. According to the *GWR Magazine*, in March 1922 a showman's traction engine weighing 17½-tons was towed by 9 horses from the Agricultural Hall in London to Paddington *en route* to Plymouth (Kelley p26), and in November 1926 a 16-ton gasometer 10ft in diameter and 15ft long on its side required a 10-horse team to take it to South Lambeth goods yard *en route* to Exeter. As the years passed, petrol-driven tractors of increasing size were bought by the GW to avoid using teams of horses and as part of a general modernising. Fifteen Fordson tractors with Muir-Hill sprung rear wheels and 15 trailers were purchased in 1926 (one tractor being fitted with pneumatic tyres); a Harvester International tractor, capable of hauling loads up to 16 tons, was acquired in the same year for the purpose of dealing with particularly heavy consignments. In 1927 a permanently-articulated Scammell heavy lorry was purchased as well as 17 more Fordson tractors.

Even so, however modern these tractors and trailers might be, the railway had no authority to cart consignments other than to/from railway depots on their way to/from a rail journey. That historical position had come about from the way the railways had been set up in Victorian times. In the years immediately following WW1, the railway companies (being obliged to employ all three road/rail/road elements in a journey) could not compete with private road hauliers for some traffic, especially over short distances. The railways had tried to get this restriction on their activities removed at the time of the 1921 Railways Act that set up the big-four main line companies, but it was not until 1928, as part of the legislation dealing with railway bus operation, that Parliament granted them authority to run road vehicles on duties that need not involve the railway as such. Thereafter 'throughout-road' haulage by the GWR substantially added to its overall revenue. In a 1933 document issued to GW staff regarding household removals using containers, the possibility is recognised of using railway containers for an all-road journey that had no rail-borne component. The rate of increase of road-borne traffic was considerable, from about 50,000 tons in 1929 to 165,000 tons in 1931, which represented earnings of £100,000 over the 3-year period. In 1931 alone, £150,000 was earned from these so-called *special cartage activities*.

'Special' was in comparison with the motor vehicles and trailers used for ordinary C&D work, so would include lorries and trailers that could be tipped, as well as really specialised kit for heavy and/or long loads (of course the GW already had some heavy-duty trailers to convey weighty or load loads brought by rail, but special cartage activities embraced much more than that). Some of these special vehicles were used by the GW's own civil engineers. The special cartage fleet increased rapidly after 1928: in that year twenty-one large capacity motor lorries and two more tractors were added to the fleet. The strength was further increased in the year following with heavy duty vehicles from Foden, Thornycroft and Scammell, some of which could tip. In this way, the railway began to handle items such as tramcar bodies, cable drums, pipes, boilers, bricks, sand, gravel, constructional steelwork and machinery for the whole of the journey, rather than having to involve a separate specialist road haulier to do part of the job.

Right **Two-wheel Eagle (of Warwick) trailer with hinged tail ramp for cable-drum traffic, and winch at front for loading and unloading, photographed in 1927. Fordson tractor fleet 199 (seems to be CME numbering). On underframe near front is 'F R E Davis Secretary/ Paddington' and 'FAW 14-0; CAW 0; RAW 17-1' for front axle, central, and rear axle weights which seems odd for a 2-wheel trailer, but may have to do with whether ramp is up or down. Also 'Speed 12 mph'. (Two-ton and 4-ton Eagle trailers were coded Dyak C and Dyak H respectively in the 1935 renumbering scheme.) Underframe was an isosceles triangle of I-beams with the axle as base, and the hitch and jockey wheel at the apex. Wheels are inside the underframe with three-plank body above. Trailer number T19 (in cream on brown plaque at extreme right hand end of central cream panel containing 'G.W.R') was later altered to T400.** ***GWR/D J Hyde collection***

A 20-ton Eagle (of Warwick) solid-tyred trailer being used for the transport of a 'Siemens London/Super Tension' cable drum at Bristol. Winch at leading end of flat trailer for loading/unloading down rear ramp. ***STEAM Swindon***

A 6-ton Scammell drop frame trailer for cable drums, coded Dyak R, of 1937. Winch to raise and lower tail board ramp (propped when vertical). Original sequential fleet number T-1021 altered to T-7704 to conform to 1935 renumbering scheme. *Author's collection*

Thornycroft A1 flatbed lorry towing an AEC trolleybus chassis with its driver on 10 August 1929. Fleet 1820, UL9384, the lorry was brand-new. *GWR/D J Hyde collection*

McCormick Deering (a brand of International Harvester) tractor YR 6529, fleet 1170 of December 1926, negotiating a narrow bridge hauling a trailer that carries a crane base. This GW tractor was the most powerful in the country at the time. The angle of the front wheels indicates the care being taken to centre the load down the middle of the bridge span. *STEAM Swindon*

Large boiler on what appears to be two end wagons of the four-wagon Pollen E 6-wheel set to Wagon Diagram A6, each wagon of which could carry 30 tons. Trailer is jacked up on timber packing and from the middle of its rear headstock has an unusual 5-link chain with a hook at its end. Hand-wheel to its left that operates brake shoes attached to massive beam across whole vehicle that engage with the back of the rear wheels. Not clear whether the boiler has come off, or is to be put on, the Pollen. *STEAM Swindon*

Associated Daimler '428' tipper in departmental grey livery, photographed after 1938 'Sand and Ballast Regulations' (by volume of by weight) came into force and to be shown by plates indicating 5cu yds on sides. Still having original solid tyres, fleet 1992, registration UU9532, joined the fleet in July 1929. Body G1188. 'Uw 4-18-0/Speed 18 mph' and 'great western railway/paddington station/london'. STEAM Swindon

Heavy-duty trailer T223 with its raised towbar at top left loaded on Rectank 17313 of Lot 892 (1921). This vehicle was in the Wagon Diagram Index at C21 and in 1947 received four bolsters and stanchions to become Bobol A (J31). The trailer is the same type shown alongside a Pollen E seen opposite page top, except that here the brake shoes on the beam across the vehicle act on the front of the rear wheels. *STEAM Swindon*

A contract to remove timber from Savernake Forest, Marlborough, in 1931 involved the use of the ex-Plynlimon bus converted to a tractor (Kelley, p166). Also involved was this 4-ton forward-control Thornycroft 'A1' GC 9156 fleet 1731 of 1930 seen negotiating muddy tracks. Cream 'G.W.R.' on brown panel at cab roof. *STEAM Swindon*

Above left **Thornycroft 6½/8-ton chassis fitted with 17ft flat body for long loads in April 1937. Restricted-width cab with sliding door. Stanchions have progressively increasing heights to allow loads to pass alongside the cab. Below the struck-out fleet number S2936 on the cab side (see Chapter 8) are the unladen weight, maximum speed and the GWR ownership.** ***GWR/P J Kelley collection***

Above right **Leyland heavy-duty tractor with winch photographed in December 1937. It replaced one of the Foden steamers. Shirt-button is a yellow-encircled yellow-GWR painted directly on to the cab door, along the bottom of which is 'gwr paddington station'. Below fleet S1086 is 'U.W. 5-13-2/SPEED 20 M.P.H.' Cream letter R on brown circular patch at top of cabside.** ***Author's collection***

Right **Latil 'Traulier' forestry tractor jointly owned by the GW and LMS, purchased in 1936. It had 4-wheel drive and 4-wheel steering together with a heavy-duty winch.** ***Ian Allan Library***

1930 for movement of transformers from works to the new power stations being built for the government country-wide electricity scheme (see *GWR Goods Wagons).* Not only was transport provided for the loads but, where appropriate, the GWR men also erected and installed the equipment. Again, Great Western men would dismantle and erect machinery in what were 'factory removals', similar in principle to 'farm removals' as discussed in *GWR Goods Train Working*. Some of these jobs were at small wayside stations where there were no mechanical facilities such as cranes and capstans, so transportable jacks and other tackle had to be used for unloading from rail to road vehicle, as well as in the work of delivery to site.

A dozen 7-ton hydraulic tipping lorries were added to the GWR cartage fleet in 1931. There were various experiments in the operation of tipping vehicles at that time owing to the inter-dependence of vehicle weight and taxation class (see Appendix 5);: in 1932 a number of 2- and 6-ton lorries were fitted with moveable rubber floors, wound by hand, which was a patent of the Principality Wagon Co in Cardiff. The moveable floor substitute for hand or hydraulic tipping was apparently so successful that 17 more were obtained in the following year, many of which were used by the GW (Civil) Engineering department. A picture taken outside the National Museum of Wales in Cathays Park, Cardiff, of a Thornycroft 'JJ' equipped with the Principality patent floor is found on p18 in Stevens-Stratten & Aldridge. The road-wagon department was asked in 1936 to provide cabs for two Morris Commercial 'Leader' normal-control 4-ton tipping chassis fitted with rubber floors. It was reported in April 1934 that difficulties were being experienced in providing suitable vehicles for roadstone, so authority was obtained to purchase for £820 five second-hand lorries and one tractor with trailer from L W Bryant (Quarries) Ltd of Shipham Gorge, Somerset. Special regulations came into force in July 1938 regarding conveyance of sand and ballast, whereby such traffic could be carried only (a) by actual weight, or (b) in vehicles calibrated to show the volume.

Articulated vehicles joined the special contract work fleet when pipe-trailers were employed behind 6-wheeled lorries. All this sort of special equipment, which included timber carriages, boiler lorries and special 20-ton or 40-ton trailers designed for carrying exceptional loads, along with Harvester, Fordson and Latil tractors fitted with winches, was usually kept at a few main depots such as London, Birmingham and Bristol, and dispatched on special tasks by rail as required. Heavy-duty tractors proved to be very useful and were used wherever possible, not only on special contract work, but also hauling trailers at agricultural shows, and assisting wheeled vehicles that had become stuck on heavy ground.

When felled timber had to be removed from the Savernake Forest near Marlborough to the station in 1931, a 6-wheeled army-type Morris tractor was used along with other road vehicles (the vehicle had been bought as part of the Government 'subsidy' scheme whereby it could be requisitioned in time of war, see Chapters 3 and 5. The Morris was a conversion from a tourist bus used in the late 1920s over Plynlimon mountain between Devil's

Latil tractor hauling a long built-up girder chained to two trailers. That hitched to the tractor is an Eagle 20-ton 6-wheeler having outside-sprung 'bogie' rear wheels, introduced in the early 1930s and subsequently coded Mentor A. ***GWR/D J Hyde collection***

Bridge and Llanidloes where there were no proper roads. Unusual for a bus, it had no hood owing to strong winds over the mountain).

In 1937, one of the Company's low-loader drop-frame trailers stationed in London was fitted with sockets, stanchions and clamps, enabling it to convey large crates of plate glass safely. An alternative set of equipment for the same trailer consisted of sides, hoopsticks and sheets, and made the vehicle suitable for livestock, usually for the big London shows. When not required for special duties, the trailer was used in ordinary cartage.

An unusual task undertaken in 1937 was the haulage of a large number of trolleybus chassis from makers to various firms for superstructures to be fitted. In some instances the chassis were conveyed to the body works by train in Asmo vans, and in others towed all the way by GW road vehicles; however, all the completed vehicles had to be brought back by road, again hauled by a cartage vehicle, as they were 'out-of-gauge' for rail.

As early as 1935, the GWR's special road services became involved in the heavy traffic associated with aerodromes, rearmament and other defence construction. Many were sited in rural areas served by branch line stations, the staff of which were called on to deal with hundreds of tons of bricks, cement, steelwork and so on. In some contracts, large petrol-tanks had to be placed on prepared foundations both on level ground and in pits up to 16 feet in depth. The tanks varied in length up to 32 feet and were 7ft to 9ft. 6in. in diameter, 87 of which were put in place in 1938.

As on rail, the carriage of long loads presented difficulties on the roads. In 1937 a 6/8-ton chassis fitted with flat body and bolsters for the carriage of girders and long sections was put into service, again in connection with aerodrome construction. A feature of this vehicle was that the body was specially lengthened and the driver's cab was half the normal width, allowing a lengthy load to project in front of the vehicle alongside the cab when necessary. Work on aerodromes showed up a weakness in the GW special contract vehicles in that many became bogged down in soft ground. This had been a problem in 1931 in the Treherbert mountain contract mentioned above. The solution was to use six-wheeled lorries with 'super-power' eight-cylinder engines, first added to the special contract fleet in 1935. They were used as double-heading tractors assisting the loaded vehicles.

'Ordinary' special contract work continued through the late 1930s. For example, in 1939 the GWR was involved with water supply pipelines from a pumping station on the river at Tewkesbury to a reservoir on the top of Churchdown Hill, and from there to Cheltenham. The bitumen-coated steel pipes for both legs were 30ft long and each weighed 30cwts. Some 2,000 tons of pipes and several hundred tons of fittings were delivered to the route which was almost entirely across open country. Six-wheeled tractors were connected to 2-wheeled trailers with a long connecting bar, rather like a pole trailer. A similar contract installed a pipeline from Chiseldon to Swindon. Government water supply schemes on behalf of rural areas involved the GW delivering pipes to isolated villages and in certain cases laying the pipes and doing all the ancillary work.

In 1939 some trailers handling heavy traffic were equipped experimentally with the vacuum brake along the lines of the train

Brockhouse 15-ton 8-wheel trailer coded Titan A (not in 1939 Telegraph Code Book). Wheels sprung in pairs. No fleet number marked on. Brake wheels at front and rear. As written on the print, the front brake handle, that is shown vertical, can be swung down and fixed below floor level without interfering with the action of the brake. At the rear there is a seat for a brakeman on the left side. Six lashing rings along raves of which the middle four separate great, western and railway that are cast on plates. ***GWR/P J Kelley collection***

Brockhouse 15-ton well-deck trailer, photographed new on 14 May 1936 in service grey with white/cream lettering. Although the fleet number T-790 is from the original sequential series, and not altered yet according to the 1935 scheme, the code Titan B is painted on according to the new scheme (see Chapter 8 for renumbering). The (solid rubber?) wheels are in four pairs, each separately sprung. There are drum brakes on the front pair operated by the hand wheel on the far side. Above 'DANGER' on hitch is the electric lead for rear lights and number plate. At the rear end is written the fleet number and also in small block capitals 'LOAD NOT TO EXCEED 15.0.0'. Along the side is 'GREAT WESTERN RLY' and there is a small shirt-button on the front beam of the well deck to the left of the fleet number. In a black panel on the forecarriage is 'G.W.R. Paddington Station London'. ***GWR/P J Kelley collection***

vacuum brake, so that in the rare event of a breakaway, the trailer was immediately brought to rest. In 1939 also, developments with heavier articulated vehicles took place when an 8-ton type was introduced, having a four-wheeled tractor unit fitted with a special Scammell coupling inter-changeable with 6 and 8-ton trailers. The vehicle was very suitable for traversing difficult ground, and could deal with heavy loads as well as take its place in the delivery of normal C&D traffic. It was employed to deliver two boilers, each weighing 10½-tons from the station yard at Ludgershall one mile by road to their installation site. The boilers had to be upended and lowered into prepared concrete pits. The GW's specially-equipped five-men gang had to erect a lifting frame and, after being raised, the boilers were skidded into position over the pit and lowered.

Heavy work continued during WW2, the loco works being asked in 1940 by the Road Transport Department to (i) 'send man to Oxford to assist in moving press castings for motor works'; and (ii) 'send man to Devizes to assist in moving three vertical boilers in the Barracks'.

Latil tractor (double axle steering) photographed in April 1943 at Chester backing to couple up to a pole trailer with double pneumatic tyres front and rear on which is loaded a petrol tank 32ft long x 9ft diameter for an aerodrome. The tractor is fleet 416 (but has no prefix letter) with brown encircled brown shirt-button on cream disc on doorside. White-edged mudguards and only one shaded headlamp on nearside for blackout regulations. *STEAM Swindon*

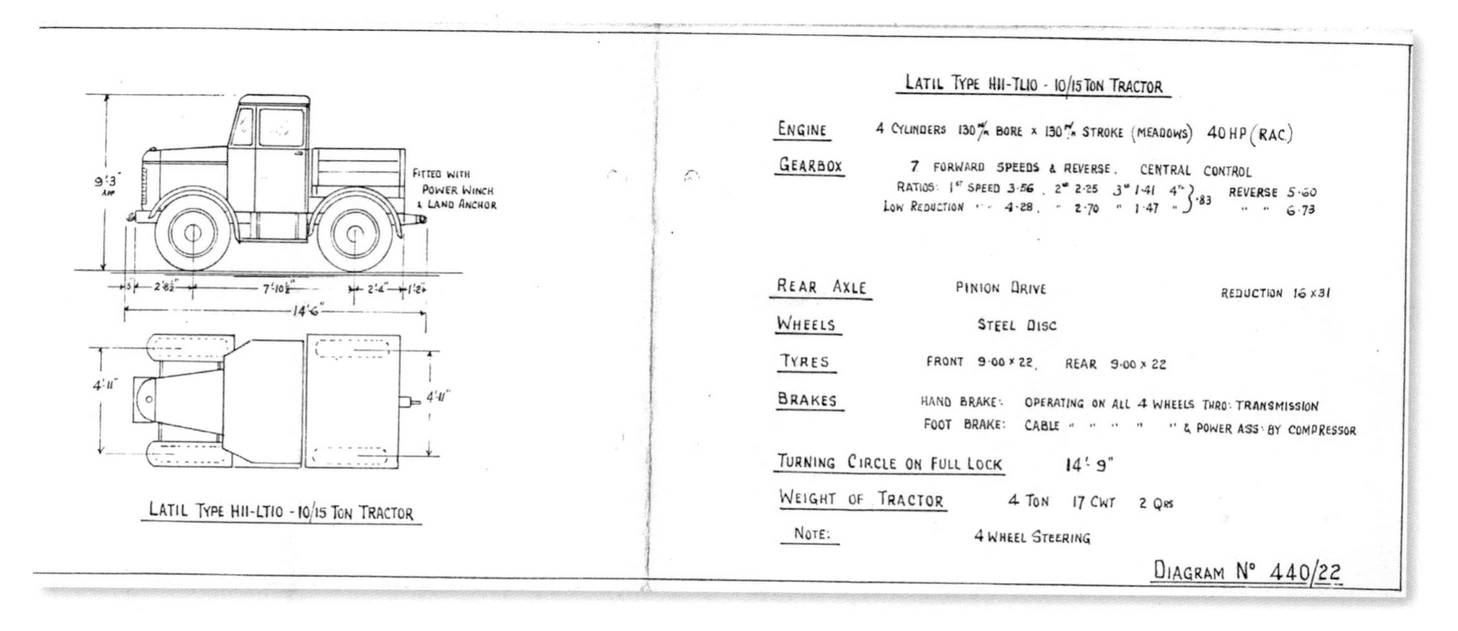

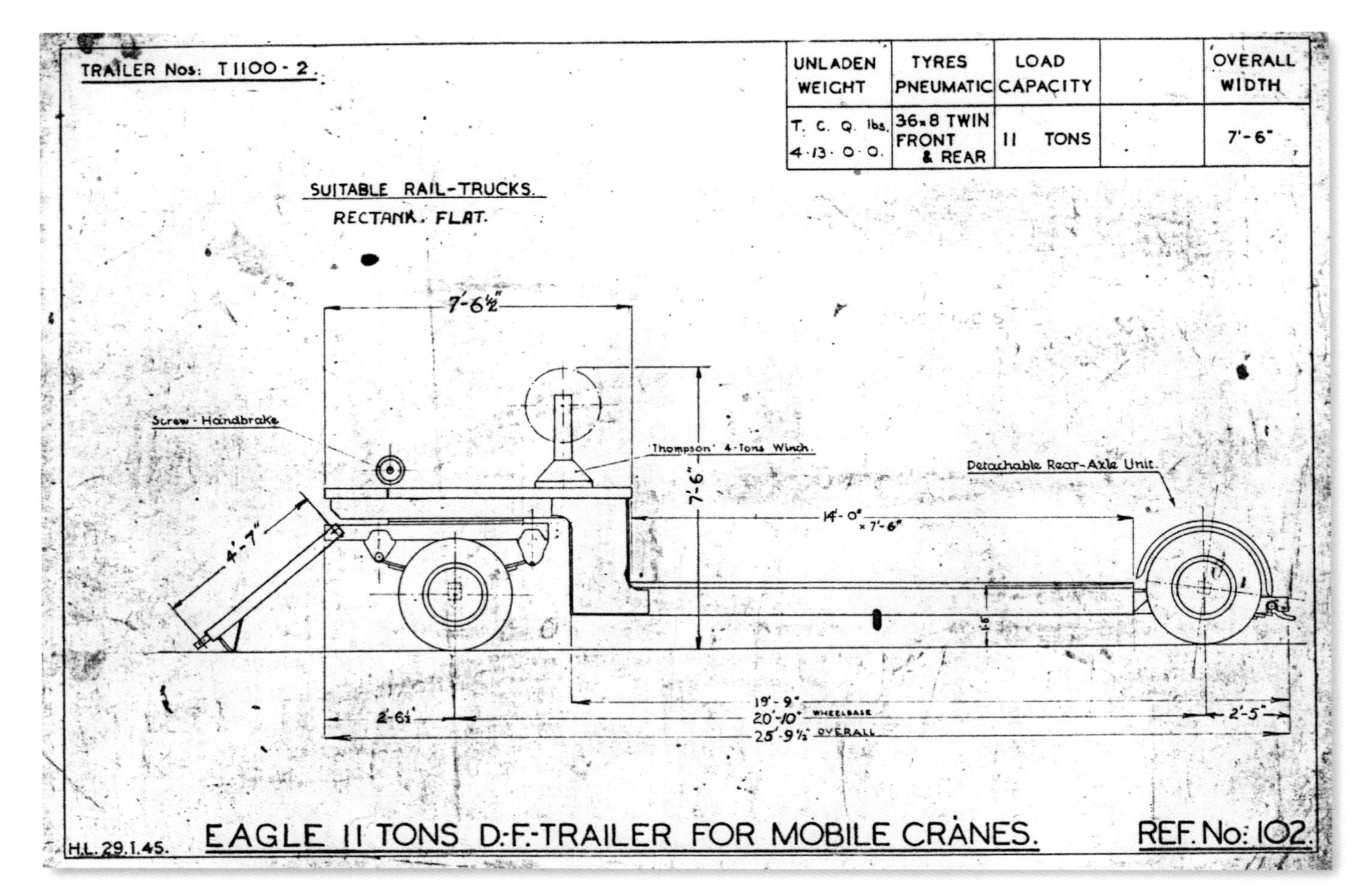

Foden timber tractor fitted with winch and ground anchor purchased by the GW in 1946. Fleet S421, HGP728, the vehicle has shirt-buttons in the form of brown encircled GWR on cream discs. *Ian Allan Library*

Early 'lift van' (i.e. container) numbered LV32 (purchased from Evans Cook Ltd of Peckham) photographed on 16 January 1928 on flatbed horse lorry (possibly to Diagram B9), fleet 1090, in Westbourne Park yard, Paddington. The lorry forecarriage has old-design naves (hubs) but the rear wheels have cast iron centres. The container overhangs the rear of the lorry and bears down on the rear springs. *GWR/D J Hyde collection*

K-type furniture container, new in March 1935, on two-horse lorry to diagram B7, fleet 2734. 'great western raily' in brown block capitals on cream panel on rave with 'Tare 1-3-1' in script at extreme right. Old pattern hubs. 'Fredavis Secy Etc' tucked away on inside of forecarrage. Given that it was already known that horse lorries were not really suitable for carrying lift vans owing to the overhang at the rear, it is not clear why this was tried again, even though the print is marked 'Heavy Trailer Experiment For K Container'. There is a bogie Macaw to the left and a van beyond that. *GWR/D J Hyde collection*

The widespread use of containers required not only motor lorries, but also appropriate flat-bed bodies on the lorry or on a trailer. The 4-ton rigid motor lorries originally employed were displaced by 6-ton lorries for container work (6 tons was the largest load for a 4-wheeled vehicle in the 1930s), and articulated trailers were increasingly used. There is little doubt that widespread use of containers would not have been possible without the considerable expansion of the GW's own motor lorry fleet.

There was rapid growth in the numbers of GW containers: 200 in 1928; 418 in 1929 (comprising 90 open, 327 covered and a single experimental insulated container for meat and other perishable traffic introduced in 1926 for the Channel Islands trade); 828 in

In October 1928, a newly-introduced GWR container B-88 (with 'To carry 4-tons /Tare 13-2' in script) being unloaded by geared hand-wound crane from 4/5-ton Thornycroft forward control lorry, at Paddington New Yard. Fleet 1336, YE5402, the lorry dates from February 1927. 'great western railway' in brown on cream panels along raves. Empty match trucks awaiting loading. *GWR/D J Hyde collection*

One of 40 'lift vans', purchased for evaluation in 1926 by the GWR from Evans Cook Ltd, being loaded on to a Thornycroft 4-ton flat lorry at Paddington New Yard in October 1928 from the GW match truck to the left of the Ransome & Rapier 2-ton mobile crane. GW container B105, built at the road wagon shop at Swindon in June 1928, with 'TO CARRY 4-TONS /TARE 13-2' in script is on a wagon on a track further over. *GWR/D J Hyde collection*

Practically new 4-ton grey-painted container BX-294 (built to Diagram BX2 in March 1929) is being loaded in April 1929 at Paddington by a Ransomes mobile crane on to a solid-tyred 6-ton 'Harrow' industrial low loader (later to be coded Dido H). Fordson pneumatic-tyred tractor fleet 391, XP2167 (one of three fleet 389-91 that came into service in September 1923 but now with later design of roof), is all-over brown with brown 'GWR' in cream panels on sides under roof. Single licence disc. Notice that even with crane rope sheave right up near top of jib, there's not much clearance to put on/lift off LMS one-planker on right. Alongside goods shed to left is the rear of a horse-drawn timber carriage fleet, 1214. *Author's collection*

1930; 1,100 in 1932; 1,423 in 1933; 1,673 in 1935; 1,900 in 1937; 2,070 in 1938; 2,150 in 1939; and 2,609 in 1947. The details of all the different types of container are given in *GWR Goods Wagons*.

The size of containers determined the sort of flat-bed trailers that were used to convey them. Small trailer wheels to lower the centre of gravity were the norm. Fifteen special trailers were purchased in 1932 for use solely with container traffic. They differed from the ordinary C&D trailer, inasmuch as they were fitted with twin pneumatic tyres on all four wheels, and had no platform floor. Suitable bearers were incorporated in the open chassis so that any type of container could be carried, and adjustable loading bars at each end prevented movement of the load. Another type of trailer built on timber-carriage lines was convertible, in that it could be used either for conveying containers, or for timber, or long loads of steel. Later 'drop-frame' trailers were employed for containers.

The use of containers on the Great Western Railway grew rapidly in the 1930s, rising at more than 10percent per annum. In 1931, 70,000 tons of traffic were carried: the number of loaded journeys in 1936 was over 62,000 with a tonnage of over 120,000 and revenue of over £220,000. In 1938, with twice as many containers as in 1931, a total of 155,000 tons were conveyed. More and more new ideas for using containers arose as the years went by. Successful experiments were carried out in the late 1930s with loads of bulbs, fish, flowers, meat, soft fruit, strawberries and Irish rabbits all employing refrigerated containers.

The opportunity of using containers for household removals was obvious and in 1933 Type K containers specially for household furniture were introduced. In a 1933 document issued to GW staff regarding household removals using containers, the possibility is recognised of using railway containers for an all-road journey that had no rail-borne component. Some of the furniture removal firms themselves had their own private-owner containers in the same way that years before they had had their own horse-drawn road vans. After the introduction of Type K containers, much of the household removal business that had been lost to road was

One of two Thornycroft 6/8-ton 'Taurus' lorries fitted with a diesel engine ordered by the GW in 1932 for trials. Extended bumper owing to weight of engine. When first delivered in January 1933 fleet 2285 GX 3365 had been fitted with a drop-sided open body (Chapter 5), but in February 1933 the sides were removed and fixing frame attached to see how the lorry would cope with containers. The M1 design of container of December 1932 relied on side- and end-louvred ventilators together with shell ventilators in the roof to keep the contents cool. In March 1933 the diesel vehicle was altered again and fitted with a van body (Chapter 6). *GWR/D J Hyde collection*

Four-ton Eagle trailer T-137 photographed at Hockley Basin on 14 November 1924. Height of hitch may be altered using frame at front of forecarriage which is braced back to the front axle. The middle rod crosspiece to stiffen the triangular-shaped towbar has become displaced as the nut-and-bolt fixings have worked loose. Supposedly for containers, this design is not listed under 'Container Trailers' in the 1939 telegraph code book, nor does it correspond with the Dido B code that was for 5-ton 4-wheel trailers. *GWR/P J Kelley collection*

T-170, a Dyson trailer for containers from the early 1930s, later coded Numa B. Double pneumatic tyres all round. Cross-bearers spaced to suit size of container, 'Great Western Railway/F R E Davis Secretary Paddington' on side rave. Sprung-loaded hitch. *Dyson Trailers, Liverpool*

There were also containers for liquids in bulk. Up until the 1930s liquids were usually transported in casks, drums, carboys and so on, all of which required handling on and off rail wagons even if taken from one rail-connected factory to another. The GWR, along with most other railways, owned relatively few tank wagons — those that they did have were the departmental vehicles listed in the DD group in the Wagon Diagram Index and used for water, oil, creosote, gas, etc. There were private owner tank wagons for acid and such, but a large increase in railway tank wagons came about with the growth of the petrol and oil industry, followed by the dairies. By the late 1930s all kinds of liquids were being transported in bulk, using either rail tank wagons or 'container demountable tanks'— the rail tank wagon without its underframe and wheels that was lifted on and off rail wagons and road vehicles by cranes.

Four-wheeled Morris tractor unloading a road-rail tank at Westbourne Park in August 1946. ***GWR/D J Hyde collection***

Six-ton Scammell mechanical horse coupled to a Garton's road-rail tank (Garton, Sons & Co Ltd had a glucose and sugar river-connected factory in Battersea). ***A G Atkins collection***

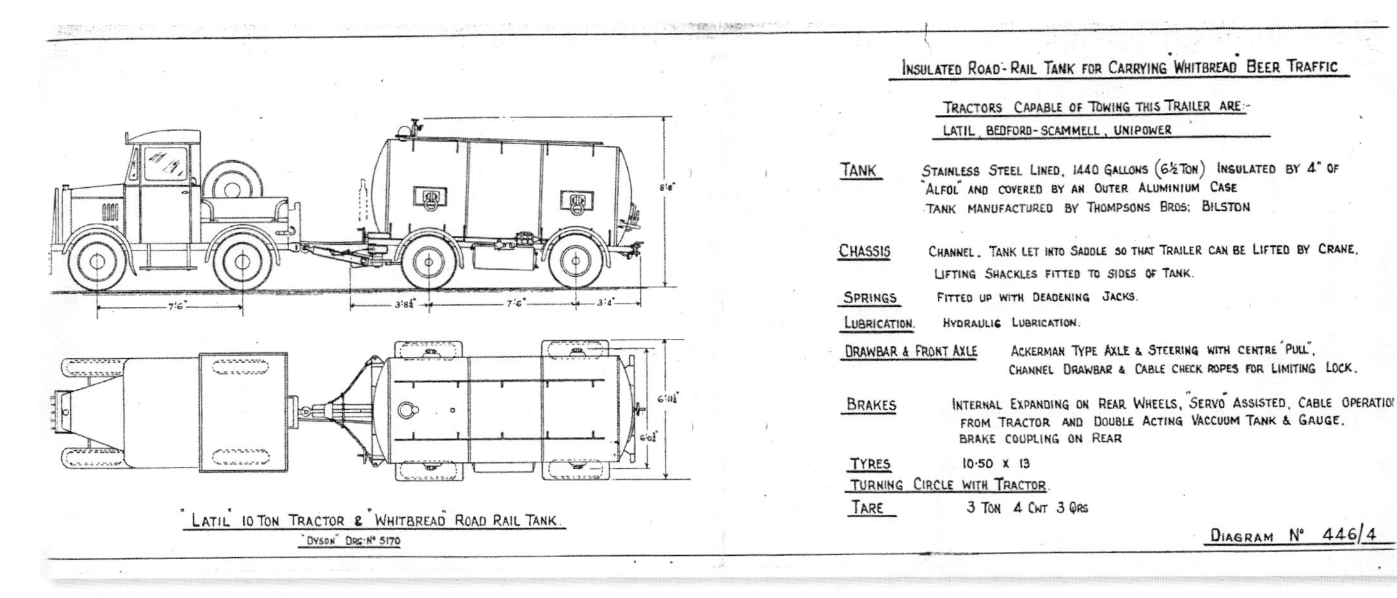

Glucose from London to Newport, liquid sugar to Paignton and vinegar from Hull to Bristol were among the commodities which began to be conveyed by the GW in demountable tanks. In 1938 the company signed a contract with Lever Brothers to hire seven wagons for the conveyance of oils, glycerine, bone-grease and tallow using demountable tanks. An interesting feature was that empty haulage was reduced in this particular arrangement by back loading, e.g. a tank filled with edible oil was, after discharge and cleaning, reloaded with bone-grease and returned to the original forwarding point. This type of transport continued through into nationalisation, the GW hiring out tank units to traders; for example, in 1947 ICI paints and varnishes were conveyed in such tanks. A variant of this scheme used road tank trailers that were carried on their wheels on rail vehicles, like the horse-drawn furniture vans of old. Some of the liquids that were taken by rail required a high temperature to be maintained during transit, which was achieved by electrical heating generated by a dynamo on the special wagons. Rail vehicles for tank road trailers were listed in the GW carriage index and those for demountable tanks in the wagon index, see Chapter 34 *GWR Goods Wagons*. Messrs Dyson of Liverpool were the builders of many of these trailers.

In the years immediately preceding WW2, containers were used to carry gas-masks, first-aid materials and Air Raid Precaution stores, as part of the re-armament and defence programmes. Some large containers had racks fitted to carry aeroplane accessories and instruments, and others were fitted for the conveyance of special items, such as machine parts. The small open SL type was good for conveying shell cases between engineering works and filling factory. Ventilated meat containers were used for oilskin decontamination clothing (hung out on the hooks).

On the outbreak of war on 3 September 1939, the GW was called upon by numerous organisations — often at very short notice — to undertake the removal of office equipment and records to emergency headquarters in areas less vulnerable to bombing. This was performed using containers, that also played a prominent part in the removal from London of valuable art treasures, books and manuscripts to places of greater safety. The fascinating story of how paintings and treasures were moved in GW containers from the National Gallery and the British Museum in London to North Wales on the outbreak of war in 1939 — eventually to Manod slate quarry near Portmeirion — is described in the October 1946 *GWR Magazine*. The Thornycroft 6/8-ton rigid-chassis lorry was found to be the best type to carry

Thornycroft 6/8-tonner arriving at Manod slate quarry from Ffestiniog station with a container of National Gallery pictures in 1941. The tarpaulin put over BX-428 is insurance against roof leakage. Cream rear raves and a 20mph disc. White-painted edges to mudguards for blackout. *National Gallery*

In WW2, containers were used in removals of the contents of buildings to safer places out in the country. Here, on 18 May 1942, an LMS container that holds effects from Harrow School has been brought by road to Greenford Station en route to Malvern School. It is being unloaded by means of the geared hand-wound yard crane. Bedford-Scammell 4-wheel tractor FLL380 is coupled to Dyak P drop frame trailer T-2079. The split-windscreen Bedford is in war guise with white edged rear mudguards and unusual white painting of front wings. Off-side headlight with mask. The fleet number C8810 is an instance of what was supposed to be prefixed by letter 'D'. ***GWR/D J Hyde collection***

containers up the mountain road and into the quarry: thirty trips were made each day from the base at Ffestiniog goods station. For the safety of staff working in the unventilated caverns, carbon monoxide fumes from the lorry exhausts had be eliminated by fitting a special device to the engines. In the event, the National Gallery in Trafalgar Square was hit by 11 high-explosive bombs in raids between 1940-41. During the war, stocks of foodstuffs were moved from the London Docks to safer places, meat and butter going in insulated containers. Ventilated M containers were in great demand to convey the increased amount of home-killed meat from West Wales and the West Country, while FX containers were continually employed for the unloading of meat boats diverted to GW ports. With the object of reducing to a minimum the movement of empty containers, all railway-owned containers were, as from 1 January 1943, brought under common-user control, and this resulted in an increase of approximately 15 percent in the number of loaded journeys compared with previous years.

An interesting example of container working late in the war was the transport of frozen pancreatic glands in refrigerated containers from ports to London laboratories for the manufacture of insulin; temperatures of from 12 to 22 °F below freezing (ie below 32°F) had to be maintained, regardless of ambient air temperature.

Six AF-containers were put into traffic in May 1938 with 10-ins thick Tropal insulation, and specially-sealed doors, to keep Walls ice cream in good condition during rail journeys. Seen being loaded at Acton in September 1947 on 6-ton trailer T-6499 coded Dyak G that bears the registration FYU40 of the mechanical horse, fleet C6318, and carries a 20mph speed limit plate. The shirt-button on the bonnet is a brown-encircled brown GWR on a cream circular patch. ***GWR/D J Hyde collection***

After the war, in 1947, the Goods Department hosted a demonstration of modern handling equipment at St Ervan's Rd yard (see *GWR Goods Services*, vol 2A). Three new types of container were on show:

(i) a light-frame construction 1-ton collapsible container for conveying market 'empties' which could take a maximum load of 120 fish boxes. Two loaded, or 6 empty and collapsed, containers fitted into an open rail wagon.

(ii) a completely weatherproof covered bulk container for cement, lime, china clay and similar traffic affected by moisture. It carried 3½ tons or 90cu ft. Three containers fitted into an open wagon. The design was approved by the Aberthaw & Bristol Channel Portland Cement Co who were to deliver 70,000 tons of cement in this type of container for building the Claerwen Dam at Rhayader in Radnorshire, Wales. The GW built 72 containers of this type, saving the transport of over a million bags of cement.

(iii) a 3½-ton open bulk container design for substances that were not affected by climate, such as road stone, gravel and sand.

Also demonstrated were stillages, 'a table with very short legs' (the forerunners of pallets). They were handled by a Scott electric elevating platform truck (the forerunner of the forklift truck).

Collapsible container, fleet 2950, loaded with fish boxes 'to be returned to Milford Haven', etc shown off at St Ervans Rd in 1947 with other devices for faster handling of freight. Its tare was 5-1-4 (in script to right of GW) and is seen loaded on the rear of trailer fleet T-8510 that has a 20mph maximum speed disc behind nearside rear wheel. At the front of the trailer, out of the picture to the right, is a collapsed container. Cables beneath trailer to rear wheel actuate brakes from mechanical horse. *Author's collection*

CHAPTER FOURTEEN

ECONOMICS AND COSTS OF CARTAGE

The illustration from the 1938 GWR *General Statistics* of cartage costs makes interesting reading. Tonnages carted/year and cartage costs/year are given for three categories, namely company horse-drawn vehicles, company motors, and agents (for which horse and motor tonnages are not separated). Comparative data for every month in the years 1929, 1936, and 1937 are provided, together with annual totals for each category in every year from 1923-1937.

The tonnage/year carted by all three categories taken together was 3.74 million tons in 1923; 4.41 million, 1925; 4.71 million, 1927; 5.09 million, 1929; 5.04 million, 1931; 5.12 million, 1933; 5.83 million, 1935; and 6.69 million tons in 1937. So there was a steady increase in the tonnage of carted goods over the period, apart from a slight blip in 1931. Even with a rise in petrol prices over that period, the price per ton to cart was lower than previously owing to better petrol consumption, and economics in horse maintenance.

Up to the very early 1930s the annual tonnage carted by horse-drawn vehicles remained roughly constant at about 2 million tons, but thereafter it gradually decreased to some 1.5 million tons in 1937. In contrast, the tonnage carted by GW motors increased progressively from 610,000 tons in 1923 to nearly 4.5 million tons in 1937. In 1923, horses carted 78 percent of all the tonnage conveyed by GW vehicles but in 1930 it had reduced to 49 percent and in 1937 was down to 25 percent.

The tonnage conveyed by GW agents hovered around 1 million tons/year up to 1929, decreased to about half a million tons in 1932, but then increased to about 750,000 tons/year in 1937. As a percentage of the *total* tonnage carted by GW horses/GW motors/GW Agents, agents' figures are about 26 percent in 1923; 16 percent in 1930; and 11 percent in 1937.

How these sums were calculated for 'cost per ton carted' is not explained, nor what was, and was not, included. Nevertheless, the general evidence is that costs/ton of cartage by GW motors was less than the cost/ton by GW horse cartage throughout 1923-1937. What is remarkable about the data, given the GW policy of dispensing with agents (Chapter 9) is that cartage costs/ton by agents was less than by GW motors. However, the figures may be misleading as discussed below.

Whether the capital cost of cartage vehicles and depreciation charges were factored into the costings is unclear and isolated figures have to be treated with caution. An example relates to the steam wagon based at Henwick employed in 1904 in the Teme Valley in Worcestershire (Chapter 4). On an occasion when the steam wagon had to be laid up owing to an accident and horse transport had to be substituted, it was said that "......costs by the steam lorry were almost a quarter of the cost of horse haulage....." Certainly fewer journeys might be required since the steam wagon could carry greater loads, but what about the initial cost of the steam wagon? This omission seems implicit in the article by Bayley (1903-4 Transactions of the *GWR Mechanics Institution*, Swindon), where it stated that it cost 3d per ton-mile of useful load to run steam wagons in general compared with 6d per ton-mile for horse-drawn lorries. Bayley's article gives interesting figures for the time: £700 for the cost of a steam wagon; coke at 15/- per ton; driver's wages 35/- per week; driver's mate at 17/6 per week. (Estimated operating costs of the Thornycroft steamer used at Hockley in 1902 were £50 per annum for repairs; 6s/week for coal and oil; and 30s/week for the driver's wages.) Notice that Bayley uses 'cost/ton-mile' rather than simply cost/ton irrespective of the distance travelled. The cost/ton for a journey of one mile has to be smaller than the cost/ton for any longer journey done at the same speed. Furthermore, shorter journeys permitted a vehicle to return to the depot and do more work. A possible reason that costs/ton for agents was less than for GW cartage would be that agents operated over shorter C&D distances.

In 1923, two million tons of goods were carried by GW horse vehicles at an average of 5s 11d per ton; 610,000 tons by GW motor vehicles at 4s 6d per ton; and 970,000 tons by agents at 4s 11d per ton. By the late 1930s, the comparable figures were 1.5 million tons at 4s 6d

17

GOODS CARTAGE—HORSES AND MOTORS.

Four Weeks Ended	Year.	Cartage by Company's Horses.		Cartage by Company's Motors.		Total.		Cartage by Agents.	
		Tonnage.	Cost per Ton.	Tonnage.	Cost per Ton.	Tonnage.	Cost per Ton.	Tonnage.	Cost per Ton.
			s. d.		s. d.		s. d.		s. d.
20th Jan.	1929	141,655	6: 6	106,473	4: 8	248,128	5: 9	60,706	4: 1
12th Jan.	1936	105,020	5: 1	261,237	4: 3	366,257	4: 6	46,389	3: 9
10th Jan.	1937	108,200	4:10	309,089	4: 0	417,289	4: 3	52,469	3: 9
9th Jan.	1938	96,216	5: 2	314,217	4: 2	410,433	4: 5	57,460	3: 7
17th Feb.	1929	168,991	5: 5	122,091	4: 4	291,082	5: 0	73,335	4: 1
9th Feb.	1936	119,235	4: 4	288.964	3:11	408,199	4: 0	55,538	3: 9
7th Feb.	1937	114,740	4: 5	319,567	3:11	434,307	4: 0	56,932	3: 8
6th Feb.	1938	99,430	4:10	342,173	4: 0	441,603	4: 2	65,413	3: 7
17th Mar.	1929	175,299	5: 3	129,492	4: 3	304,791	4:10	72,348	4: 1
8th Mar.	1936	116,879	4: 5	296,296	3:10	413,175	4: 0	55,571	3: 9
7th Mar.	1937	117,551	4: 4	333,250	3:11	450,801	4: 0	60,011	3: 9
6th Mar.	1938	97,446	4:10	348,073	3:11	445,519	4: 1	61,555	3: 7
14th Apr.	1929(*a*)	170,761	5: 6	126,198	4: 6	296,959	5: 1	69,433	4: 1
5th Apr.	1936	125,392	4: 3	318,673	3: 9	444,065	3:10	61,227	3: 8
4th Apr.	1937(*a*)	113,321	4: 7	321,065	4: 0	434,386	4: 2	54,435	3: 9
3rd Apr.	1938								
12th May	1929	187,862	5: 1	148,386	4: 4	336,248	4: 9	79,712	4: 0
3rd May	1936(*a*)	114,989	4: 7	289,302	3:11	404,291	4: 1	55,145	3: 9
2nd May	1937	127,391	4: 1	364,737	3: 9	492,128	3:10	61,642	3: 9
1st May	1938(*a*)								
9th June	1929(*b*)	175,459	5: 5	136,926	4: 7	312,385	5: 1	72,969	4: 1
31st May	1936(*b*)	125,991	4: 3	316,229	3:10	442,220	3:11	58,263	3: 9
30th May	1937(*b*)‡	111,034	4: 7	316,694	4: 1	427,728	4: 2	53,247	3: 9
29th May	1938								
7th July	1929	180,932	5: 4	146,832	4: 6	327,764	4:11	77,633	4: 0
28th June	1936(*b*)	115,415	4: 7	291,336	4: 1	406,751	4: 3	58,143	3: 8
27th June	1937	118,283	4: 4	341,687	4: 0	459,970	4: 1	58,312	3: 9
26th June	1938(*b*)								
4th Aug.	1929	176,990	5: 4	147,488	4: 5	324,478	4:11	77,028	4: 1
26th July	1936	118,835	4: 5	306,303	3:11	425,138	4: 1	57,475	3: 9
25th July	1937	113,399	4: 6	333,569	4: 0	446,968	4: 2	58,351	3: 8
24th July	1938								
1st Sept.	1929	158,085	5:11	136,184	4: 9	294,269	5: 5	65,664	4: 1
23rd Aug.	1936	107,644	4: 8	290,637	4: 0	398,281	4: 2	51,163	3: 8
22nd Aug.	1937	102,314	4:11	315,844	4: 1	418,158	4: 4	51,194	3: 8
21st Aug.	1938								
29th Sept.	1929	180,098	5: 2	154,103	4: 5	334,201	4:10	73,150	4: 1
20th Sept.	1936	120,551	4: 4	318,807	3:11	439,358	4: 0	57,280	3: 9
19th Sept.	1937	114,540	4: 6	352,146	3:11	466,686	4: 1	61,246	3: 8
18th Sept.	1938								
27th Oct.	1929	185,664	5: 1	171,341	4: 2	357,005	4: 7	77,351	4: 1
18th Oct.	1936	129,060	4: 1	341,708	3: 9	470,768	3:10	61,277	3: 9
17th Oct.	1937	119,578	4: 5	372,239	3:10	491,817	4: 0	63,772	3: 9
16th Oct.	1938								
24th Nov.	1929	186,105	5: 1	169,952	4: 3	356,057	4: 9	79,045	4: 0
15th Nov.	1936	130,794	4: 1	358,885	3: 8	489,679	3: 9	60,304	3: 9
14th Nov.	1937	117,724	4: 4	379,159	3: 9	496,883	3:11	66,957	3: 9
13th Nov.	1938								
22nd Dec.	1929	185,764	5: 2	165,968	4: 5	351,732	4:10	76,884	4: 0
13th Dec.	1936	131,269	4: 3	360,416	3: 8	491,685	3:10	59,674	3: 9
12th Dec.	1937	115,523	4: 6	373,024	3:10	488,547	4: 0	62,001	3: 8
11th Dec.	1938								
Total	1923	2,156,645	5:11	609,982	4: 6	2,766,627	5: 7	969,934	4:11
Total	1924	2,306,502	5: 7	801,434	4: 5	3,107,936	5: 3	999,414	4: 8
Total	1925	2,435,759	5: 4	926,796	4: 2	3,362,555	5: 0	1,048,782	4: 6
Total	1926§	2,343,622	5: 3	982,077	4: 3	3,325,699	5: 0	961,534	4: 5
Total	1927	2,439,532	5: 2	1,215,540	3:11	3,655,072	4: 9	1,055,460	4: 3
Total	1928	2,298,163	5: 6	1,413,933	4: 1	3,712,096	4:11	962,824	4: 2
Total	1929	2,273,665	5: 5	1,861,434	4: 5	4,135,096	4:11	955,258	4: 1
Total	1930	2,112,918	5: 5	2,214,436	4: 8	4,327,354	5: 1	824,848	4: 1
Total	1931†	1,998,355	5: 1	2,369 096	4: 5	4,367,451	4: 8	674,441	4: 1
Total	1932	1,733,742	5: 1	2,511,886	4: 4	4,245,628	4: 8	564,456	4: 0
Total	1933	1,658,638	4: 9	2,878,957	4: 2	4,537,595	4: 4	586,041	3:10
Total	1934	1,703,011	4: 6	3,292,384	3:10	4,995,395	4: 1	645,403	3:10
Total	1935	1,587,529	4: 8	3,575,951	3:11	5,163,480	4: 2	662,731	3: 9
Total	1936	1,561,074	4: 5	4,038,793	3:10	5,599,867	4: 0	737,449	3: 9
Total	1937	1,493,598	4: 6	4,432,070	3:11	5,925,668	4: 1	760,569	3: 9
Total	1938								

For Notes, *see* page 3.

Extract from the 1938 GW General Statistics volume. *Author's collection*

(GW horse); 4.4 million tons at 3s 11d (GW motor); and 760,000 tons at 3s 9d (agents). The tonnage of goods taken by horse-drawn transport thus fell over that period by 500,000 tons (i.e. by 25 percent of the 1923 figure) but the tonnage taken by GW motor vehicles rose by the amazing figure of 3.79 million tons (a 621 percent increase over 1923). The costs per ton, by both horse and by motor, fell for both the railway and for its agents. It is perhaps worthy of note that the agents' cost per ton for carrying goods in the late 1930s at 3s 9d was lower than the GW motor fleet cost per ton (3s 11d). We do not know the relative make-up of the agents' fleets (ratio of horse-drawn vehicles to motors) to enable a calculation of an average agents' cost, but the implication is that the agents employed by the GWR either had no horse-drawn vehicles or were particularly efficient at that time.

Costs to the GW were affected when shed and cartage staff at large depots worked on bonus schemes. The scheme instituted at Paddington on 1st January 1900 and in use elsewhere before WW1 specified the following minimum weights to be moved per team of horses per week:

4-horse teams	60 tons
3-horse	50 and 58 tons
2-horse	24, 27, 30 and 33 tons
1-horse	12 and 15 tons

Loads above these qualified for bonuses which (in 1908) were 10d/ton to carmen and 3d/ton to van guards. The varying weights expected per team reflected (i) the nature of the traffic dealt with; (ii) the district (flat or hilly); and (iii) the distance to and from the station. GW cartage staff were able to augment their weekly wages by sums varying from a few pennies up to 18/- or more. Overall the cost to the company of handling goods diminished after the bonus scheme got underway. For example, in 1908, it had reduced to 13.61d/ton in the shed and, on the cartage side, costs were reduced by 8d/ton. Furthermore £15,000 was saved by not having to hire extra cartage vehicles that year.

Parcels carried by passenger train were charged at a higher rate than if carried by ordinary goods train, and it was possible for the railway to make as much money from carriage of fewer parcels as from loads of lower-rated heavy goods. Hence, when motors were first introduced, parcels vans featured prominently in the small fleet; they were designed to replace one-horse light vans. These motors ensured quick delivery and pick-up and were emblazoned with 'Express Parcels Service' on their sides. The working cost per mile for the parcels vans was 2.5d which was said to be actually cheaper than the normal cost/mile of horse-drawn vehicles, unless the horse was working all the time to its maximum capacity. As explained by Coventry in his 1910 *GWR Mechanics Institute* paper, the figures were much more in favour of the motor van when the extra work that could be done by the staff and the quicker deliveries were considered – but there were still problems about 'idle time'.

The capital costs of motor lorries were, of course, considerably more than traditional horse-drawn vehicles, although the running costs were said to be comparable. The perceived wisdom in the early 1920s was that delivery rounds involving a short mileage with a considerable number of calls were better covered by horses, since the advantage of the greater speed of the more-costly motor lorry was nullified in practice by the standing time which prevented the vehicles from being worked more efficiently. Furthermore, since at that time few motor lorries operated with trailers, considerable time was spent with the motor lorry having to wait while loading and unloading at depots. To attack this problem, experiments were begun using tractors and trailers, and also 'demountable vehicle bodies' (Chapter 6). Bulkeley in 1921 reported the savings made by a haulage contractor who had substituted tractors and semi-trailers (articulated trailers) for horse-drawn transport: a 2-horse team could haul about 3 tons per trip at a cost of 7/6 per ton; but a petrol tractor and semi-trailer hauled just over 8 tons at a cost of just under 4/- per ton. Bulkeley made the point that a few motors mixed into a fleet consisting mostly of horses would not yield efficient results, and he gives formulae for deciding what type of vehicle is going to be best for cartage working of a depot as a whole.

There were heavy increases in all costs during WW1, including the provision and maintenance of the cartage establishment. When rates charged to customers for goods transport by rail included charges for cartage at one or both ends of a journey, there was nothing that the railways could do to keep pace with increased costs since these rates were fixed by government at 1913 levels. Only when cartage charges were separate from rail charges in a quotation could rates be increased. By 1915 the various Cart-owner Associations throughout the country had already put up their rates. Immediately after WW1, it was agreed by the new Ministry of Transport that something would have to be done to restore the railways to their 1913 'Standard Revenues'. Not only was the Victorian 'Classification of Goods' revised, but also all rates were revised (see Chapter 4 of Volume 1 of *GWR Goods Services*). The 'Appointed Day' for the revisions to come into effect was 1 January 1928. At the outset, attempts had been made to institute rates varying with costs. This would, however, have resulted in appreciably increasing the overall cost in many cases. After much discussion in the years up to the Appointed Day, the question was settled in favour of a uniform scale applicable at all stations *except* those on the Southern Railway, and in London and Liverpool. It was also agreed to continue existing exceptional rail rates, many of which included collection and delivery.

A substantial deficit under the heading of C&D occurred annually in the GW's balance sheet – about £200,000 in 1930. The costs/ton of goods and cost per 100 parcels were virtually identical for all the four main line companies. While the LMS and LNER also declared losses, the Southern Rly showed a small profit because of their varying C&D rates for different stations. The GW losses did not result from excessive operating costs, rather because the standard amounts credited to cartage were inadequate. It was always held that railway cartage charges kept well below cost were justified so as to deter outside hauliers and traders from performing their own cartage to and from goods stations. Were that to occur, it would lead to congestion and delay in goods depots, the answer to which would have to be for the railway to build new warehouses and accommodation at costs far exceeding the loss on the cartage account. The same deficit was found where the work was done by agents, since the amounts paid to them were greater than the notional sums used in the GW balance sheets.

Even before the above simplified charging scheme had come into play, the GW in its Country Lorry service (Chapter 10) had not used the complicated Victorian general classification of goods for

GREAT WESTERN RAILWAY.

GOODS DEPARTMENT.

CENSUS OF WAGES STAFF. MARCH, 1914.

GRADES (SUPERVISORY) NOT COVERED BY THE CONCILIATION BOARDS.

GRADE.	NUMBER OF MEN EMPLOYED AT EACH RATE OF WAGES.																																						Number of Men.	Average Weekly Rate of Wages.	Average Weekly Earnings.
	25/-	26/-	27/6	28/-	29/-	30/-	31/-	32/-	32/6	33/-	34/-	35/-	35/6	36/-	37/-	37/6	38/-	38/6	39/-	40/-	40/6	41/-	41/6	42/-	42/6	43/-	44/-	45/-	46/-	46/6	47/-	47/6	50/-	52/6	55/-	57/6	58/-	60/-			
Inspectors :—																																									
C.G.M.O. Travelling	–	–	–	–	–	–	–	–	–	–	–	–	–	–	–	–	–	–	–	–	–	–	–	–	–	–	–	2	–	–	–	–	–	–	–	–	–	–	2	45/-	45/-
Chief	–	–	–	–	–	–	–	–	–	–	–	–	–	–	–	–	–	–	–	–	–	–	–	–	–	–	–	–	–	–	–	–	2	–	–	–	1	1	4	54/6	54/6
District	–	–	–	–	–	–	–	–	–	–	–	–	–	–	–	–	–	–	–	1	–	–	–	–	–	–	–	–	–	–	–	1	5	1	1	–	–	1	10	50/6	50/6
District Assistant	–	–	–	–	–	–	–	–	–	–	–	–	–	–	–	–	1	–	–	–	–	–	–	–	–	–	–	–	–	–	–	–	–	–	–	–	–	–	1	38/-	38/-
Shed	–	–	–	–	–	–	–	–	–	–	–	–	–	–	–	–	1	–	1	–	1	–	1	1	–	–	–	–	–	–	–	1	2	–	1	–	–	–	9	44/10	44/10
Shed Assistant	–	–	–	–	–	–	–	–	–	–	–	–	–	–	–	–	–	–	–	–	–	–	–	–	2	–	–	–	–	–	–	–	–	–	–	–	–	–	2	42/6	42/6
Yard	–	–	–	–	–	–	–	–	–	–	–	–	–	–	–	–	–	1	–	2	–	1	1	–	–	1	1	2	1	–	–	–	2	–	–	–	–	–	12	43/8	43/8
Yard, Sub	–	–	–	–	–	–	–	–	–	–	–	–	–	–	–	1	–	–	–	–	–	–	–	–	–	–	–	–	–	–	–	–	–	–	–	–	–	–	1	37/6	37/6
General	–	–	–	–	–	–	–	–	–	–	1	1	–	1	–	1	–	–	1	1	–	–	3	–	3	1	1	6	–	–	1	1	6	1	2	–	–	1	32	45/3	45/3
Cartage	–	–	–	–	–	–	–	–	–	–	–	1	–	1	–	–	1	–	–	5	–	–	–	1	1	–	–	1	–	–	–	4	1	–	–	–	–	–	16	42/5	42/5
Market	–	–	–	–	–	–	–	–	–	–	–	–	–	1	–	–	–	–	–	1	–	–	–	–	1	–	–	1	–	–	–	–	2	–	–	–	–	–	6	43/7	43/7
Show	–	–	–	–	–	–	–	–	–	–	–	–	–	–	–	–	–	–	–	1	–	–	–	–	–	–	–	–	–	–	–	–	–	–	–	–	–	–	1	40/-	40/-
Platform	–	–	–	–	–	–	–	–	–	–	–	–	–	–	–	–	–	–	–	1	–	–	–	–	–	–	–	–	–	–	–	–	–	–	–	–	–	–	1	40/-	40/-
Cattle	–	–	–	–	–	–	–	–	–	–	–	–	–	–	2	–	–	–	–	–	–	–	–	–	–	–	–	–	–	–	–	–	2	–	–	1	–	–	5	46/4	46/4
Timber	–	–	–	–	–	–	–	–	–	–	–	–	–	–	1	1	–	–	–	2	–	–	1	–	–	–	–	2	–	1	–	–	–	–	–	–	–	–	8	41/7	41/7
Live Stock	–	–	–	–	–	–	–	–	–	–	–	1	–	–	–	–	–	–	–	–	–	–	–	–	–	1	–	–	–	–	–	–	–	–	–	–	–	–	2	39/-	39/-
Outwards	–	–	–	–	–	–	–	–	–	–	–	–	–	–	–	–	–	–	–	1	–	–	–	–	–	–	–	–	–	–	–	–	–	–	–	–	–	–	1	40/-	40/-
Inwards	–	–	–	–	–	–	–	–	–	–	–	–	–	–	–	–	–	–	–	–	–	–	–	–	–	–	–	1	–	–	–	–	–	–	–	–	–	–	1	45/-	45/-
Docks	–	–	–	–	–	–	–	–	–	–	–	1	–	–	–	–	–	–	–	–	–	–	1	–	–	1	–	4	–	–	–	–	–	1	–	–	–	–	8	44/-	44/-
Docks, Assistant	–	–	–	–	–	–	–	–	–	–	–	–	–	–	–	–	–	–	–	–	–	–	1	–	–	–	–	–	–	–	–	–	–	–	–	–	–	–	1	41/6	41/6
Shipping	–	–	–	–	–	–	–	–	–	–	–	–	–	–	1	–	–	–	–	–	–	–	–	–	–	1	–	–	–	–	–	–	–	–	–	–	–	–	2	39/3	39/3
Ships' Stores	–	–	–	–	–	–	–	–	–	–	–	–	–	–	–	–	–	–	–	–	–	–	–	–	1	–	–	–	–	–	–	–	–	–	–	–	–	–	1	42/6	42/6
Coal Shipping	–	–	–	–	–	–	–	–	–	–	–	–	–	–	–	–	–	–	–	–	–	–	1	–	–	–	–	–	–	–	–	–	–	–	–	–	–	–	1	41/6	41/6
Canal	–	–	–	1	–	2	–	–	2	–	–	–	–	–	1	–	–	–	1	–	–	–	–	–	–	–	–	–	–	–	–	–	–	–	–	–	–	–	7	32/9	32/9
Advertising	–	–	–	–	–	–	–	–	1	–	–	–	–	–	–	–	–	–	–	1	–	–	–	–	–	–	–	–	–	–	–	–	–	–	–	–	–	–	2	36/3	36/3
Canvassing	–	1	2	–	–	–	–	–	–	–	–	–	–	–	–	1	–	–	–	1	–	–	–	–	1	–	–	–	–	–	–	–	–	–	–	–	–	–	6	33/7	33/7
Flat	–	–	–	–	–	–	–	1	–	–	–	–	–	–	–	–	–	–	–	–	–	–	–	–	–	–	–	–	–	–	–	–	–	–	–	–	–	–	1	32/-	32/-
Grain	–	–	–	–	–	–	–	–	–	–	–	–	–	–	–	–	–	–	–	1	–	–	–	–	–	–	–	–	–	–	–	–	–	–	–	–	–	–	1	40/-	40/-
Tobacco	–	–	–	–	–	–	–	–	–	–	1	–	–	–	–	–	–	–	–	–	–	–	–	–	–	–	–	–	–	–	–	–	–	–	–	–	–	–	1	34/-	34/-
Horse	–	–	–	–	–	–	–	–	–	–	–	–	–	–	–	–	–	–	–	2	–	–	–	–	–	–	–	–	–	–	–	–	–	1	1	–	–	–	4	46/11	46/11
Queenstown Agent	1	–	–	–	–	–	–	–	–	–	–	–	–	–	–	–	–	–	–	–	–	–	–	–	–	–	–	–	–	–	–	–	–	–	–	–	–	–	1	25/-	25/-
Sub.	–	–	–	–	–	–	–	–	–	–	1	1	–	–	1	1	2	–	1	3	1	–	1	–	4	–	–	1	–	–	–	–	–	–	–	–	–	–	17	39/9	39/9
Police	–	–	–	–	–	–	–	–	–	–	–	–	–	–	–	–	–	–	–	–	–	–	–	–	–	–	–	1	–	–	–	–	–	1	–	–	–	–	2	48/9	48/9
Enquiry	–	–	–	–	–	–	–	–	–	–	–	–	–	–	–	1	–	–	–	1	–	–	–	–	–	–	–	–	–	–	–	–	–	1	–	–	–	–	3	43/4	43/4
Receiving Office	–	–	–	–	–	–	–	–	–	–	–	–	–	–	–	–	–	–	–	2	–	–	–	–	1	–	–	–	–	–	–	–	–	–	–	–	–	–	3	40/10	40/10
Berthing Masters (Inspectors)	–	–	–	–	–	–	–	–	–	1	–	–	–	–	–	–	–	–	–	–	–	–	–	–	–	–	–	–	–	–	–	–	–	–	–	–	–	–	1	33/-	33/-
Total No. of Inspectors	1	1	2	1	–	2	–	1	3	1	3	5	–	3	6	6	5	1	4	26	2	1	10	2	14	5	2	21	1	1	1	7	22	6	5	1	1	3	176	43/10	43/10
Uniform Goods Agents	–	–	–	–	–	–	–	–	–	–	–	–	–	1	–	–	–	–	–	–	–	–	–	–	–	–	–	1	–	–	–	–	–	–	–	–	–	–	2	40/6	40/6
Berthing Masters	1	–	–	1	1	3	–	–	–	–	–	–	–	–	–	–	–	–	–	–	–	–	–	–	–	–	–	–	–	–	–	–	–	–	–	–	–	–	6	28/8	28/8
Dock Gatemen (Foreman)	–	–	–	–	–	1	–	–	–	–	–	–	–	–	–	–	–	–	–	–	–	–	–	–	–	–	–	–	–	–	–	–	–	–	–	–	–	–	1	30/-	30/-
Foremen	–	1	–	6	6	15	21	44	1	43	21	32	1	18	19	–	61	–	–	–	–	–	–	–	1	–	–	1	–	–	–	–	–	–	–	–	–	–	291	34/2	35/5
SUPERVISORY GRADES \ TOTAL	2	2	2	8	7	21	21	45	4	44	24	37	1	22	25	6	66	1	4	26	2	1	10	2	15	5	2	23	1	1	1	7	22	6	5	1	1	3	476	37/9	38/5

2358a. 2

GREAT WESTERN RAILWAY.

Rates of Pay of Railway Staff.

General Manager's Office
Paddington Station, W.

July, 1921.

Traffic Staff (Continued).

Grade	Area	Class	Standard Rate per wk.	Temporary rate, subject to Sliding Scale operating from Jan. 1st, 1921.	Apl. 1st 1921.	July 1st 1921.	Oct. 1st 1921.	Jan. 1st 1922.	Apl. 1st 1922.
Stableman, Stableman in Charge ...	To be paid rates agreed upon stations in Goods Depart-			for men in same grade at the same or adjacent ment.					
Station Foreman ...	All	1	65/-	84/6	80/6	75/6			
		2	58/-	77/-	73/-	68/-			
Ticket Collector ...	London & Industrial	1	58/-	79/-	75/-	70/-			
	do.	2	54/-	74/6	70/6	65/6			
	Rural ...	1	58/-	76/-	72/-	67/-			
	do.	2	54/-	71/6	67/6	62/6			
Ticket Collector (Train) ...	London & Industrial	—	60/-	79/-	75/-	70/-			
	Rural ...	—	60/-	76/-	72/-	67/-			
Timekeeper	To be paid rates agreed upon stations in Goods Depart-			for men in same grade at the same or adjacent ment.					
Traffic Regulator ...	All	—	75/-	95/6	91/6	86/6			
Train Attendant ...	London & Industrial	—	50/-	74/-	70/-	65/-			
	Rural ...	—	50/-	71/6	67/6	62/6			
Yard Foreman ...	All	1	75/-	94/6	90/6	85/6			
		2	70/-	91/-	87/-	82/-			

ALLOWANCES TO MEN WORKING TWO OR MORE HORSES AT THE SAME TIME.

Men working two horses at the same time, to be paid an allowance at the rate of 2/- per week over their ordinary rate of pay, and a further allowance at the rate of 2/- per week to be made for each additional horse.

11

15

GOODS & CARTAGE STAFF.

Grade	Area	Class	Standard Rate per wk.	Temporary rate, subject to Sliding Scale operating from Jan. 1st, 1921.	Apl. 1st 1921.	July 1st 1921.	Oct. 1st 1921.	Jan. 1st 1922.	Apl. 1st 1922.
Caller Off ... ... (see List B)	London ...	—	52/-	76/-	72/-	67/-			
	Industrial	—	49/-	75/-	71/-	66/-			
	Rural ...	—	43/-	70/-	66/-	61/-			
Carter (see List E) ... Single Horse.	London ...	—	53/-	77/6	73/6	68/6			
	Industrial	—	50/-	75/-	71/-	66/-			
	Rural ...	—	46/-	70/6	66/6	61/6			
Leading or Head	London ...	—	57/-	79/6	75/6	70/6			
	Industrial	—	54/-	77/6	73/6	68/6			
	Rural ...	—	49/-	71/6	67/6	62/6			
Checker (see List C)	London ...	—	57/-	79/6	75/6	70/6			
	Industrial	—	54/-	77/6	73/6	68/6			
	Rural ...	—	47/-	72/6	68/6	63/6			
Horsekeeper-in-Charge	London ...	—	62/-	85/-	81/-	76/-			
	Industrial	—	59/-	82/-	78/-	73/-			
	Rural ...	—	52/-	75/6	71/6	66/6			
Motor Driver:— Electric	London ...	—	56/-	80/6	76/6	71/6			
	Industrial	—	53/-	79/6	75/6	70/6			
Petrol or Steam ...	London ...	—	60/-	82/-	78/-	73/-			
	Industrial	—	57/-	80/6	76/6	71/6			
Porter (see List A) ...	London ...	—	47/-	73/6	69/6	64/6			
	Industrial	—	44/-	72/6	68/6	63/6			
	Rural ...	—	40/-	67/-	63/-	58/-			
Stableman-in-Charge	London ...	—	62/-	85/-	81/-	76/-			
	Industrial	—	59/-	82/-	78/-	73/-			
	Rural ...	—	52/-	75/6	71/6	66/6			
Working Foreman ... (see List D)	London ...	—	62/-	85/-	81/-	76/-			
	Industrial	—	59/-	82/-	78/-	73/-			
	Rural ...	—	52/-	75/6	71/6	66/6			

ALLOWANCES TO MEN WORKING TWO OR MORE HORSES AT THE SAME TIME.

Men working two horses at the same time to be paid an allowance at the rate of 2/- per week over their ordinary rate of pay, and a further allowance at the rate of 2/- per week to be made for each additional horse.

Goods & Cartage Staff (Continued).

List A.

To be paid at rates applying to Goods Porters.
Gatemen (including Crossing Keepers).
Watchmen.

List B.

To be paid at rates applying to Callers Off.
Callers Off.
Cranemen (other than Steam Cranemen and men operating Electric and Hydraulic Cranes exceeding 5 tons capacity).
Number Takers.
Scalesmen.
Office-men, e.g., to embrace:—
Invoice Distributors.
Bill Distributors.
Book Room Porters.
Book Room Attendants.
Messengers at Stations.
Loaders.
Sheeters, Sheetmen, Ropers and Ropemen.
Capstanmen (Goods Yard).
Shunt Horse (a) Drivers.
(b) Brakesmen.
Rope Splicers.
Traverser Hookers.
Traverser Workers.
Round Timber Loaders.

List C.

To be paid at rates applying to Checkers.
Chief Number Takers.
Check Weighers.

Goods & Cartage Staff (Continued).

List C.—(Continued).

Chaff Cutters (tending machines).
Timber Measurers.
Coopers and Repairers.
Cranemen (in charge of Steam Cranes and Electric and Hydraulic Cranes exceeding 5 tons capacity).
Timekeepers.
Weighbridgemen at Goods Depots.

List D.

To be paid at rates applying to Working Foremen.
Working Foremen.
Searchers and Tracers (at Stations), to embrace Clearing Men and Discrepancy Men.
Senior Checkers.

List E.

To be paid at rates applying to Carters (Single Horse).
Stablemen, Ostlers } Not in Charge.
Horsekeepers, }
To embrace:—
Horsedressers.
Horse Removers.
Manger Washers
Collarmen.
Harness Cleaners.
Coachmen.
Chain Horse Drivers.
Provender Stores Loaders and Drivers.
Road Motor Attendants.
Van Setters.

GREAT WESTERN RAILWAY.

CENSUS OF STAFF EMPLOYED DURING THE WEEK ENDED MARCH 9th, 1929.

GOODS DEPARTMENT.

Great Western Railway.

AUTHORISED STAFF ESTABLISHMENT.

GOODS DEPARTMENT.

Conciliation Grades. STATEMENT "A"

GRADE.	Office or District.																	Total.
	C.G.M.O.	London.	Reading.	Bristol.	Exeter.	Plymouth.	Gloucester.	Cardiff.	Cardiff Valleys.	Swansea.	Worcester.	Birmingham.	Shrewsbury.	Central Wales.	Liverpool.	Manchester.	Ireland.	
allers Off	6	142	23	35	12	9	3	50	8	16	22	37	5	—	32	—	—	400
apstanmen	—	68	3	7	—	—	—	5	3	—	—	28	—	—	—	—	—	114
arters, Leading	—	1	1	1	1	—	—	—	—	—	—	1	—	—	2	—	—	7
arters	—	530	27	260	20	33	31	98	—	28	22	412	11	—	27	59	—	1,558
hain Horse Drivers	—	47	—	—	—	—	—	—	—	—	—	—	—	—	—	—	—	47
,, ,, Boys	—	—	—	—	2	—	—	—	—	—	1	—	—	—	—	—	—	3
heckers	4	266	45	183	30	26	29	121	29	76	26	181	15	—	78	—	14	1,123
heckers, Senior	—	36	—	5	—	—	—	4	4	—	—	—	—	—	5	—	1	55
ooper and Repairer	—	1	—	—	—	—	—	—	—	—	—	—	—	—	—	—	—	1
ranemen	—	1	2	—	—	—	—	—	—	—	—	2	—	—	2	—	—	7
oremen, Bookroom	—	1	—	—	—	—	—	—	—	—	—	—	—	—	—	—	—	1
,, Working	—	24	4	2	2	1	4	9	1	2	3	1	—	—	1	—	—	54
,, Yard	—	2	—	5	—	—	—	—	—	—	—	2	1	—	—	—	—	10
atemen	—	—	—	—	—	—	2	—	—	3	—	—	—	—	1	—	—	6
oaders	—	241	8	61	1	—	10	32	3	15	—	51	—	—	38	11	—	471
essengers, Lad	—	72	5	23	4	1	2	19	4	10	8	28	1	—	17	8	1	203
otor Drivers	—	94	2	31	10	6	4	20	—	8	9	74	2	—	30	11	—	301
umbertakers, Adult	—	12	2	3	—	—	—	7	1	7	—	8	—	—	1	—	—	41
,, Junior	—	3	—	3	2	3	—	4	4	6	1	12	—	—	3	—	—	41
licemen	1	27	3	6	—	2	—	5	—	2	—	11	—	—	3	2	1	63
rters, Adult	—	627	100	210	65	44	47	170	42	89	56	391	25	—	232	1	26	2,125
,, Junior	—	70	15	28	7	3	15	21	1	16	9	22	3	—	34	1	1	246
ad Motor Attendants, Adult	—	—	—	—	1	2	—	—	—	—	—	3	—	—	—	8	—	14
,, ,, ,, Junior	—	—	—	—	8	—	—	—	—	—	—	—	—	—	—	—	—	8
pe Splicers	—	2	—	—	—	—	—	—	—	—	—	—	—	—	—	—	—	2
eeters and Ropers	—	4	—	35	—	—	4	33	6	—	—	—	—	—	—	—	—	82
unters, Class 1	—	27	—	23	—	—	4	—	—	—	—	23	3	—	7	—	—	87
,, ,, 2	—	2	—	—	—	—	—	—	—	—	—	19	—	—	—	—	—	21
,, ,, 3	—	36	—	31	—	—	4	—	—	—	—	19	5	—	7	—	—	102
,, ,, 4	—	—	—	2	—	—	—	—	—	—	—	14	—	—	2	—	—	18
unt Horse Drivers	—	—	—	—	1	—	2	—	—	—	10	8	2	—	12	—	—	35
unting Engine Drivers	—	2	—	—	—	—	—	—	—	—	—	—	—	—	—	—	—	2
pper Boys	—	—	—	—	1	—	—	1	—	—	2	6	—	—	10	—	—	20
nekeepers	—	9	—	5	—	—	—	—	—	—	—	3	—	—	3	2	—	22
cers	4	10	—	7	—	1	—	1	—	—	—	3	—	—	—	—	—	26
nguards	—	600	—	32	—	—	—	18	—	3	—	100	1	—	—	34	—	788
nsetters	—	—	—	—	—	—	—	—	—	2	—	—	—	—	—	8	—	10
tchmen	—	—	—	—	—	—	—	—	—	—	—	5	—	—	—	—	—	5
ighbridgemen	—	21	—	11	1	—	—	3	—	5	—	—	1	—	3	—	—	45
TALS Adults	15	2,233	220	923	144	124	144	558	97	253	148	1,296	70	—	486	102	42	6,855
TALS Juniors	—	745	20	86	24	7	17	63	9	35	21	168	5	—	64	43	2	1,309
TALS Adults and Juniors	15	2,978	240	1,009	168	131	161	621	106	288	169	1,464	75	—	550	145	44	8,164

Shop and Miscellaneous Staff. STATEMENT "B"

GRADE.	C.G.M.O.	London.	Reading.	Bristol.	Exeter.	Plymouth.	Gloucester.	Cardiff.	Cardiff Valleys.	Swansea.	Worcester.	Birmingham.	Shrewsbury.	Central Wales.	Liverpool.	Manchester.	Ireland.	Total.
tmen	—	—	—	—	—	—	—	—	—	—	—	7	—	—	—	—	3	10
ck Gatemen	—	1	—	—	—	—	—	—	—	—	—	—	—	—	—	—	—	1
,, Leading	—	1	—	—	—	—	—	—	—	—	—	—	—	—	—	—	—	1
emen	—	5	—	—	—	—	—	—	—	—	—	—	—	—	—	—	—	5
,, Leading	—	1	—	—	—	—	—	—	—	—	—	—	—	—	—	—	—	1
ssengers, Adult	4	1	—	1	—	—	—	—	—	—	—	—	—	—	—	—	—	6
,, Junior	14	3	2	3	—	1	2	4	2	4	1	1	1	—	2	1	1	42
Totals	18	12	2	4	—	1	2	4	2	4	1	8	1	—	2	1	4	66

39.

GOODS DEPARTMENT.

SECTION 7B.

CONCILIATION STAFF.

(Under Agreements with the National Union of Railwaymen and Associated Society of Locomotive Engineers and Firemen).

GRADE.	ADULTS - Number at each Rate. 40/-	42/-	44/-	47/-	48/-	49/-	50/-	52/-	53/-	54/-	57/-	59/-	60/-	62/-	65/-	68/-	Total	Average wages.	Average Earnings.
Caller-off ...	-	-	-	-	-	4	253	139	-	-	-	-	-	-	-	-	396	50/8	58/4
Capstanman, London	-	-	-	-	-	-	-	64	-	-	-	-	-	-	-	-	64 }	52/- }	55/11 }
" Class 1 ('A' Rate	-	-	-	-	-	-	38	-	-	-	-	-	-	-	-	-	38 } 103	50/- } 50/- } 51/3	54/4 } 54/2 } 55/[illegible]
" " ('B' Rate	-	-	-	-	-	1	-	-	-	-	-	-	-	-	-	-	1 }	49/- }	48/- }
Carter ('A' Rate	-	-	-	-	-	-	978	-	461	-	-	-	-	-	-	-	1439 } 1473	51/- } 50/11	56/- } 55/10
" ('B' "	-	-	6	-	-	-	28	-	-	-	-	-	-	-	-	-	34 }	48/11 }	49/5 }
" Leading ...	-	-	-	-	-	-	-	-	-	5	1	-	-	-	-	-	6	54/6	58/6
Chain Horse Driver ('A' Rate	-	-	-	-	-	-	3	-	59	-	-	-	-	-	-	-	62 } 66	52/10 } 52/10	54/9 } 54/9
('B' "	-	-	-	-	-	-	-	-	4	-	-	-	-	-	-	-	4 }	53/- }	54/6 }
Checker ...	-	-	-	-	-	-	2	-	-	832	257	-	-	-	-	-	1091	54/8	59/4
" Senior ...	-	-	-	-	-	-	-	-	-	-	-	19	-	34	-	-	53	60/11	60/10
Craneman in charge of steam electric or hydraulic crane exceeding 5 tons capacity ...	-	-	-	-	-	-	-	-	-	-	1	-	-	-	-	-	1	57/-	72/-
Craneman (other than above) ...	-	-	-	-	-	-	5	-	-	-	-	-	-	-	-	-	5	50/-	72/10
Craneman (Petrol Electric Mobile)	-	-	-	-	-	-	-	-	-	-	5	-	7	-	-	-	12	58/9	57/6
Fireman ...	-	-	-	-	-	-	-	-	-	-	-	-	5	-	-	-	5	60/-	78/9
" Leading ...	-	-	-	-	-	-	-	-	-	-	-	-	-	-	1	-	1	65/-	77/-
Foreman, Working...	-	-	-	-	-	-	-	-	-	-	-	37	-	15	-	-	52	59/10	59/5
Gateman (at Depot Gates) ...	-	-	-	-	2	-	-	-	-	-	-	-	-	-	-	-	2	48/-	47/-
Loader ('A' Rate	-	-	-	-	-	-	265	240	-	-	-	-	-	-	-	-	505 } 540	50/11 } 51/-	59/7 } 59/3
('B' "	-	-	-	-	-	5	-	30	-	-	-	-	-	-	-	-	35 }	51/7 }	55/4 }
Motor Driver Leading	-	-	-	-	-	-	-	-	-	-	-	-	-	-	-	1	1	68/-	65/-
Motor Driver (a) Petrol or Steam	-	-	-	-	-	-	-	-	-	-	322	-	140	1	-	-	463	57/11	70/4
Number-taker ...	-	-	-	-	-	2	37	8	-	-	-	-	-	-	-	-	47	50/4	51/6
" " Chief	-	-	-	-	-	-	-	-	-	1	-	-	-	-	-	-	1	54/-	53/-
Officeman ('A' Rate	-	-	-	-	-	-	33	24	-	-	-	-	-	-	-	-	57 } 59	50/10 } 50/10	52/6 } 52/6
('B' "	-	-	-	-	-	1	-	1	-	-	-	-	-	-	-	-	2 }	50/6 }	52/- }
Porter ('A' Rate	-	-	-	-	1285	416	-	-	-	-	-	-	-	-	-	-	1701 } 1998	48/3 } 47/9	53/10 } 53/1
('B' "	1	2	177	117	-	-	-	-	-	-	-	-	-	-	-	-	297 }	45/2 }	49/2 }
Repairer ...	-	-	-	-	-	-	-	-	-	1	1	-	-	-	-	-	2	55/6	57/6
Road Motor Attendant	-	-	1	-	1	-	17	-	-	-	-	-	-	-	-	-	19	49/7	53/0
Roper... ...	-	-	-	-	-	-	-	2	-	-	-	-	-	-	-	-	2	52/-	50/6
Sheeter ...	-	-	-	-	-	-	75	6	-	-	-	-	-	-	-	-	81	50/2	51/1
Shunt Horse Driver Class 1 ('A' Rate	-	-	-	-	-	-	31	3	-	-	-	-	-	-	-	-	34 } 36	50/2 } 50/1	53/1 } 52/10
" " ('B' "	-	-	-	-	-	2	-	-	-	-	-	-	-	-	-	-	2 }	49/- }	49/- }
Timekeeper ...	-	-	-	-	-	-	-	-	-	9	11	-	-	-	-	-	20	55/8	57/6
Tracer ...	-	-	-	-	-	-	-	-	-	-	-	11	-	14	-	-	25	60/8	59/6
Van Setter ...	-	-	-	-	-	-	8	-	-	-	-	-	-	-	-	-	8	50/-	52/11
Watchman ...	-	-	-	-	4	-	-	-	-	-	-	-	-	-	-	-	4	48/-	52/9
Weighbridgeman ...	-	-	-	-	-	-	-	-	-	26	18	-	-	-	-	-	44	55/3	54/7
TOTAL (Adults)	1	2	184	117	1292	431	1773	517	524	874	616	67	152	64	1	1	6616	51/4	57/-

SECTION 7B.

CONCILIATION STAFF (Continued).

GRADE.	JUNIORS. Number at each Rate. 16/-	20/-	25/-	30/-	35/-	Total.	Average Wages.	Average Earnings.
Chain Horse Driver ...	-	1	1	-	2	4	28/9	28/-
Number-taker	1	2	13	15	20	51	30/-	31/9
Officeman	56	40	32	38	51	217	25/-	24/8
Porter	29	45	46	44	64	228	26/8	26/5
Slipper Lad	4	1	2	-	5	12	25/9	25/11
Vanguard	202	153	138	131	184	808	24/11	28/4
Shunt Horse Driver ...	1	1	1	-	-	3	20/4	19/8
TOTAL (Juniors) ...	293	243	233	228	326	1,323	25/5	27/6

SECTION 7A & 7D[1].

TRAFFIC AND LOCOMOTIVE DEPARTMENTS CONCILIATION GRADES UNDER THE CONTROL OF THE GOODS DEPARTMENT.

GRADE.	Number at each Rate. 16/-	20/-	25/-	30/-	35/-	50/-	53/-	54/-	55/-	60/-	62/-	65/-	72/-	75/-	Total.	Average Wages.	Average Earnings
Bookroom Foreman ...	-	-	-	-	-	-	-	-	-	-	1	-	-	-	1	62/-	60/-
Bus Driver - Motor - Public Omnibus	-	-	-	-	-	-	-	-	-	-	1	-	-	-	1	62/-	73/-
Foreman, Yard, Class 1	-	-	-	-	-	-	-	-	-	-	-	-	-	9	9	75/-	76/-
Parcel Porter ...	-	-	-	-	-	2	-	-	-	-	-	-	-	-	2	50/-	49/-
Parcel Vanman, Horse (London) Adults	-	-	-	-	-	-	12	-	-	-	-	-	-	-	12	53/-	52/1
" " " Juniors	3	1	3	2	6	-	-	-	-	-	-	-	-	-	15	27/6	28/8
" " Motor (Petrol)	-	-	-	-	-	-	-	-	-	5	-	-	-	-	5	60/-	63/2
Shunter, Goods, Class 1 ...	-	-	-	-	-	-	-	-	-	-	-	90	-	-	90 }		
" " " 2 ...	-	-	-	-	-	-	-	-	-	22	-	-	-	-	22 } 238	58/11	63/5
" " " 3 ...	-	-	-	-	-	-	-	-	110	-	-	-	-	-	110 }		
" " " 4 ...	-	-	-	-	-	16	-	-	-	-	-	-	-	-	16 }		
Driver (Petrol Shunting Engine) 7D[1]	-	-	-	-	-	-	-	-	-	-	-	-	2	-	2	72/-	70/6
TOTAL - Adults ...	-	-	-	-	-	18	12	-	110	27	2	90	2	9	270	59/3	63/4
Juniors ...	3	1	3	2	6	-	-	-	-	-	-	-	-	-	15	27/6	28/8

SUMMARY - CONCILIATION STAFF.

Section	Number at each Rate. 16/-	20/-	25/-	30/-	35/-	40/-	42/-	44/-	47/-	48/-	49/-	50/-	52/-	53/-	54/-	55/-	57/-	59/-	60/-	62/-	65/-	68/-	72/-	75/-	Total	Average Wages.	Ave. Earn
7B Adults	-	-	-	-	-	1	2	184	117	1292	431	1773	517	524	874	-	616	67	152	64	1	1	-	-	6616	51/4	[illegible]
7B Juniors	293	243	233	228	326	-	-	-	-	-	-	-	-	-	-	-	-	-	-	-	-	-	-	-	1323	25/5	[illegible]
7A Adults	-	-	-	-	-	-	-	-	-	-	-	18	-	12	-	110	-	-	27	2	90	-	-	9	268	59/2	[illegible]
7A Juniors	3	1	3	2	6	-	-	-	-	-	-	-	-	-	-	-	-	-	-	-	-	-	-	-	15	27/6	[illegible]
7D.1. Adults	-	-	-	-	-	-	-	-	-	-	-	-	-	-	-	-	-	-	-	-	-	-	2	-	2	72/-	[illegible]
TOTAL: - Adults	-	-	-	-	-	1	2	184	117	1292	431	1791	517	536	874	110	616	67	179	66	91	1	2	9	6886	51/8	[illegible]
Juniors	296	244	236	230	332	-	-	-	-	-	-	-	-	-	-	-	-	-	-	-	-	-	-	-	1338	25/5	[illegible]

GOODS DEPARTMENT.

SECTION 8.

DOCK AND QUAY STAFF.

(Other than Supervisors and Staff Afloat).

GRADE.	Number at each Rate. 50/-	54/-	57/-	59/-	60/-	62/-	63/-	64/-	66/-	72/-	80/-	83/-	85/-	90/-	Total	Average Wages.	Average Earnings
(A) Under Agreement applicable Dockers following Lord Shaw Award, dated May 5th, 1920:-																	
Boatman... ...	-	-	-	-	-	-	-	-	5	-	-	-	-	-	5	66/-	81/2
Capstanman ...	-	-	-	-	-	-	-	-	-	-	-	29	-	-	29	83/-	97/9
Checker ...	-	-	-	-	-	-	-	-	2	-	-	-	-	-	2	66/-	79/6
Ganger	-	-	-	-	-	-	-	-	1	-	-	-	-	-	1	66/-	84/-
Ganger - Jetty ...	-	-	-	-	-	-	-	-	-	-	-	-	17	-	17	85/-	98/4
Labourers (including Dock and Casual Stevedores)	-	-	-	-	-	26	-	-	-	5	20	-	60	18	129	79/7	93/2
Silo Worker ...	-	-	-	-	-	-	-	-	-	-	-	-	8	-	8	85/-	99/3
(B) Under Agreement dated August 4th, 1920:-																	
Checker ...	-	-	-	51	-	-	-	-	-	-	-	-	-	-	51	59/-	60/1
" Senior ...	-	-	-	-	-	-	1	-	-	-	-	-	-	-	1	63/-	62/-
Crane Driver ...	-	-	-	-	2	-	-	-	-	-	-	-	-	-	2	60/-	94/-
Dockgateman ...	-	-	-	1	-	-	-	-	-	-	-	-	-	-	1	59/-	82/-
" Leading	-	-	-	-	-	-	-	1	-	-	-	-	-	-	1	64/-	88/-
Loader... ...	-	-	1	-	-	-	-	-	-	-	-	-	-	-	1	57/-	59/-
Porter ... ...'A' Rate	-	97	-	-	-	-	-	-	-	-	-	-	-	-	97 } 98	54/- } 54/-	56/9 } 56/[illegible]
'B' "	1	-	-	-	-	-	-	-	-	-	-	-	-	-	1 }	50/- }	52/- }
TOTAL - Adults	1	97	1	52	2	26	1	1	8	5	20	29	85	18	346	69/4	78/3

OTHER GOODS DEPARTMENT STAFF.

Section of Census.	GRADE.	Number at each Rate.																																			Total	Average Wages.	Average Earnings
		2/-	8/-	13/-	16/-	20/-	25/-	27/-	30/-	33/-	35/-	40/-	42/-	43/-	44/-	45/-	46/-	48/-	50/-	50/6	51/-	53/-	54/-	56/-	59/-	60/-	61/-	63/-	64/-	65/-	67/-	68/-	69/-	72/-	74/-	82/-			
	MALE STAFF.																																						
10B	Policeman	-	-	-	-	-	-	-	-	-	-	-	-	-	-	-	-	-	-	-	-	-	-	-	-	-	-	1	-	-	-	-	-	-	-	-	1	63/-	62/-
13B7	Blacksmith ...	-	-	-	-	-	-	-	-	-	-	-	-	-	-	-	-	-	-	1	-	-	-	-	-	-	-	-	-	-	-	-	-	-	-	-	1	51/-	51/-
15B1	Boatman ...	-	-	-	-	-	-	-	-	-	-	-	-	-	-	-	-	-	-	-	-	6	-	-	-	-	-	-	-	-	-	-	-	-	-	-	6	53/-	68/8
16B	Caretaker ...	1	-	-	-	-	-	-	-	-	-	-	-	-	-	-	-	-	-	-	-	-	-	-	-	-	-	-	-	-	-	-	-	-	-	-	1	2/-	2/-
"	Cattleman ...	-	-	-	-	-	-	-	-	-	-	-	-	-	-	-	-	-	-	-	-	-	-	-	-	-	-	-	-	-	-	-	4	-	-	-	4	69/-	71/9
"	Cattle Truck Cleaner	-	-	-	-	-	-	-	-	-	-	-	-	-	-	-	-	-	-	-	-	-	-	-	-	-	-	-	1	-	-	-	-	-	-	1	2	73/-	71/6
16A	Furnace Attendant...	-	-	-	-	-	-	-	-	1	-	-	-	-	-	-	-	-	-	-	-	-	-	-	-	-	-	-	-	-	-	-	-	-	-	-	1	33/-	39/-
16B	Jetty Attendant ...	-	-	-	-	-	-	-	-	-	-	-	-	-	-	-	-	-	-	-	-	-	-	-	-	1	-	-	-	-	-	-	-	-	-	-	1	60/-	60/-
16A	Lavatory Attendant	-	1	-	-	-	-	-	-	-	-	-	-	-	-	-	-	-	-	-	-	-	-	-	-	-	-	-	-	-	-	-	-	-	-	-	1	8/-	7/-
16A	Messenger (Head or District Office) (Adult)	-	-	-	-	-	-	-	-	-	-	2	-	-	1	-	-	-	1	-	1	2	1	2	-	-	-	-	-	1	-	-	-	-	-	-	11	51/1	51/7
"	" " " (Junior)	-	-	-	9	5	7	-	4	-	18	-	-	-	-	-	-	-	-	-	-	-	-	-	-	-	-	-	-	-	-	-	-	-	-	-	43	27/2	26/7
16B	Mess Room Attendant	-	-	-	-	-	-	-	-	-	-	-	-	-	-	-	-	-	-	-	-	-	-	1	-	-	-	-	-	-	-	-	-	-	-	-	1	56/-	56/-
16A	Round Timber Loader (District Office)	-	-	1	-	-	-	1	-	-	-	-	-	2	-	2	2	2	-	-	-	-	-	-	1	-	1	-	-	1	1	1	-	1	10	-	26	59/1	57/4
16B	Round Timber Loader (Station or Depot)	-	-	-	-	-	-	-	-	-	-	-	-	-	-	-	-	-	-	-	-	2	-	1	-	-	-	-	-	-	-	-	-	-	-	-	3	54/-	52/4
"	Tonnage Porter ...	-	-	-	-	-	-	-	-	-	-	-	-	-	-	-	-	-	-	-	-	-	-	1	-	-	-	-	-	-	-	-	-	-	-	-	1	56/-	56/-
"	Weighbridge Porter	-	-	-	-	-	-	-	-	-	-	-	1	-	-	-	-	-	-	-	-	-	-	-	-	-	-	-	-	-	-	-	-	-	-	-	1	42/-	41/2
	TOTAL (Adults)	1	1	1	-	-	-	1	-	1	-	2	1	2	1	2	2	2	1	1	1	10	1	5	1	1	1	1	1	2	1	1	4	1	10	1	61	55/3	56/3
	" (Juniors)	-	-	-	9	5	7	-	4	-	18	-	-	-	-	-	-	-	-	-	-	-	-	-	-	-	-	-	-	-	-	-	-	-	-	-	43	27/2	26/7

Section of Census.	GRADE.	Number at each Rate.																											Total	Average Wages.	Average Earnings.
		2/-	3/-	4/-	5/-	6/-	7/-	8/-	9/-	10/-	11/-	12/-	13/-	14/-	15/-	16/-	18/-	19/-	20/-	21/-	23/-	25/-	26/-	27/-	28/-	40/-	41/-	46/-			
20	Charwoman ...	2	5	7	2	3	6	16	9	10	4	12	1	1	3	37	9	6	3	2	4	2	1	1	3	1	1	-	151	13/4	12/11
"	Gatekeeper ...	-	-	-	1	-	-	1	-	1	-	-	-	-	-	-	-	-	-	-	-	-	-	-	-	-	-	-	3	7/8	7/4
"	Office keeper ...	-	-	-	-	-	-	-	-	-	-	-	-	-	-	-	-	-	-	-	-	-	-	-	-	-	-	1	1	46/-	45/-

GOODS DEPARTMENT.

Section of Census.	GRADE.	1921	1922	1923	1924	1925	1926	1927	1928	1929
	SALARIED STAFF, WEEKLY PAID CLERKS AND SUPERVISORS.									
1	Officers and other Staff in receipt of £500 per annum and upwards	51	45	52	53	54	57	60	60	59
2A	Male Clerical Staff - Adults	2,632	2,580	2,697	2,698	2,756	2,818	2,806	2,813	2,836
	" " " Juniors	194	247	352	419	315	208	160	202	177
2B	Unappointed Clerks - Adults	163	149	165	147	137	106	92	108	85
	" " Juniors	4	6	5	1	2	1	-	-	-
2C	Clerical Staff Redundant ...	7	1	-	1	-	-	2	50	4
3	Goods Agents, etc. ...	114	117	133	137	137	134	131	133	133
4A	Railway Supervisory Staff ...	565	530	545	546	550	550	535	535	552
4B	Dock " " ...	-	4	7	6	2	1	1	1	1
13A	Workshop " " ...	22	15	11	10	10	10	-	-	-
15A	Canal " " ...	5	4	-	-	-	-	-	-	-
17	Women Clerks - Adults ...	681	498	528	587	575	573	611	633	644
	" " Juniors ...	24	4	21	29	21	24	75	83	38
	TOTAL - Adults ...	4,245	3,943	4,138	4,185	4,221	4.249	4,238	4,333	4,314
	Juniors ...	222	257	378	449	338	233	235	285	215
	CONCILIATION STAFF.									
7B	Caller-off	299	308	327	372	373	391	393	403	396
	Capstanman, London ...	32	33	33	32	63	65	66	67	64
	" - Class 1 'A' rate	43	41	45	44	44	44	46) 47	43) 44	38) 39
	" " 'B' "	-	-	-	-	-	-	1)	1)	1)
	Carter ... 'A' rate	1,397	1,299	1,454	1,591	1,567	1,590	1593) 1598	1525) 1534	1439) 1473
	" 'B' "	-	-	-	-	-	-	5)	9)	34)
	" Leading	10	6	7	9	9	7	7	6	6
	Chain Horse Driver - 'A' rate	21	38	34	46	46	58	61) 62	65) 67	62) 66
	" " " 'B' "	-	-	-	-	-	-	1)	2)	4)
	" " " Juniors	-	2	4	4	4	3	5	4	4
	Checker	1,097	1,054	1,126	1,162	1,130	1,149	1,122	1,100	1,091
	" Senior	1	1	7	13	47	53	51	52	53
	Craneman (Petrol Electric Mobile)	-	-	-	-	-	-	9	9	12
	Cranemen, in charge of steam cranes, or of electric and hydraulic cranes, exceeding 5 tons capacity ...	1	3	2	2	2	6	1	1	1
	Craneman (other than steam craneman and men operating electric and hydraulic cranes exceeding 5 tons capacity)	3	-	3	3	3	5	4	4	5
	Fireman	4	3	2	2	2	2	5	5	5
	" Leading	-	-	1	1	1	1	1	1	1
	Foreman, Working, i.e. men who for more than 50 per cent. of their time are occupied on non-supervisory duties	24	23	49	52	51	52	47	54	52
	Gateman (at Depot Gates) ...	5	5	2	2	2	2	2	2	2
	Loader 'A' rate	257	245	266	287	445	472	491) 495	470) 505	505) 540
	" 'B' "	-	-	-	-	-	-	14)	35)	35)
	Motor Driver, Leading ...	-	-	-	-	-	-	-	-	1
	" " (a) Petrol or Steam. ...	128	156	184	250	290	331	367	390	463
	" " (b) Electric ...	4	2	3	8	9	3	-	-	-
	Number-taker - Adults ...	51	61	57	61	51	43	38	41	47
	" " Juniors ...	75	65	62	55	46	49	54	50	51
	" " Chief ...	2	2	2	2	1	1	1	1	1
	Officeman - 'A' rate ...	107	79	76	68	67	66	68) 69	60) 61	57) 59
	" 'B' " ...	-	-	-	-	-	-	1)	1)	2)
	" Juniors ...	204	138	200	204	202	201	204	210	217
	Porter - 'A' rate ...	2,207	1,968	2,139	2,420	2,227	2,173	2004) 2140	1880) 2112	1701) 1998
	" 'B' "	-	-	-	-	-	-	136)	232)	297)
	" Juniors	282	340	218	212	207	220	219	221	228
	Provenderman	10	-*	-	-	-	-	-	-	-
	Repairer	1	1	1	1	1	1	1	2	2
	Road Motor Attendant - Adults	50	16	15	13	15	14	16	19	19
	" " " Juniors	-	11	-	-	-	-	-	-	-
	Roper	2	8	7	2	2	2	2	2	2
	Round Timber Loader ...	-	-	-	-	2	-	-	-	-
	Sheeter	48	69	74	78	91	98	80	84	81
	Shunt Horse Driver, London ...	1	1	1	1	1	-	-	-	-
	" " " Class 1 'A' rate	46	41	39	38	38	38	35	32	34) 36
	" " " " 'B' "	-	-	-	-	-	-	-	-	2)
	" " " Class 2									
	Adults	1	-	-	1	1	-	1	-	-
	" " " " Juniors	4	4	-	-	-	-	-	3	3
	Slipper Boy	16	15	23	21	23	16	16	13	12
	Stableman (not in charge) - Adults	382	-*	1	1	-	-	-	-	-
	" " Juniors	18	-*	-	-	-	-	-	-	-
	Stableman-in-charge ...	9	-*	1	-	-	-	-	-	-
	Timber Measurer	-	-	-	-	1	-	-	-	-
	Timekeeper	36	28	24	25	22	22	22	20	20

*Transferred to Road Transport Department on its inception, February, 1922.

44.

GOODS DEPARTMENT.

Section of Census.	GRADE.	1921	1922	1923	1924	1925	1926	1927	1928	1929	1930
7B (Continued)	Conciliation Staff - (Continued).										
	Tracer	22	23	28	28	28	26	26	25	25	
	Vanguard	657	516	600	737	796	794	795	792	808	
	Van Setter ...	10	10	10	-	10	11	9	9	8	
	Watchman	20	16	18	13	10	6	4	4	4	
	Weighbridgeman - Adults	52	50	52	54	57	51	49	46	44	
	" Juniors	1	-	-	-	-	-	-	-	-	
	TOTAL - Adults ...	6,383	5,590	6,090	6,682	6,709	6,783	6,770	6,702	6,616	
	" Juniors	1,257	1,091	1,107	1,233	1,278	1,283	1,293	1,293	1,323	
7A	Bookroom Foreman ..	-	-	-	-	-	1	1	1	1	
	Bus Driver, Motor Public Omnibuses	-	-	-	-	-	-	-	-	1	
	Parcel Vanman, Horse, London - Adults	16	16	15	15	15	16	15	14	12	
	Juniors ...	15	16	15	16	11	15	17	17	15	
	Parcel Vanman, Motor (Petrol)	-	-	1	1	1	1	2	3	5	
	Parcel Porter ...	-	-	-	-	-	2	2	2	2	
	Shunter, Goods, Class 1	86	79	83	84	87	89	90	89	90	
	" " " 2	25	22	19	22	19	22	22	22	22	
	" " " 3	101	97	91	107	105	106	104	107	110	
	" " " 4	25	25	23	21	19	19	19	19	16	
	Yard Foreman, Class 1	13	9	11	9	9	11	11	10	9	
7D.1	Driver (Petrol Shunting)	-	-	-	-	-	-	2	2	2	
	TOTAL - Adults ...	266	248	243	259	255	267	268	269	270	
	" Juniors	15	16	15	16	11	15	17	17	15	
	DOCK AND QUAY STAFF.										
8A	Under Agreement following Lord Shaw's Award, dated 5.5.20 -										
	Boatman	-	-	-	-	-	6	5	4	5	
	Capstanman ...	-	-	28	32	29	30	29	25	29	
	Checker	-	11	7	12	2	2	2	2	2	
	Crane Driver ...	-	-	-	-	-	1	-	-	-	
	Ganger	-	-	-	-	-	-	-	1	1	
	" Jetty ...	-	-	20	19	19	18	18	19	17	
	Labourers (including dockers and casual stevedores) - Adults...	40	115	183	236	174	150	207	99	129	
	" " " Juniors	-	1	1	2	-	-	-	-	-	
	Silo worker ...	-	-	6	10	8	8	8	6	8	
8B.	Under Agreement dated 4.8.20.										
	Berthingman	9	9	9	-	-	-	-	-	-	
	Checker ...	34	37	38	45	38	49	55	49	51	
	Checker (Senior) ...	-	-	-	-	-	-	1	1	1	
	Crane Driver ...	-	-	-	-	-	-	-	3	2	
	Dockgatemen	4	4	4	5	5	1	1	1	1	
	" Leading	2	2	2	2	2	1	1	1	1	
	Foreman (working)...	-	-	-	-	-	1	-	-	-	
	Loader	-	-	-	-	-	-	-	1	1	
	Porter A Rate	47	50	52	68	66	84	102	97	97) 98	
	" B "	-	-	-	-	-	-	-	-	1)	
	Ropeman	-	1	1	1	-	-	-	-	-	
	Weighbridgeman ...	-	1	1	1	-	-	-	-	-	
8C	Staff engaged in bunkering and shipping coal other than under Lord Shaw's Award -										
	Tipper	20	20	3	6	6	-	-	-	-	
	TOTAL - Adults ...	156	250	354	437	349	351	429	309	346	
	" Juniors	-	1	1	2	-	-	-	-	-	
	SHOP & ARTISAN STAFF (MALE).										
13B(6)	Boiler Attendant ...	-	-	-	-	1	1	-	-	-	
	Chargeman	1	-	-	-	1	1	-	-	-	
	Dresser	21	18	12	11	18	15	-	-	-	
	Engineman	2	2	2	2	2	2	-	-	-	
	Examiner and Labourer	16	16	-	-	-	-	-	-	-	
	" " Leading	1	-	-	-	-	-	-	-	-	
	Examiner	10	18	-	-	-	-	-	-	-	
	Labourer	35	35	-	-	-	-	-	-	-	
	" Leading ...	2	-	-	-	-	-	-	-	-	
	" Grade 1 ...	-	-	11) 47	10) 48	10) 62	11) 50	-	-	-	
	" " 2 ...	-	-	36)	38)	52)	39)				
	Marker - Adults ...	7	9	1	1	4	5	-	-	-	
	" Juniors ...	9	3	4	4	-	1	-	-	-	
	Messroom Attendant ...	1	1	2	2	2	2	-	-	-	
	Mixer	2	2	2	1	2	2	-	-	-	

45.

GOODS DEPARTMENT.

Section of Census.	GRADE.	1921	1922	1923	1924	1925	1926	1927	1928	1929
13B (6) (Continued)	SHOP & ARTISAN STAFF (MALE) - (Continued).									
	Repairer - Adults	203	241	188	184	206	191	-	-	-
	" Juniors	89	12	16	9	12	3	-	-	-
	Ropeman	4	-	3	2	2	2	-	-	-
	Saddler	26	-*	-	-	-	-	-	-	-
	Shoeing-smith	47	-*	-	-	-	-	-	-	-
	Shunt Horse Driver	-	-	-	-	1	1	-	-	-
	Type Cutter	1	-	-	-	-	-	-	-	-
	Watchman	6	6	2	3	1	1	-	-	-
13B (7)	Blacksmith	-	-	1	1	1	1	1	1	1
	TOTAL (Male) - Adults	385	348	260	255	304	274	§ 1	1	1
	" " Juniors	98	15	20	13	12	4	-	-	-
	SHOP AND ARTISAN STAFF (FEMALE).									
19	Forewoman	-	-	1	1	1	1	-	-	-
	Machinist - Adults	17	18	9	12	13	8	-	-	-
	" Juniors	2	1	2	-	-	2	-	-	-
	MISCELLANEOUS GRADES.									
10B	Policeman	-	-	-	-	-	-	-	1	1
	Male Staff -									
16A‖	Furnace Attendant	1	1	1	1	1	1	1	1	1
	Lavatory "	-	1	-	1	1	1	1	-	1
	Messenger - Adults	23	15	11	11	11	13	15	15	11
	" Juniors	30	35	28	34	36	36	39	37	43
	Round Timber Loader	20	17	22	40	35	34	31	25	26
15B (1)	Boatman	4	-	7	7	7	8	8	3	6
16B†	Caretaker	-	-	-	1	1	1	1	1	1
	Cattle Man	4	4	4	5	4	2	4	3	4
	" Truck Cleaner	2	3	3	3	3	2	2	2	2
	Chain Horse Lad	2	-	-	-	-	-	-	-	-
	Foreman, Working (Canal)	1	-	-	-	-	-	-	-	-
	Jetty Attendant	-	-	1	1	1	1	1	1	1
	Labourer	10	-	2	-	-	-	-	-	-
	Mess Room Attendant	-	-	1	1	1	1	1	1	1
	Porter (Canal)	1	-	-	-	-	-	-	-	-
	Round Timber Loader	31	22	23	25	5	6	7	4	3
	Tonnage Porter	6	12	23	28	19	14	3	1	1
	Weighbridge Porter	-	-	-	-	-	-	-	1	1
	TOTAL (Male) - Adults	103	75	98	124	89	84	75	59	60
	" " Juniors	32	35	28	34	36	36	39	37	43
	Female Staff -									
20	Charwoman	122	136	141	137	144	143	144	149	151
	Checker	-	-	1	-	-	-	-	-	-
	Office Keeper	1	1	1	1	1	1	1	1	1
	Gatekeeper	-	-	3	3	3	3	3	3	3
	Porter, Junior	1	-	-	-	-	-	-	-	-
	TOTAL (Female) - Adults	123	137	146	151	148	147	148	153	155
	" " Juniors	1	-	-	-	-	-	-	-	-

‖Head and District Offices.

† Stations and Depots.

* Transferred to Road Transport Department on its inception February, 1922.

§ Sheet Department transferred to Stores Department as from 1st July, 1926.

rail-borne traffic that was based on the value of the cargo, but instead used a flat rate for all traffic, charges being based on weight (between 7lbs and 1 ton) and actual road mileage. This made the scheme affordable for farmers. Country Lorry charges were:

	4-ton loads, per ton	2-ton loads, per ton
Up to 2 miles	2s 6d	3s
Over 2 and up to 3 miles	2s 6d	4s
3 to 5	3s 6d	5s 6d
5 to 7	5s	7s
7 to 9	6s 6d	8s 6d
9 to 12	8s	10s 6d

The only exceptions to the simplified charging scheme applied to items such as coal or bricks, where extra handling was required or where, as in the case of agricultural machines, the goods were very bulky and perhaps required craneage. Similarly, when Railheads were introduced (which, like Country Lorries, again depended entirely on motor vehicles), simplified methods of charging were introduced whereby it was made available at a flat rate per ton, irrespective of distance.

The *Road and Rail Traffic Act* of 1933 officially recognised 'agreed charges' between railway and regular customer whereby all kinds of goods could be charged at a flat rate per ton, or per package, irrespective of distance, the charge being the average of the whole of the firm's forwardings during 2 representative months. This was very important for the railways in fighting road competition. By the end of 1937 the scheme had been taken up by 433 firms dealing with the GW, and over 1,000 negotiations were then currently underway before being finalised and submitted to the Railway Rates Tribunal for authorisation. Traffic needing widespread national distribution lent itself to the simplified charging of this scheme.

The substitution of motors for horses at the large goods depots speeded up collection and delivery work, particularly to and from premises at the outer edges of cartage areas, and was welcomed by traders. Costs of carting under all-motor schemes were less than those of a mixed fleet of horses and motors. For example, at South Lambeth the cost per ton of carting goods was 6s 6d just before horses were dispensed with in 1930; by 1931, the cost/ton had dropped to 5s 10d per ton.

According to the GWR *Guide to Economical Transport,* collection of milk up to 5 miles could be undertaken for 1s 2d per gallon, including the cartage of empty churns. The *Guide* was issued in 1936 to replace an earlier pamphlet entitled *How to Send and How to Save* which became out of date owing to the introduction of more up-to-date facilities in the late 1920s/early 1930s.

In the between-wars campaign to put competition between private road hauliers and railways on the same footing, the GW often made the case that even when restricted in what it could do, it still offered remarkably cheap transport for goods; for example, that Cornish broccoli, each weighing 2lb on average, was brought by express goods train to London in excellent condition next morning for less than ½d each. And that the rail-element cost of country-lorry type goods haulage at 1½d per ton per mile was already cheap, yet it was "stolen" by road hauliers.

References

Bill Aldridge and Alan Earnshaw 2000 *Great Western Road Vehicles*. Trans-Pennine Publishing.
Tony Atkins and David Hyde 2000 *GWR Goods Services*. (Part 1 An Introduction.) Wild Swan.
Tony Atkins 2007 *GWR Goods Services.* (Part 2A Goods Depots and their Operation.) Wild Swan.
Tony Atkins 2009 *GWR Goods Services.* (Part 2B Goods Depots and their Operation.) Wild Swan.
Tony Atkins 2014 *GWR Docks & Marine*. Noodle Books.
Tony Atkins 2016 *GWR Goods Train Working.* (Volume 1 From Development to Guard Duties.) Crecy.
Tony Atkins 2017 *GWR Goods Train Working* (Volume 2 From Control Offices to Exceptional Loads.) Crecy.
A G Atkins, W Beard and R Tourret (1975/6/86/98/2013) *GWR Goods Wagons*. OPC-Ian Allan (most recent publisher).
V Bayley 1903-4 *Steam Freight-Carrying Vehicles.* Pamplet No 51 GWR Swindon Junior Engineering Society.
George Bulkeley 1921 *Mechanical Appliances for handling Railway Traffic*. London: The Railway Gazette.
Rex Christiansen and R W Miller 1967 *The Cambrian Railways* Volume II. David & Charles.
John Cummings 1980 *Railway Motor Buses and Bus Services in the British Isles 1902-33* Volume 2. Oxford Publishing Co.
F C A Coventry 1910-11 *The GWR Road Motor Car Department.* Pamphlet No 104 GWR Swindon Engineering Society.
A E C Dent 1931-2 *Maintenance Methods of the GWR Road Transport Department*. Pamphlet No 183 GWR Swindon Engineering Society.
A E C Dent 1934-5 *Further Notes on Road Transport Maintenance*. Pamphlet No 202 GWR Swindon Engineering Society.
Alan Earnshaw 2008 *Great Western Road Vehicles – Part II.* Trans-Pennine Publishing.
G Grant 1930 *Reminiscences of a Retired Great Western Railway Superintendent*. Railway Magazine.
Kelley, Philip J 1973 *Road Vehicles of the Great Western Railway*. Oxford Publishing Co.
Kelley, Philip J 2002 *Great Western Road Vehicles*. Oxford Publishing Co.
Rod Priddle and David Hyde 1996 *GWR to Devizes.* Millstream Books.
J K L Russell 1995 *Great Western Horse Power.* Oxford Publishing Co.
J Simmons and G Biddle (Editors) 1997 *The Oxford Companion to British Railway History.* Oxford University Press.
J N Slinn *Great Western Way.* 1978 Historical Model Railway Society.
S W Stevens-Stratten and W J Aldridge 1987 *Railway-Owned Commercial Vehicles.* Ian Allan.

Appendix 1 : Fleet Numbers

John Cummings's Ledger (with some emedations) Courtesy of Philip Kelley
THESE FLEET NUMBERS ARE THOSE FROM BEFORE THE RENUMBERING SCHEME OF 1935
In 'Issued by' column "G'terLondon" means Greater London and London CC means London County Council
For further details of GWR buses, see book by John Cummings

FLEET NUMBER	REGISTRATION	ISSUED BY	MAKER	BODY TYPE	DATE INTRODUCED	PAGE NUMBER IN KELLEY	NOTES
1	AF 37	Cornwall	Milnes-Daimler 16 HP	BUS	17/08/03		From Newnes, Ilfracombe
2	AF 36	"	"	"	17/08/03		From Newnes, Ilfracombe
3	AF 38	"	"	"	31/10/03		
4	AF 61	"	Milnes-Daimler 20 HP				
Fleet 5-33 were all Milnes-Daimler BUSES, sold on by 1920							
First users of 34-6 were Clarkson STEAM BUSES; their fleet numbers were taken over by Milnes-Daimler BUSES							
37	A 7645	London	Milnes-Daimler	5-ton LORRY	Oct-04	35	1st GW motor lorry
39	AF 280	Cornwall	Wolseley	2-ton VAN	1907		
40	LC 1083	G'terLondon	Wolseley	PARCELS VAN	Jun-05	38	1st GW parcels van
Fleet 41-3 were Milnes-Daimler BUSES							
44	CO 112	Plymouth	Milnes-Daimler	5-ton LORRY	Feb-05	37	2nd GW motor lorry
Fleet 45-7 were Milnes-Daimler BUSES of 1905, of which fleet 46 (O 1213) became a LORRY							
48	DA 100	W'hampton	Durkopp 20 HP	BUS	Aug-05		Withdrawn June, 1910
	LC 3636	G'terLondon	Milnes-Daimler 20 HP	5-ton LORRY	1911	42	
Fleet 49/50 were Milnes-Daimler BUSES, of 1905 (CO 125 and LC 1171), both later LORRIES.							
Fleet 51/2 were Maudslay BUSES of April-05							
53	LC 189	G'terLondon	Maudslay 12 HP	BUS	May-05		
	K 1564	Liverpool	Milnes-Daimler 20 HP	PARCELS VAN	1914		Van converted to bus; see 181 from 2/22. At Tregenna Castle Hotel, St Ives, 1914-20.
54	O 1774	Birmingham	Wallis & Steevens	4½-ton STEAM TRACTOR	1904		became S4. then S1; sold 1924
55	O 1761	"	"	3½-ton STEAM TRACTOR	1904		became S5, then S2
56		unknown	Aveling & Porter	3 ton STEAM TRACTOR	Nov-04		Sold to Parry of Bilston, 1906
	AF 272	Cornwall	Milnes-Daimler 30 HP	BUS	Jun-07		
Fleet 57-80 were all BUSES of 1905/6 (Milnes-Daimler; Durkopp; Wolseley; and Straker-Squire)							
81	U 308	Leeds	Yorkshire Steam Motor Co	3 ton STEAM WAGON	1905	36	Became S1. Sold 1913
82	LC 4338	G'terLondon	Anglo-American Electric	ELECTRIC PARCELS VAN	Feb-06	38	
Fleet 83-94 were all Milnes-Daimler BUSES of 1906/7. A detail is					Mar-05		
92	AF 277	Cornwall	Milnes-Daimler 30 HP	BUS	Jul-07		To Swindon Works Fire Brigade, 1922
95	BH 020	Bucks	Electric	ELECTRIC PARCELS VAN	Mar-08	39	
	HA 202	Smethwick	Straker-Squire	1 ton PARCELS VAN	Apr-18		
Fleet 96-105 were all Milnes-Daimler BUSES of 1908							
106	CM 392	Birkenhead	Straker-Squire	15 cwt PARCELS VAN	1909		
107	CM 393	"	"	"	"		Temporary bus
108	CM 394	"	"	"	"		"
109	O 4504	Birmingham	"	"	"	41	
110	O 4505	"	"	"	"		Sold to Mahoney, Newport
111	O 4506	"	"	"	"		
Fleet 112-8 were all Milnes-Daimler BUSES of 1909/10							

FLEET NUMBER	REGISTRATION	ISSUED BY	MAKER	BODY TYPE	DATE INTRODUCED	PAGE NUMBER IN KELLEY	NOTES
119	LD 7190	G'terLondon	Goodchild Auto Carrier	TRICYCLE PARCELS EXPRESS 1910	222		
120	LD 7191	"	"	"	"		
121	LD 7192	"	"	"	"		
Fleet 122 was a Straker-Squire BUS of 1910							
123	LA 3092	G'terLondon	Straker-Squire	15 cwt PARCELS VAN	Sep-10		Sold to Mahoney, Newport
124	LD 4380	G'terLondon	"	"			Sold to Saul, Manchester, 1924
125	LA 3299	G'terLondon	"	"			Replaced by 325 (F2)
126	O 5539	Birmingham	"	"			Replaced by 326 (F3)
127	O 5540	"	"	"			Replaced by 594
128	O 5715	"	"	"			
129	BO 595	Cardiff	"	"			Sold to Mahoney, Newport
130	O 7013	Birmingham	"	"			
131	O 7044	"	"	"			
132	K 5411	Liverpool	"	"			Sold to Williams, Bristol; replaced by 592
133	O 7064	Birmingham	"				"
134	DW 347	Newport	"	"	Oct-11		Sold to Williams, Bristol
135	AE 2604	Bristol	"	"			
136	LD 6282	G'terLondon	"	"			Sold to Mahoney, Newport
137	CO 529	Plymouth	"				"
138	K 5445	Liverpool	"	"			Sold to Mahoney, Newport; replaced by 596
139	O 7146	Birmingham	"				"
140	DW 353	Newport	"	"	Dec-11		Sold to Mahoney, Newport
141	LB 7335	G'terLondon	"	"			
142	AF 781	Cornwall	"	"	Feb-12		Run on coal gas in WW1; temporary bus
143	BO 604	Cardiff	"	"			Sold to Saul, Manchester, 1924
144	AE 2632	Bristol	"	"			
145	AF 752	Cornwall	"	"	Dec-11		
146	LE 4167	G'terLondon	"	"			
147	BO 610	Cardiff	"	"			
148	LE 4168	G'terLondon	"	"			Sold to Williams, Bristol
149	N 6289	Manchester	"	"			Sold to Mahoney, Newport
150	N 6300	"	"	"			Sold 1924; replaced by 595
151	AF 801	Cornwall	"	"	Mar-12		
152	DW 354	Newport	"	"	Dec-11		Sold 1924; replaced by 593
Fleet 153-162 were Dennis BUSES of 1911							
163	LE 9606	G'terLondon	Commer	3½-ton LORRY	Aug-11		
164	LE 9625	"	"	"	"		
165	LE 9609	"	"	"	"		
166	LE 9658	"	"	"	"		
167	LE 9633	"	"	"	"		
Fleet 168-171 were Milnes-Daimler BUSES of 1911							
172	K 1603	Liverpool	Milnes-Daimler 30 HP	5-ton LORRY	1912		
173	K 1604	"	"	"	"		
174	K 1605	"	"	"	"		
175	LC 5034	G'terLondon	Maudslay 30 HP	"	"		Sold to Shaw, Helston

176	LC 8698	"	"	"	"		
Fleet 177 was a Vulcan CAR registered number AB 566 (Worcester)							
178	T 3592	Devon	Maudslay 30 HP	BUS	Nov-13		moved to 201
	O 8640	Birmingham	Straker-Squire	15 cwt PARCELS VAN	1916		
179	T 3594	Devon	Maudslay 30 HP	BUS	Nov-13		moved to 202
	LT 3509	G'terLondon	Knox	TRACTOR	Apr-18	61	Purchased from Rudd, Poplar. Withdrawn 1931
180	DE 605	Pembroke	Maudslay 30 HP	BUS	Dec-13		moved to 203
	HA 202	Smethwick	Straker-Squire	1 ton PARCELS VAN	Apr-18		
	LT 9966	G'terLondon	AEC 45 HP	3½-ton LORRY	1919		moved to 401
	LL 787	G'terLondon	Adler	CAR			Unlicensed car in Salvage Dept Paddington taken in lieu of unpaid fees; sold to Mahoney, Newport
181	LU 8655	G'terLondon	AEC 45 HP	LORRY	1919		moved to 402
	K 1564	Liverpool	Milnes-Daimler 30 HP	BUS	Feb-22		ex-53; renumbered 2/22; replaced by 521
182	LT 9936	G'terLondon	AEC 45 HP	3½-ton LORRY	1919		moved to 403
	CM 1770	Brkenhead	General Electric	5 ton ELECTRIC LORRY	1920	44	E5
183	LT 9896	G'terLondon	AEC 45 HP	3½-ton LORRY	1919		moved to 404
	CM 1768	Birkenhead	General Electric	5 ton ELECTRIC LORRY	1920		E6
184	LT 9897	G'terLondon	AEC 45 HP	3½-ton LORRY	1919		1st ex-army lorry. moved to 405
	CM 1769	Birkenhead	General Electric	5 ton ELECTRIC LORRY	1920		E7
185	LT 9938	G'terLondon	AEC 45 HP	3½-ton LORRY	1919		moved to 406
	CM 1767	Birkenhead	General Electric	5 ton ELECTRIC LORRY	1920		E8
186	LT 9937	G'terLondon	AEC 45 HP	3½-ton LORRY	1919		moved to 407
	DX 2146	Ipswich	Ransome, Sims & Jeffries	3½-ton ELECTRIC LORRY	1920		E9
187	LT 9939	G'terLondon	AEC 45 HP	3½-ton LORRY	1919		moved to 408
	DX 2147	Ipswich	Ransome, Sims & Jeffries	3½-ton ELECTRIC LORRY	1920		E10
188	LT 9968	G'terLondon	AEC 45 HP	3½-ton LORRY	1919		moved to 409
	DX 1985	Ipswich	Ransome, Sims & Jeffries	2½-ton ELECTRIC LORRY	1920	43	E11
189	LT 9965	G'terLondon	AEC 45 HP	3½-ton LORRY	1919		moved to 410
	DX 1987	Ipswich	Ransome, Sims & Jeffries	2½-ton ELECTRIC LORRY	1920		E12
190	LT 9967	G'terLondon	AEC 45 HP	3½-ton LORRY	919		moved to 411
	DX 1988	Ipswich	Ransome, Sims & Jeffries	2½-ton ELECTRIC LORRY	1920	44	E13
191	AF 80	Cornwall	AEC 45 HP	BUS	Jun-19		moved to 225
	DX 1986	Ipswich	Ransome, Sims & Jeffries	2½-ton ELECTRIC LORRY	1920	44	E14
192	AF 101	Cornwall	AEC 45 HP	BUS	Jun-19		moved to 224
193	AF140	Cornwall	AEC 45 HP	BUS	Jun-19		moved to 223
	XK 1561	London CC	Austin 20 HP	BUS	Aug-22		
194	AF 174	Cornwall	AEC 45 HP	BUS	Jun-19		moved to 222
	BO 3510	Cardiff	Willys-Overland	15-cwt VAN			ex-Cardiff Rly
195	BX 917	Carmarthen	AEC 45 HP	BUS	Jun-19		moved to 221
	XL 9625	London CC	Austin 12 HP	CAR			
196	BX 918	Carmarthen	AEC 45 HP	BUS	Jul-19		moved to 220
	XL 9624	London CC	Austin 20 HP	BUS	Aug-22		
197	T 6674	Devon	AEC 45 HP	BUS	Apr-19		moved to 219
	XM 1025	London CC	Austin 20 HP	BUS	Sep-22		
198	T 6676	Devon	AEC 45 HP	BUS	Apr-19		moved to 218
	XM 1026	London CC	Austin 20 HP	BUS	Sep-22		
199	T 6678	Devon	AEC 45 HP	BUS	Apr-19		moved to 217

FLEET NUMBER	REGISTRATION	ISSUED BY	MAKER	BODY TYPE	DATE INTRODUCED	PAGE NUMBER IN KELLEY	NOTES
	XM 101	London CC	Fordson	TRACTOR	Sep-22	161	1st GW Ford tractor
Fleet 200 not used							
201	T 3542	Devon	Maudslay 30 HP	BUS	Nov-13		ex 178
202	T 3594	"	Maudslay 30 HP	BUS	Nov-13		ex 179
203	DE 605	Pembroke	Maudslay 30 HP	BUS	Dec-13		ex 180
Fleet 204-15 were Maudslay BUSES of 1914. Some details are							
210	T 4420	Devon	Maudslay 30 HP	BUS	Jul-14		At Ebbw Jct Newport, 1919
211	T 4422	"	"	"	"		"
213	T 4444	"	"	"	Aug-14		"
Fleet 216-87 were AEC BUSES of 1919-24, except for fleet 268 XL 4859 (London CC) which was a LORRY; others later became 4/5-ton LORRIES							
288	AN 0690	Berkshire	AEC 45 HP	3½-ton LORRY	1926		ex 1101
289	AN 0501	"	"	"	"		ex 1102
290	AN 0511	"	"	"	"		ex 1103
Fleet 291-94 were AEC BUSES of 1927; later becme LORRIES							
295	LY 8663	G'terLondon	AEC 45 HP	3½-ton LORRY	1927		From Agent Daniel Davies, Ty Isha Farm, Llanelly
Fleet 296-300 were not used.							
Fleet 301-324 were Straker-Squire 1-ton PARCELS VANS with LL (Greater London) and Y (Somerset) number plates, introduced in 1914. Some details are							
304	LL 4219	G'terLondon	Straker-Squire	1-ton PARCELS VAN			Sold to Shaw, Helston
311	Y 2629	Somerset	"	"	Jul-14		Mar-15 Swindon Works Fire Brigade (later at Ebbw Jct); replaced at Swindon by Fleet 1707
315	Y2643	Somerset	"	"	Sep-14		Also to Swindon Wlorks Fire Brigade
325	?		Ford	1-ton	Apr-21		F2; withdrawn before 1931
326	?		"	"	"		F3; withdrawn before 1931
327	XF 5043		"	"	"		F1; withdrawn before 1931
328	?		"	"	"		F5 was HT 3451
329	?		"	"	"		
330	?		"	"	"		
Fleet 331-342 were Ford 1-ton LORRIES, with XK 1361-XK 1372 (London County Council) sequential number plates introduced in March 1922; 341/2 scrapped before 1931						52	
343	BO 3003	Cardiff	Leyland	4/5-ton LORRY			See 363
Fleet 344-346 were Burford 15-cwt LORRIES of August 1924 with XU (London Conty Council) number plates; 344/6 scrapped before 1931						223	
347	XU 2154	London CC	Chevrolet 22 hp	LORRY	Jul-24		Sold Jul-28
348	XU 2155	"	"	"	"		Sold Sept-27
349	XU 2156	"	"	"	"		Sold Dec-31
350	XU 2157	"	"	"	"		Sold Oct-26
351	XU 2158	"	"	"	"		"
352	XU 2159	"	"	"	"		Sold Nov-28
353	XU 2160	"	"	"	"		Went to Western National as a bus Dec-28
Fleet 354-356 were Chevrolet BUSES, with sequential London CC number plates XU 2161-63.							
357	XW 8579	London CC	Burford	15-cwt LORRY	Jan-25		at Swindon Works
358	XE 3312	London CC	Ford	1-ton LORRY	Nov-22		ex Alexandra Docks Rly; repainted brown and cream, August 1925.
359	DW 2610	Newport	"	"	"		"
360	T 7167	Devon	"	"	Feb-25		From Agent Gilley Bros, Torquay. Withdrawn by 1931
361	TA 4219	"	"	"	"		"
362	CO 2512	Plymouth	Thornycroft 'J' 40 HP	LORRY	Feb-25		"

1403	YU 9307	"	"	"	"		ex-1033
1404	UC 5329	"	"	"	"		GW & GC Joint (chair traffic)
1405	YU 5101	"	"	"	Apr-28		
1406	(GK 6018)	"	"	"	(July-31)		Guernsey, 1928 (Gurnsey registration unknown) ; returned to mainland 1931
Fleet 1407-1459 were all Thornycroft 'A1' LORRIES with YW and YX (Greater London) number plates, introduced between June-28 and Jan-30. Some details are						86	
1413	(GK 6019)	G'terLondon	Thornycroft 'A1'	2-ton LORRY	Jul-31		Guernsey, 1928 (Gurnsey registration unknown) ; returned to mainland 1931
1415	(GK 6062)	"	"	"	Aug-31		Jersey, 1928 (Jersey registration unknown); returned to mainland 1931
1457	UV 9542	"	"	"	Jun-29		GW & GC Joint (chair traffic)
1458	UW 9785	"	"	"	Nov-29		GW & GC Joint
1459	GC 9039	"	"	"	Jan-30		GW & LMS Joint
Fleet 1460-1499 of 1928/9 all used Thornycroft 'A1' chassis. Most were BUSES, some of which were delivered directly to Western National. Those listed below (and 1497/99) have known cartage bodies.							
1467	YX 1530	G'terLondon	Thornycroft 'A1'	2-ton VAN	Jul-28		Cadbury contract
1493	GJ 2372	G'terLondon	"	"	Jul-30		GW & GC Joint
Fleet 1494-99 came from Hall-Lewis in Cardiff, all with Cardiff UH number plates. A detail is							
1497	UH 3462	Cardiff	Thornycroft 'A1'	2-ton LORRY			Stores lorry
Fleet 1500 not used							
Fleet 1501-1598 were BUSES of 1928/9 on Maudslay ML3 chassis (1587 on ML4A chassis), some of which were delivered directly to Western National. Others became LORRIES such as							
1512	YV 8570	G'terLondon	Maudslay	LORRY	Jun-28		Chair traffic; ex Strachan-bodied bus
1550	YV 5431	"	"	"	May-28		Livestock lorry; ex-Vickers-bodied bus
Fleet 1599 not used?							
Fleet 1600-1615 were Guy, Gilfold and Thornycroft BUSES of 1929.							
Fleet 1616-1619 not used?							
Fleet 1620-1631 were all Maudslay BUSES of 1929							
Fleet 1632-1638 not used?							
1639	KV 1927	Coventry	unknown	unknown	1929		GW & LMS Joint
1640	KV 5714	"	"	"	"		"
1641	KV 6139	"	"	"	"		"
Fleet 1642/3 were not used?							
1644	JO 2674	Oxford	Bedford	2-ton			from Agent Quartly. Thame
1645	KX 7759	Bucks	"	2-ton HORSEBOX		104	"
1646	KV 1528	Coventry	"	"		104	"
1647	GX 3371	G'terLondon	Guy	ROADSWEEPER	Oct-32		
1648	MW 7588	Wilts	Chevrolet	1-ton (LORRY?)			from Agent Mrs B L Hawkins, Swindon
1649	MW 7589	"	"	(LORRY?)			
Fleet 1650-1680 were BUSES and CARS of 1929/30; Guy OND fleet 1651 with Greater London registration UU 975 later became a LORRY							
1681	AXN 142	London CC	Austin	VAN	1930		
Fleet 1682-3 were Ford CARS of 1930 with Greater London registrations AXN 143 and AXX 466							
1684	MW 3902	Wilts	Raleigh	MOTORCYCLE			
Fleet 1685-1688 were Ford and Hillman CARS of 1930 with Greater London plates							
Fleet 1689-1693 not used?							
Fleet 1694-1699 were Morris Cowley CARS with Greater London plates							
Fleet 1700-1751 were all Thornycroft 'PB' 4/5-ton LORRIES with XV (London CC), UL, UW, GC (Greater London) number plates of 1928/9. A detail is						p4	
1706	XV 5526	G'terLondon	Thornycroft 'PB'	4/5-ton LORRY	Feb-29		fitted for Coventry system demountable flat

FLEET NUMBER	REGISTRATION	ISSUED BY	MAKER	BODY TYPE	DATE INTRODUCED	PAGE NUMBER IN KELLEY	NOTES
1707	UL 9287	G'terLondon	"	"	Feb-29		Replaced Fleet 318 in the Swindon Factory Fire Brigade
Some of Fleet 1752-1791 were not used, but 1754 was a Bramco tractor							
1792	BL 8437	Berkshire	Thornycroft "j" 40 HP	4/5-ton LORRY	1931		from Agent Quartly, Thame
1793	LU 9823	G'terLondon	"	"	"		from Austin Greene, Cardiff; sold to Rogers, Cardiff
Fleet 1794-1799 of January/Febrauary 1930 with GC (Greater London) number plates finished the run of Thornycroft 'PB' 4/5-ton LORRIES							
Fleet 1800-1882 were all Thornycroft 'A1' 2-ton LORRIES with XV (London CC), UL, GU and UU (Greater London) number plates, introduced between Nov-28 and Aug-29. A detail is							
1815	UL 9136	G'terLondon	Thornycroft 'A1'	4/5-ton LORRY	Feb-29		fitted for Coventry system demountable flat
Fleet 1883-1898 were not used?							
1899	GP 9003	G'terLondon	Thornycroft 'A8' 8-wheeled rigid- chassis	LORRY			
Fleet 1900 -1993 were Associated-Daimler 4/5-ton LORRIES and VANS with UL, GU and UU number plates introduced between Mar-29 and July-29							
1994	GK 6180	G'terLondon	AEC 'Mammoth' 8-wheeled rigid- chassis	LORRY	1929		
1995	GK 6181	"	"	"	"		
Fleet 1996-1999 were not used?							
2000	UW 9701	G'terLondon	Thornycroft A1	2-ton VAN	Nov-29	54	LMS and GW Joint at Cardiff
Fleet 2001-2019 were Thornycroft A1 2-ton VANS having UW or GC (Greater London) number plates,introduced in Nov/Dec-29						128	
Fleet 2020-2048 were Thornycroft A1 4/5-ton LORRIES having UW or GC (Greater London) numberplates, introduced Nov/Dec-29							
Fleet 2049-2096 were either VANS or LORRIES on 2-tonThornycroft A1 chassis having GC (Greater London) number plates, introduced Nov/ Dec-29						99	
2097	GC 9863	G'terLondon	Thornycroft A1	2-ton LORRY	Dec-29		
2098	GC 9864	"	"	"	"		
2099	GC 9865	"	"	"	"		
Fleet 2100-2173 were all Thornycroft 'PB' 4/5-ton LORRIES with GC, GF or GK (Greater London) number plates introduced in the early 1930's						101	
Fleet 2174-2199 were not used?							
Fleet 2200-2284 were all Thornycroft 'JJ' 6/8-ton LORRIES with GK or GX (Greater London) number plates, introduced in early 1930's.						109	
2227	GK 6127	G'terLondon	Thornycroft	6/8-ton LORRY (later VAN)	1930		Livestock vehicle
2247	GK 6147	"	"	6/8-ton LORRY	"	102	Tipper
2249	GK 6149	"	"	"			"
2267	GX 3347	"	"	"			flatbed
2285	GX 3365	"	Thornycroft 'Taurus' Diesel	6/8-ton LORRY (later VAN)	1930		
2286	GX 3366	"	"	6/8-ton LORRY	"		
Fleet 2287-2298 were all Thornycroft 'JJ' LORRIES with ALN467-ALN478 (Greater London) sequential number plates							
2299	CG 2263	G'terLondon	Thornycroft	6/8-ton LORRY			Returned to Thornycroft. Was on trial only
2300	not registered		Rushton	TRACTOR			Replaced Tractor 389
2301	GF 2769	G'terLondon	"	"			Returned to Rushton
2302	GJ 2332	G'terLondon	"	"			
2303	not registered		Fordson	TRACTOR			
Fleet 2304-2315 were all Fordson TRACTORS with GK 6188-GK 6199 (Greater London) sequential number plates, introduced in 1930						168	
2316	not registered		Fordson	ROADLESS TRACTOR	1930	166	Bought originally for mountain work at Treorchy
Fleet 2317-2320 were all unregistered Fordson TRACTORS of th early 1930s							
2321	ALN 487	G'terLondon	Latil	TRACTOR			
2322-2329 were not used?							
Fleet 2330-2339 were Dennis 2-ton LORRIES/VANS with GJ and GK number plates. Some details are							
2330	GJ 2315	G'terLondon	Dennis	2-ton VAN	1930	81	Cadbury contract
2331	GJ 2316	"	"	"	1931	83	Kemp contract

GREAT WESTERN RAILWAY.

~~SWS/EB~~

Telephone:
PADDINGTON 7000.
EXTEN. ~~2142~~

OFFICE OF CHIEF OF POLICE,
PADDINGTON STATION.

7th July, 1947.

Your reference:—
M.7783.

Please quote this reference:—
SP. C.

Dear Sir,

Accident to Police Car.

I am obliged by your letter of the 3rd instant. Reviewing the circumstances carefully I feel myself in agreement with the view that it should have been possible to bring the car to a stand without hitting the tree and I can only come to the conclusion that in the fluster of the accident the driver unwittingly accelerated instead of braking.

The enclosed report from Superintendent Jordan stresses that the gear lever on examination after the accident was found to be in second gear. The fact of the car being in second gear together with the retarding effect of the broken spring should have enabled the car to have been stopped quite easily.

What really transpired will, I am afraid, not be definitely established but the human element seems to have failed when the emergency presented itself. Naturally this is theory but as Sergeant Edmonds has been driving various types of vehicles for years it is, perhaps, fair to say that the structural defect which suddenly manifested itself presented a situation which by its very unexpectedness and the extremely small margin of time between the driver being conscious of the trouble and the moment of impact (not more than five seconds) was psychologically too much for him, as indeed it might have been for most drivers.

Yours faithfully,

A.E.C.Dent,Esq.,
SLOUGH.

Index